IMAGES
of America

LANCASTER

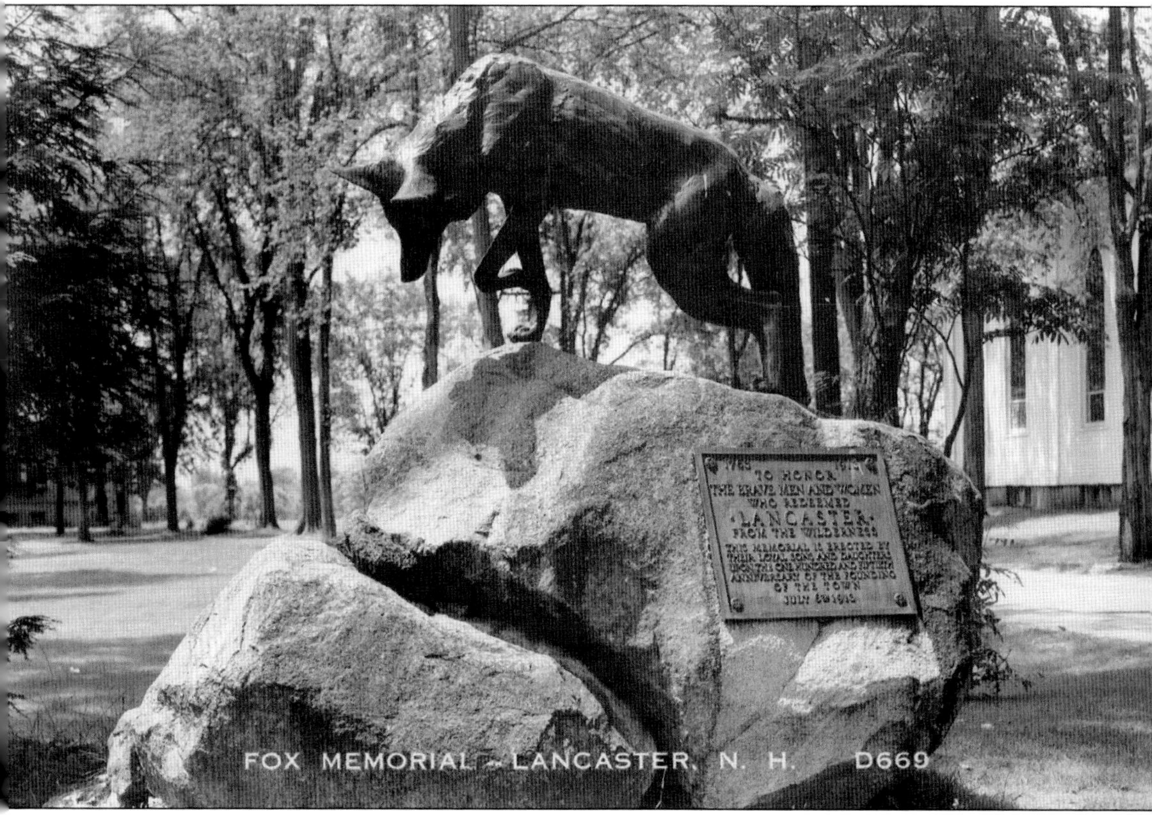

One of the highlights of the 150th anniversary celebration of Lancaster was the dedication of the Fox Memorial, which was sculpted by Anna Vaughn Hyatt of New York and graces the corner of Centennial Park. It was donated by the Unity Club. The stone and bronze fox are a tribute to "The Brave Men and Women Who Redeemed Lancaster from the Wilderness." (Courtesy of the Lancaster Historical Society.)

On the Cover: Crossing Israel's River on Main Street, this double-barreled bridge with covered walkways on each side was constructed in 1862 to replace an uncovered wooden bridge. It was a Paddleford truss style, featuring curved openings with ornamental carvings. This bridge was damaged by the flood of 1870 and was repaired, but it was ultimately destroyed in the flood of 1886, when the sash and blind factory building floated into it shortly after this photograph was taken. It was replaced by the first iron bridge in Lancaster. (Courtesy of the Lancaster Historical Society.)

IMAGES
of America

LANCASTER

The Lancaster Historical Society

ARCADIA
PUBLISHING

ISBN 978-1-4671-2077-7

Published by Arcadia Publishing
Charleston, South Carolina

Printed in the United States of America

Library of Congress Control Number: 2013942634

For all general information, please contact Arcadia Publishing:
Telephone 843-853-2070
Fax 843-853-0044
E-mail sales@arcadiapublishing.com
For customer service and orders:
Toll-Free 1-888-313-2665

Visit us on the Internet at www.arcadiapublishing.com

To the brave men and women who redeemed Lancaster from the wilderness

Contents

Acknowledgments 6

Introduction 7

1. Around Town 9
2. Downtown 21
3. Lodging and Entertainment 39
4. Celebrations 55
5. Homes and Businesses 69
6. Transportation 81
7. Winter Activities 93
8. Education 99
9. Disasters 103
10. Rural Life 111

ACKNOWLEDGMENTS

Since the Lancaster Historical Society was founded in 1963, scores of volunteers have contributed thousands of hours to preserve the history of Lancaster and the surrounding area. It is impossible to thank all those volunteers individually, but without their hard work and love of history, this book would not have been possible. The Lancaster Historical Society's library, archives, and collections offer a wealth of stories and information about the town's history. The board members and volunteers who maintain these collections have earned our immeasurable gratitude. Unless otherwise noted, all images appearing in this book were provided by the Lancaster Historical Society.

We also wish to thank our editor at Arcadia Publishing, Caitrin Cunningham, for her expert guidance and encouragement (when needed). Special thanks go to board members Anne Morgan and Bob Hunt, who devoted countless hours in locating the photographs and researching and writing the captions for this collection. Also, thanks go to William Thompson and Betty Newell for their keen memories, and Midge Rosebrook, Lawrence "Gomer" Powell, and the P.J. Noyes Company for the use of their photographs. We would also like to thank Murray Vashaw, Wilber Hartford, Connie Cardinal, and Althea Donovan for helping clear up numerous little mysteries, as well as the Weeks Memorial Library librarian, Barbara Robarts, for help in researching this book.

Introduction

Lancaster celebrates its 250th anniversary in 2014. The charter was granted by New Hampshire governor Benning Wentworth to David Page of Petersham, Massachusetts, in 1763. Emmons Stockwell, Page's indentured servant, enlisted in the army at the time of the French and Indian War. He passed through the "Upper Cohoss," returning to Petersham with accounts of meadows along the Connecticut River. In 1761, Page had been among the grantees of the town of Haverhill, but had felt cheated in the division of town lands. It may have been at Stockwell's suggestion that he resigned his rights in Haverhill and applied for a grant of the meadows of Upper Coos.

The grant was made on July 6, 1763, in the name of Lancaster, after the towns of that name in Massachusetts and England. Young Stockwell and David Page Jr. set out to take possession of the land, arriving in time to build a log hut somewhere along the riverbank, probably near the present Holton house. By April 1764, a total of 12 acres had been cleared and planted with corn. It grew rapidly; by August 25, it was 12 feet high and in full milk. Unfortunately, the prospect of a good crop was destroyed by a killing frost on August 26, but perseverance was the norm for our forefathers. They managed to keep their cattle through the winter by cutting grass on open land near Beaver Brook. The nearest mill was at Fort No. 4, in Charlestown, but the settlers did not depend on it for food for their daily use. Emmons Stockwell made a huge mortar that held two bushels. Corn, beans, and rye were put into it and pounded with a great wooden pestle. Cooked potatoes and vegetables were mixed with the contents of the mortar and baked. This was called "thump" and was considered a delicious dish.

The first woman that came to Lancaster was Ruth Page. Her father, Governor Page, who was so called by way of distinction, never resided in Lancaster but was somewhat of a director of the settlement. David Page and David Page Jr. were his brother and nephew. On August 25, the night before the great frost, Governor Page and Ruth, who were traveling to Lancaster from Petersham, slept in the woods in Orford. They arrived in Lancaster to find the little settlement somewhat disheartened, but the settlers were no doubt cheered to know a woman had come to make their homes more comfortable. The year after Ruth's arrival, she was married to Emmons Stockwell and began housekeeping. She was 18 and he was 23. Ruth Stockwell was a woman of great determination and character. She could do everything that was necessary, and she did it well. It was said that in the days of the American Revolution, she was the salvation of the settlement. The hardships and dangers that surrounded them weakened the resolutions of the settlers. They met at Emmons Stockwell's house to discuss the abandonment of the town. Ruth Stockwell declared that she would not go away; that she knew no such thing as failure. Others were strengthened by the decision of the Stockwells, and the settlement was saved. Emmons and Ruth Stockwell lived together for more than 55 years and had 15 children, seven sons and eight daughters, all of whom grew to maturity.

Emmons Stockwell had a vigorous mind, a great deal of common sense, and he possessed incredible strength. He could neither read nor write until he was taught by his wife. For many years, there was no school or schoolhouse. Ruth Stockwell, who was a very good scholar for the time, taught the children of the settlement in her own house. The year after Ruth Stockwell's marriage, Edward Bucknam, one of the young settlers, married a sister of Ruth's who had probably come to visit her sister. The Bucknams settled at the mouth of Beaver Brook, a stream that runs through Martin meadows, and had six children. Their oldest daughter, Eunice, was the first child born in Lancaster.

It was a long time before any roads were built. Canoes were the only transportation in the early days, and they were made from the trunks of large trees. The women could row these canoes up and down the river with great skill. They could also handle rifles and fishing poles with expertise. As the rivers and streams were full of fish, and the forest was home to moose and other game, the tables of the settlers could be supplied something besides "thump."

Edward Bucknam was a very useful man to the new settlement. He was a good surveyor, and could "draw teeth" and "let blood," as well as perform the marriage service. He laid out a large portion of the town and many of the highways.

In 1803, Coos County was set off from Grafton County and a courthouse was built. Many prominent lawyers, including Daniel Webster, presided here. At the head of Main Street stands the Wilder-Holton House. Now the headquarters of the Lancaster Historical Society, this house is believed to be the first two-story frame structure in Coos County. Times have changed since the cellar hole was dug in 1780, and Lancaster has been home to many notable people since, including New Hampshire governor, US congressman, and US senator Jared W. Williams, New Hampshire governor Chester B. Jordan, US congressmen Jacob Benton and Ossian Ray, US senators John Wingate Weeks and Irving W. Drew, secretary of commerce Sinclair Weeks, and noted Civil War colonels Edward E. Cross and Francis L. Town.

The Lancaster Historical Society has selected images from its archives to illustrate the rich architectural, commercial, and agricultural history of Lancaster over the past 250 years. It has also used information from previous works published by the society as well as *The Lancaster Sketch Book*, by Persis F. Chase, first published in 1887 and reissued by the society in 1975.

This book is intended to entertain and inspire a new generation of citizens with an interest in preserving the past. It is not a history, nor does it claim to be a complete record. Please visit the Lancaster Historical Society or the Weeks Memorial Library to learn more. The authors would be interested in additional information about any of the images in the book.

One

Around Town

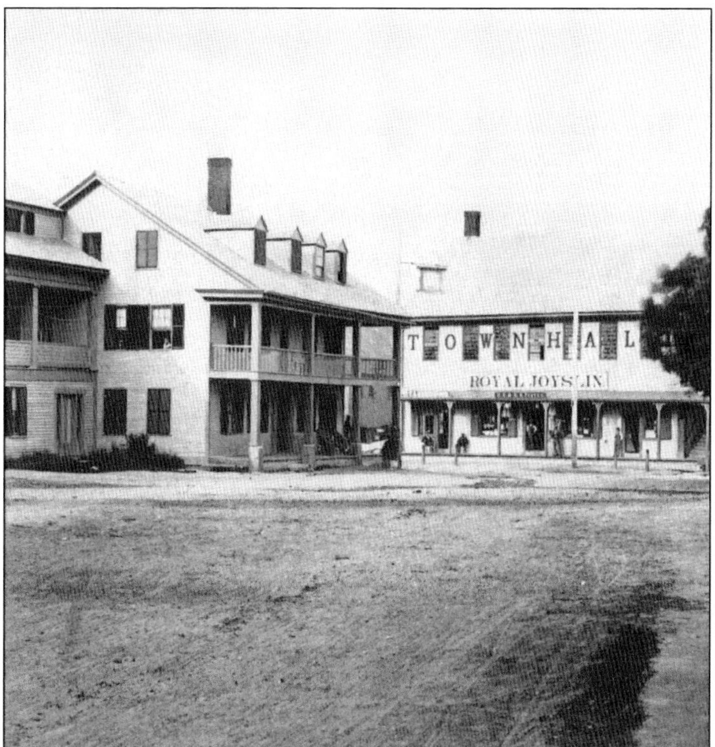

This 1876 stereotype photograph shows the town hall, on Elm Street. The building, a former meetinghouse, was moved down from Soldiers' Park and renovated with stores on the first floor and the town hall on the second. Later, "spacious and elegant" quarters for the Masons were added, making a third story. The building burned on July 16, 1900, and the present town hall was erected on the same site. Also seen is the American House Hotel, built in 1812 by Sylvanus Chessman.

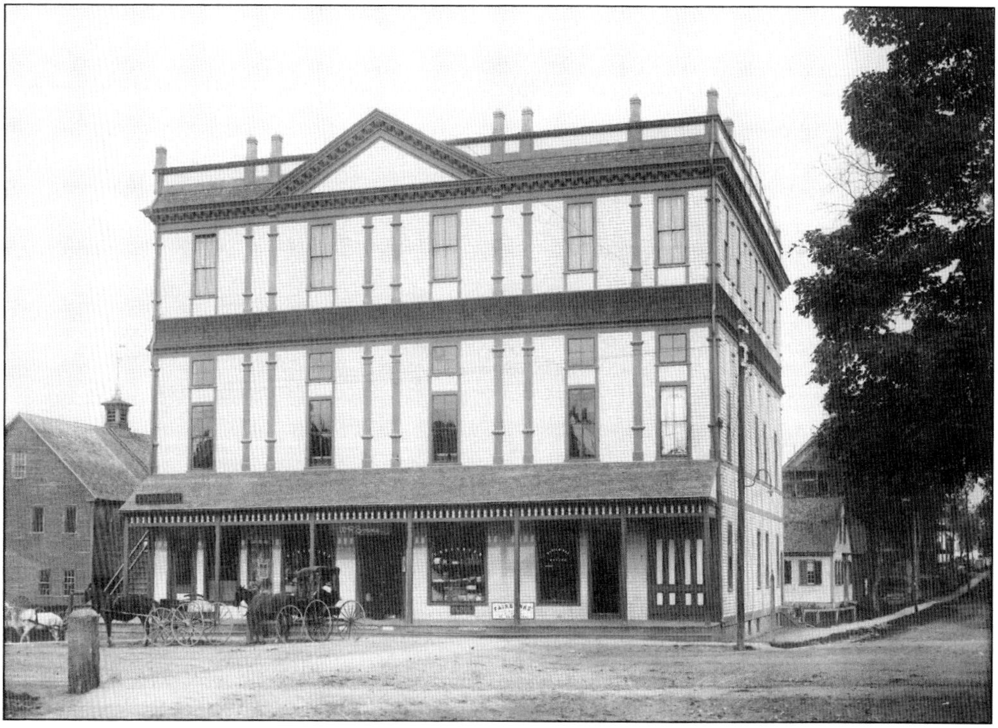

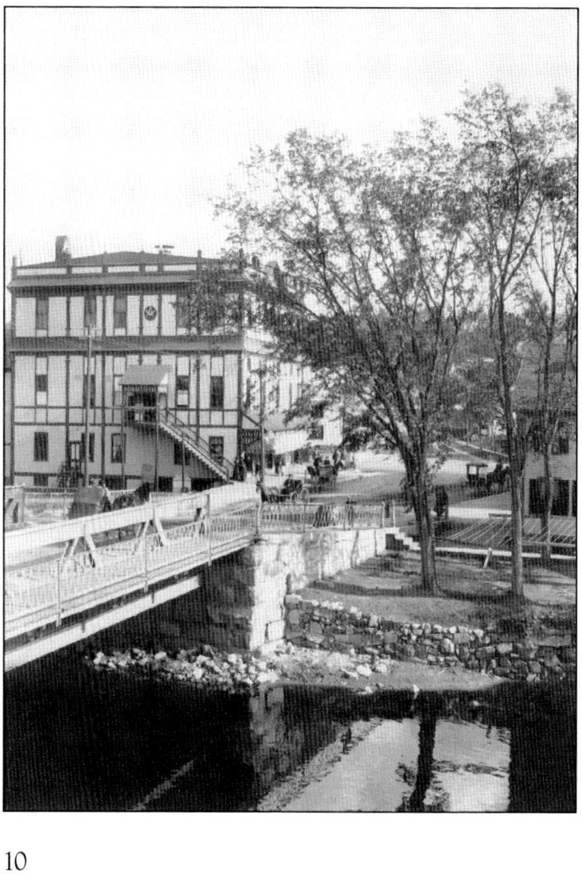

Poles for electricity were set in Lancaster in 1889, so the photograph above of the newly renovated town hall and Masonic temple dates from the early 1890s. Water mains were not laid until 1892, and the Benton Fountain had not yet been erected. It was on the corner by 1900, when the building burned.

A new iron bridge replaced the double covered bridge, which washed away in the flood of 1886. Alas, this new bridge suffered the same fate in 1895. The town hall is at the end of the bridge, complete with the new third floor that was added for the North Star Masonic Lodge.

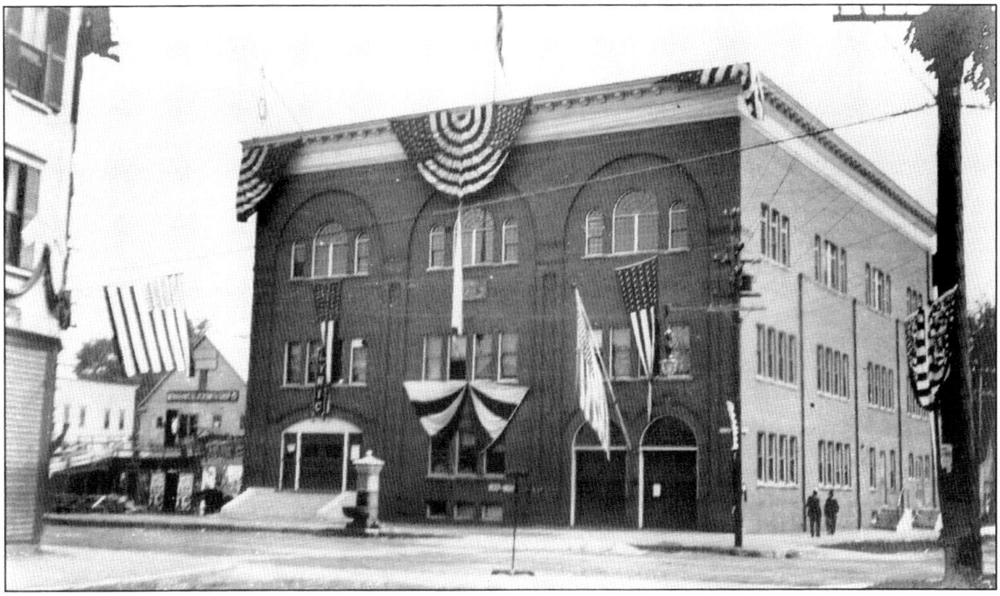

Built in 1901 and dedicated in May 1902, the new town hall replaced the old one, which burned, along with many town records, in July 1900. As in the previous building, the Masons occupied the third floor. The town and the North Star Corporation collaborated on the construction. The building also contained an auditorium and quarters for the town office and the police and fire departments.

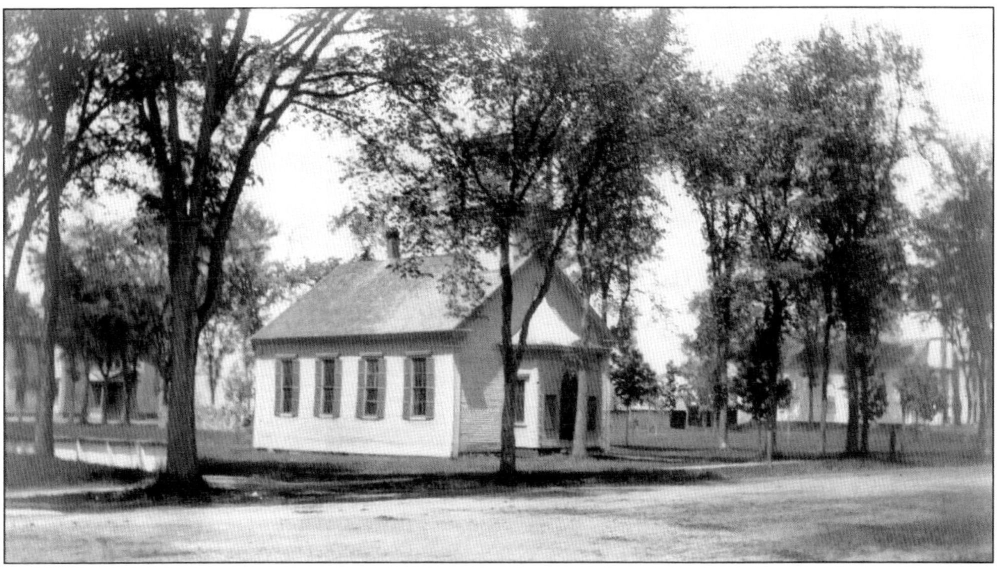

This is a rare view of the first courthouse, erected on the corner of Main and Bridge Streets in 1806. After 1829, Lancaster Academy shared the space and funerals were also held there, as the old meetinghouse was large and not easily heated. The building was moved many times and was used as a Baptist church, a public library, an armory, and a schoolhouse.

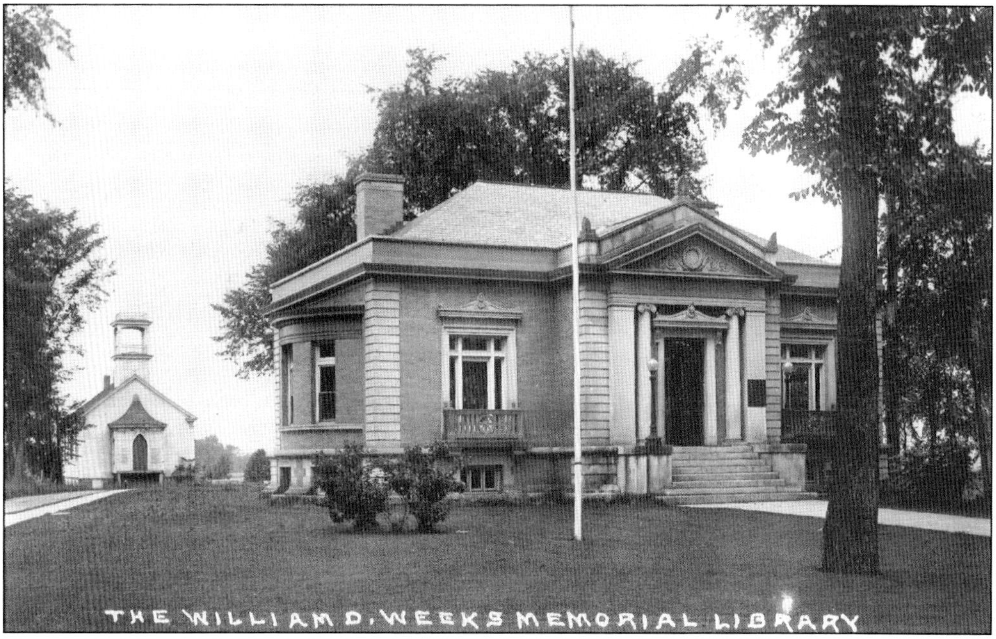

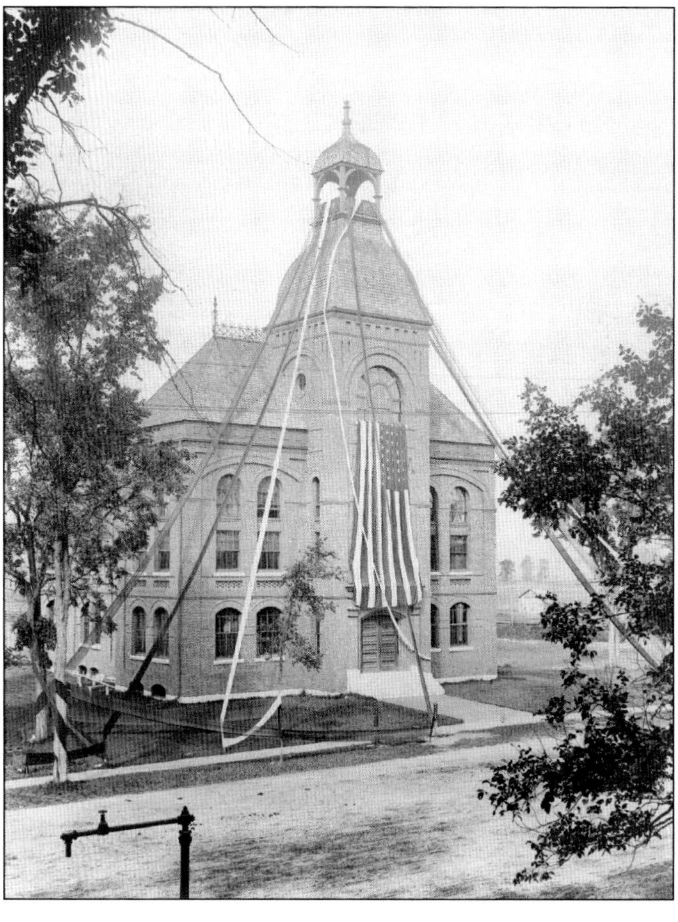

In 1900, John Wingate Weeks offered to build a new library for the town in memory of his father. Construction of the William D. Weeks Memorial Library (above) began in 1906, and the new building opened in 1908.

The "old courthouse" was built in 1887 to replace the 1869 courthouse that was lost in the disastrous fire of November 1886. In the fire, all county records dating back to 1805 were lost. This photograph was taken soon after the new building was erected. Now privately owned, it is currently the home to a branch of Guardian Angel Credit Union and other businesses.

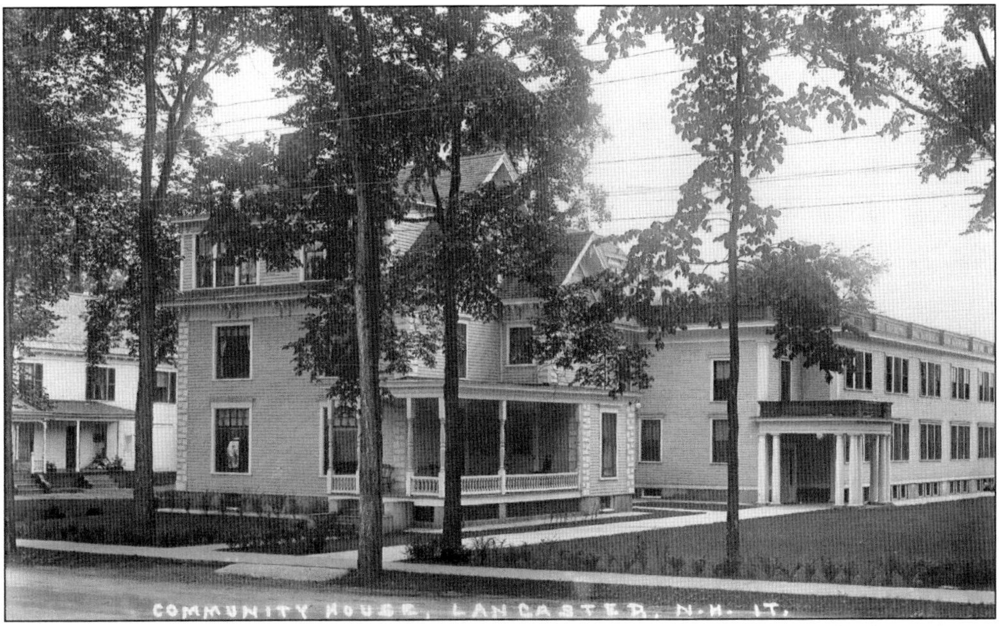

After Civil War colonel Francis L. Town died, he left his estate to be "used for the better living of the people of Lancaster, with emphasis on the youth." His house became the Colonel Town Community House, and a gymnasium was added to the property. The house is also known as the Bugbee-Town house and is the site of the Bugbee-Town murder mystery of the 1880s.

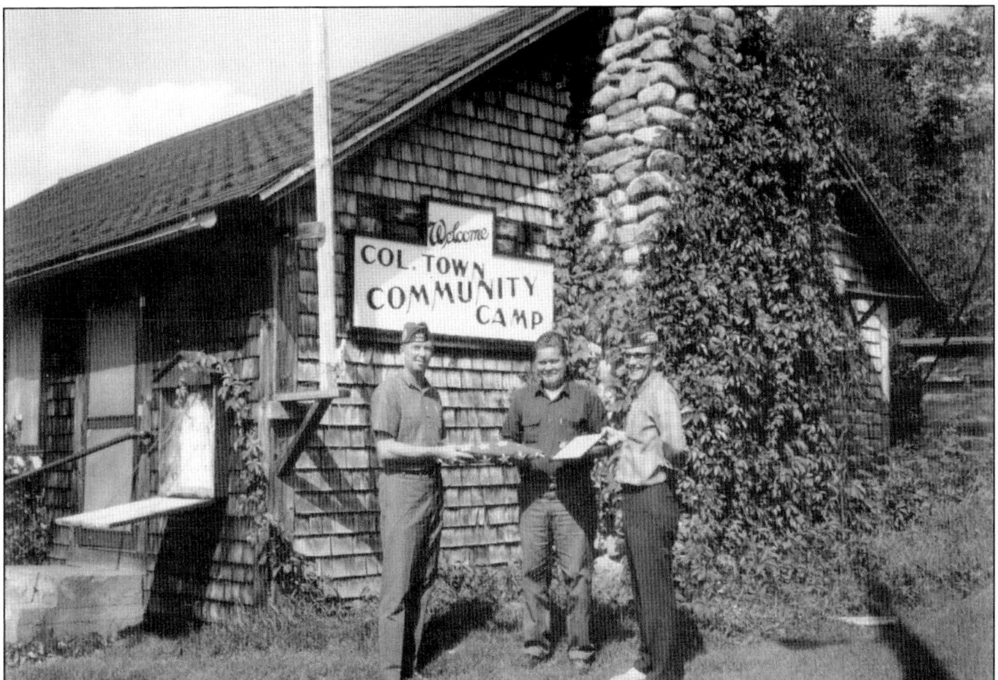

Part of Colonel Town Recreation, the community camp is located "out east," off Pleasant Valley Road near where the Kilkenny Railroad used to run. It is available to residents for picnics, reunions, camping, and recreation.

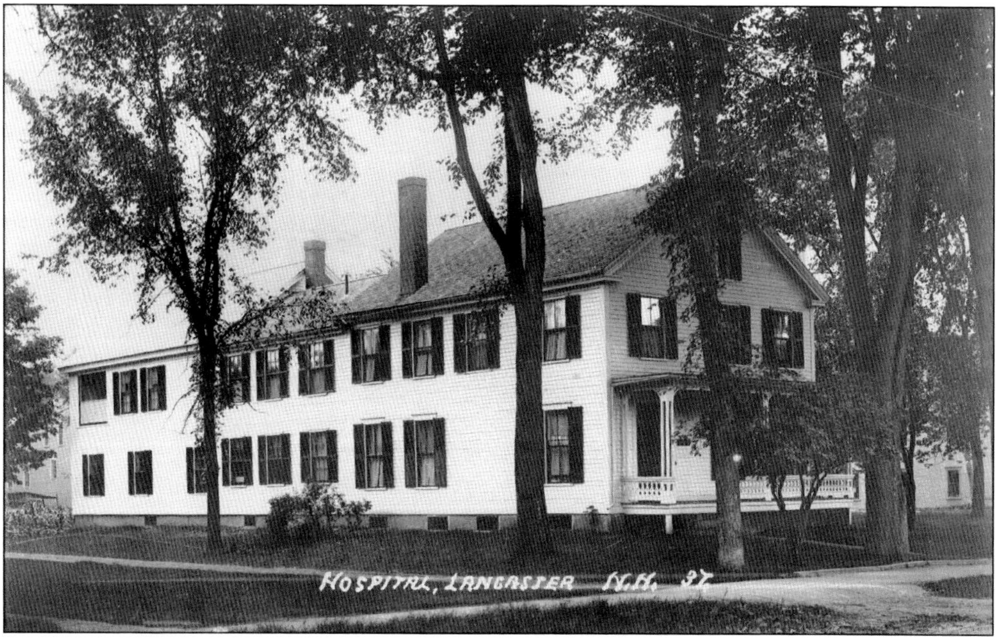

In 1913, Dr. Homer Smith established a hospital in the former J.A. Smith property on Main Street. It became a community hospital in 1919 and was used for that purpose until 1947. Later opened as a bowling alley and restaurant by Glenn "Babe" Smith, it was demolished in the 1990s.

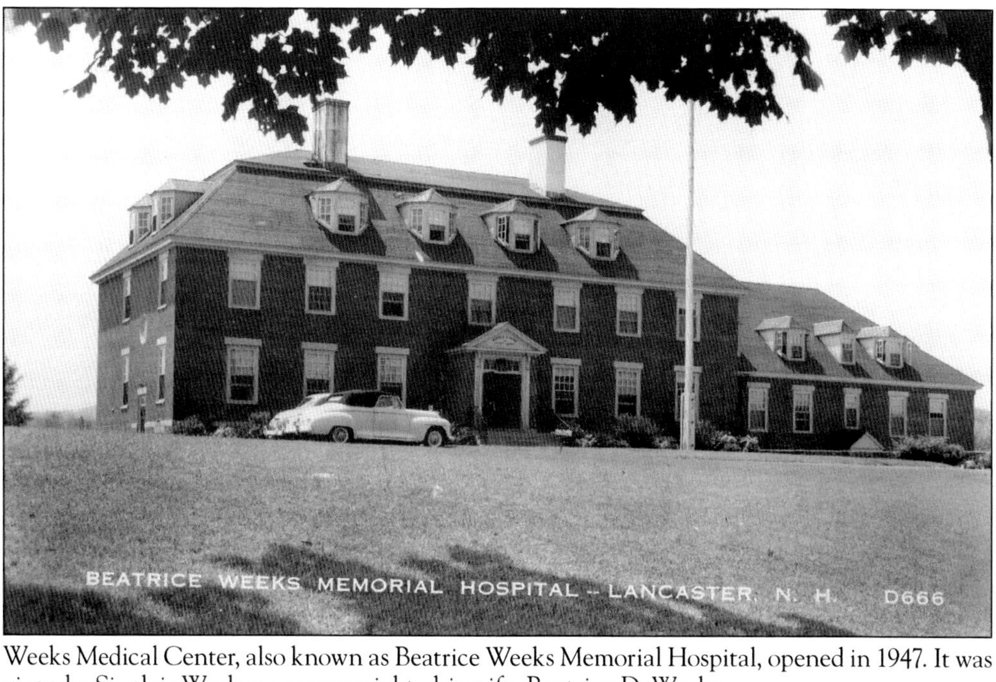

Weeks Medical Center, also known as Beatrice Weeks Memorial Hospital, opened in 1947. It was given by Sinclair Weeks as a memorial to his wife, Beatrice D. Weeks.

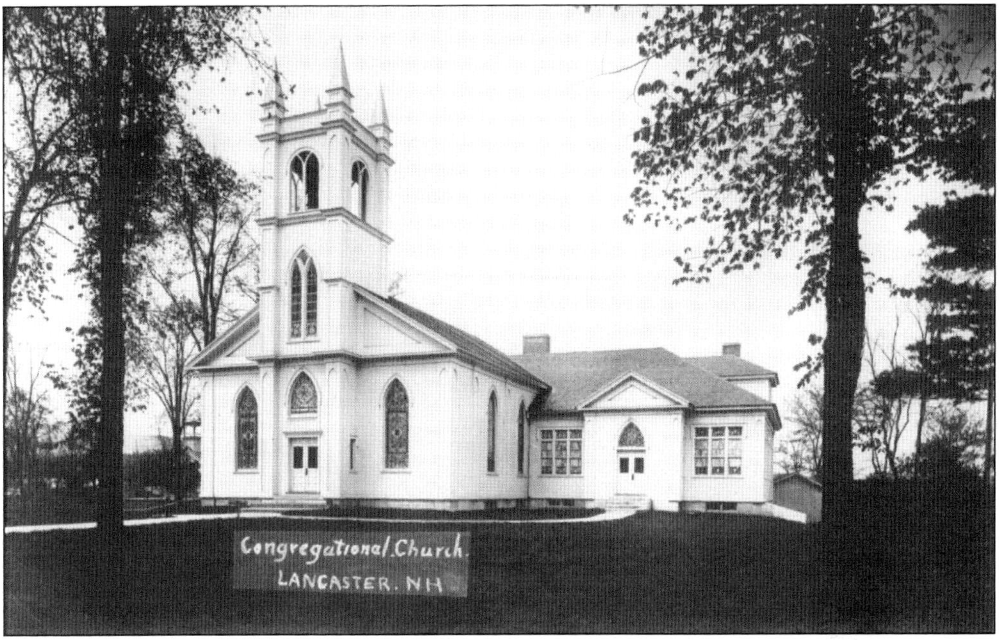

The first church in Lancaster was the Congregational church, organized on July 17, 1794, under the leadership of Parson Joseph Willard. It met in the old meetinghouse on Sand Hill. Eventually, factions separated from this group and built the church above in 1840 on the site of the present church.

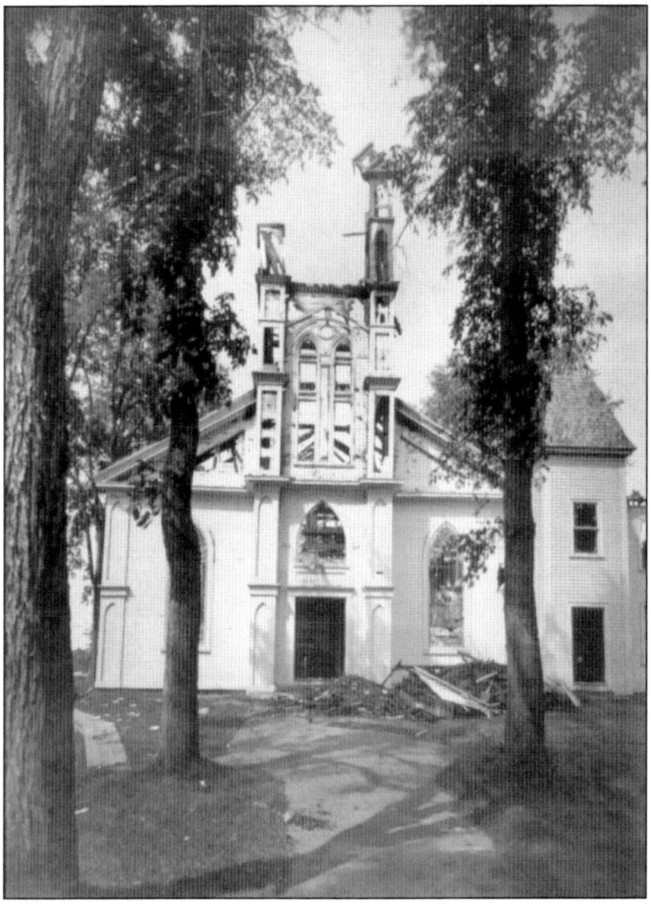

June 25, 1910, saw the members and minister of Lancaster Congregational Church celebrating the final payment on their mortgage with a potluck supper. In the early hours of the next morning, the fire alarm was raised that the church was on fire. It appeared that the cause was an overheated chimney that caught the wood around it on fire. Fortunately, the stained-glass windows and the organ were saved. One year later, the cornerstone for a new church was laid.

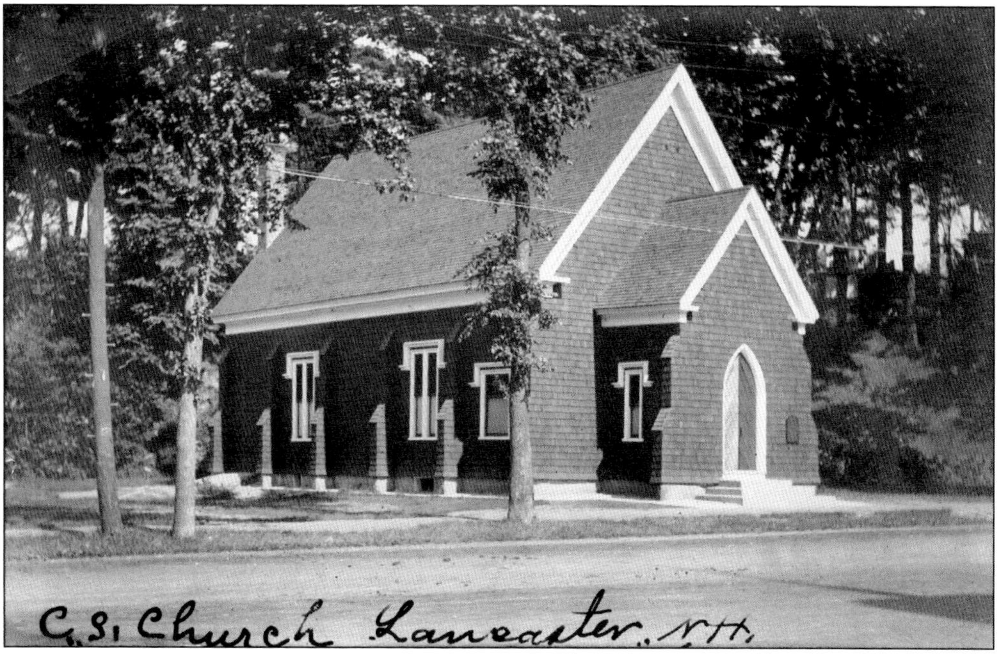

The Unitarian Society of Lancaster was formed on February 22, 1854, and its new church (above) was ready for worship in two years. It is on Main Street next to Wilder Cemetery and is now a Christian Science church and reading room.

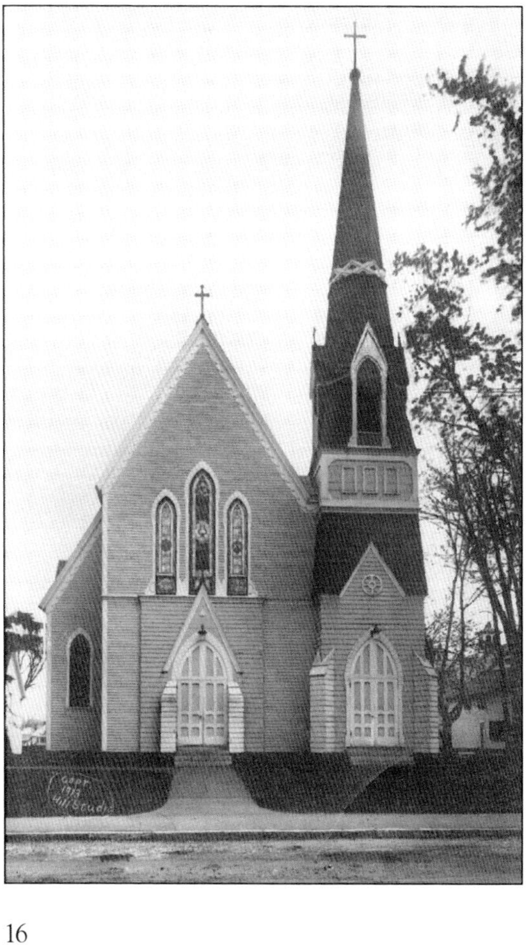

The first Catholic mass was celebrated in the home of Patrick Connary on May 4, 1850. In 1856, Fr. Isadore H. Noisseaux made his home on the present church site and added a chapel, where services were held until 1877. Two years later, the present church building was constructed.

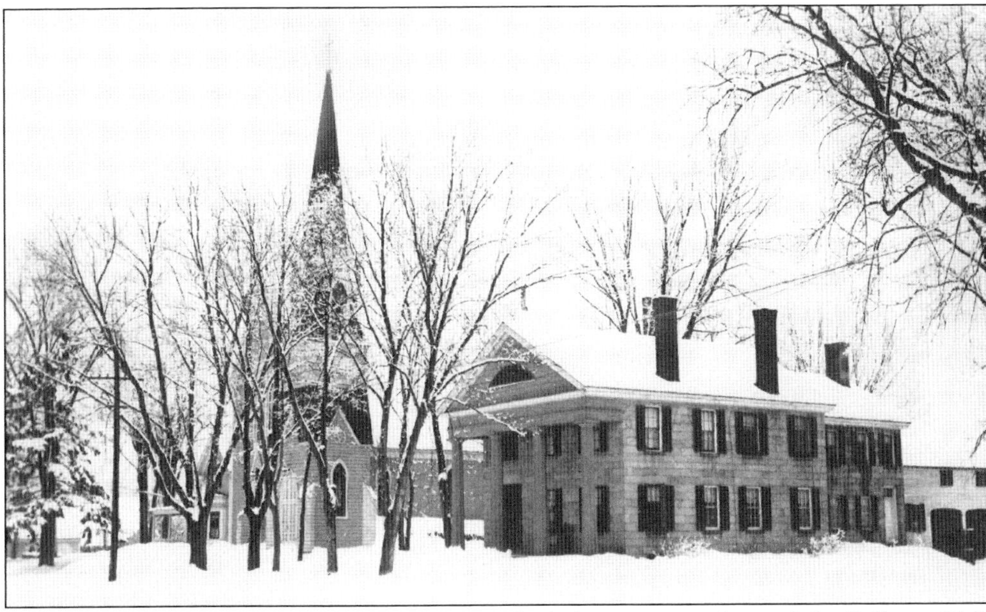

The landmark Stone House, on Main Street, was built for prominent lawyer John Sullivan Wells between 1835 and 1840. This beautiful house was constructed from one solid block of granite found near the Lancaster-Northumberland line. It is lined with brick. It is currently owned by the Gaynor-Knecht family.

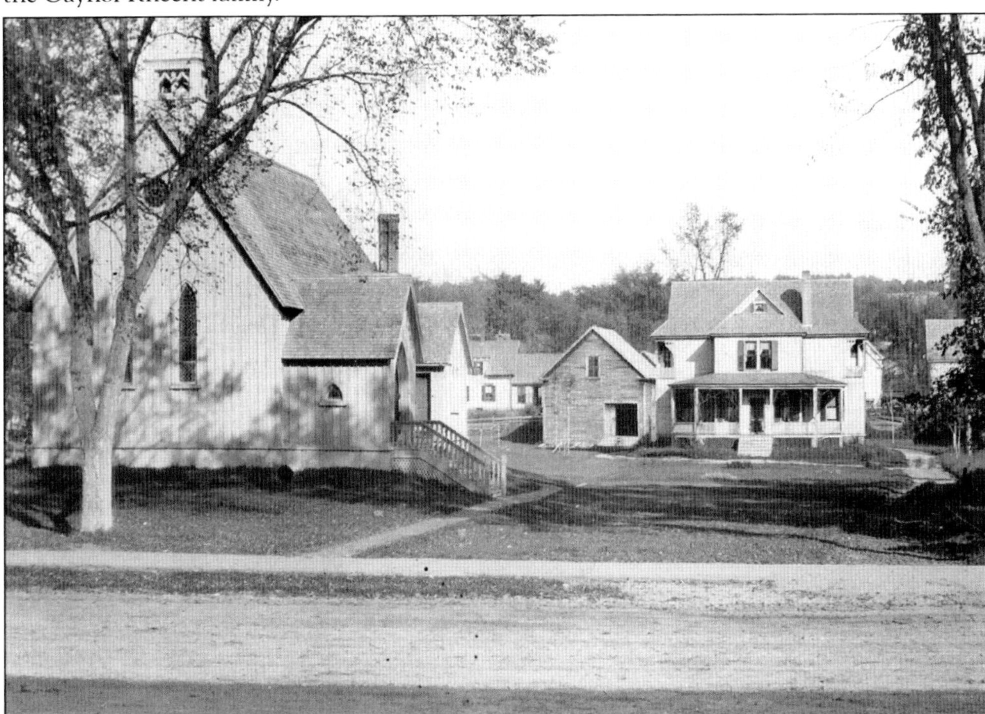

The first known Episcopal service was held on August 6, 1856, by Bishop Charlton Chase. Succeeding services were conducted by visiting ministers. The present church, St. Paul's, was erected in 1876 on a large lot that also includes a rectory at the rear.

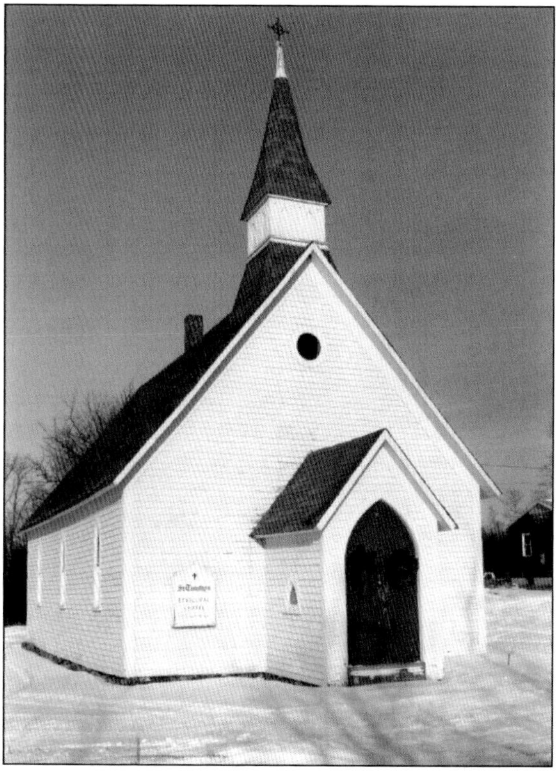

St. Timothy's Episcopal Church was built about 1893 in the eastern section of Lancaster, known as Lost Nation. This small, picturesque church is still used and maintained by St. Paul's Episcopal Church.

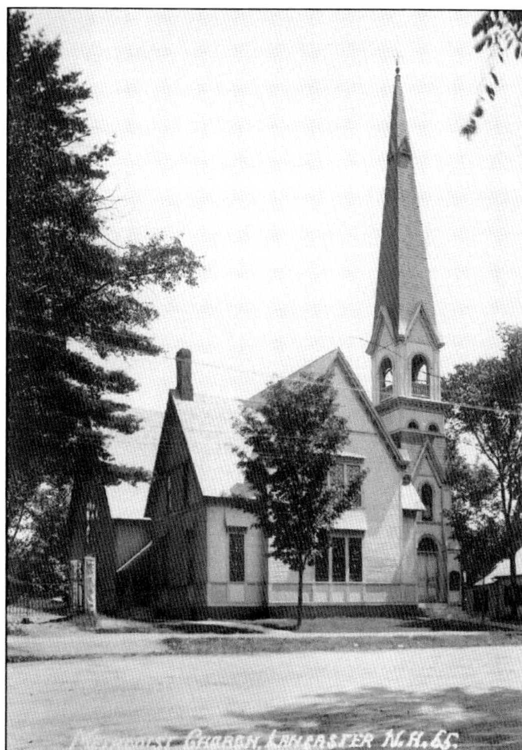

The new Methodist church, seen here, was dedicated on March 20, 1889, after the previous building of worship, on Middle Street, was divided in two, with half on Bunker Hill Street and the other on Cemetery Street. This new building was lighted by a Wheeler reflector with 16 lamps.

To honor the men who served in the Civil War, the Women's Relief Corps was instrumental in the creation of the Soldiers Memorial Monument, dedicated "In Remembrance of Those Who Served" in 1907. It sits in Soldiers' Park, at the south end of the village between Routes 2 and 3.

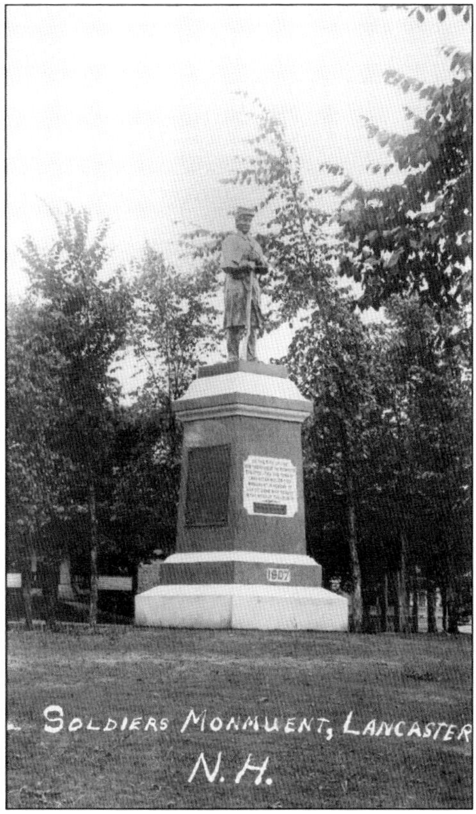

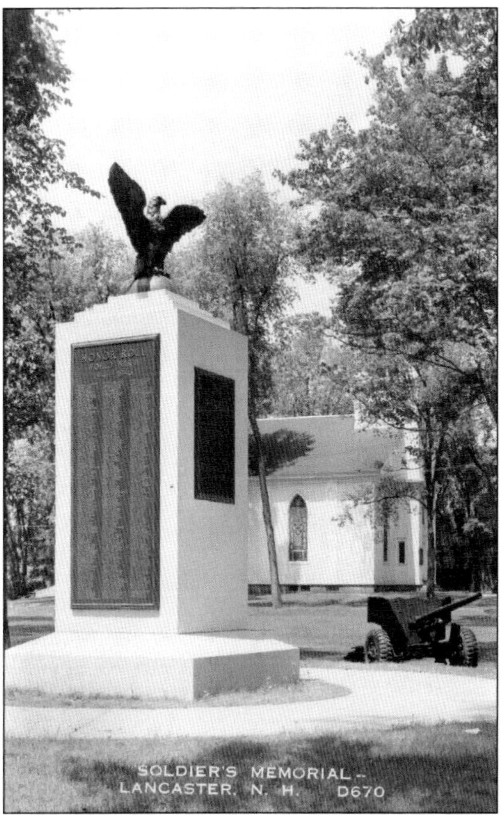

Memorial Day in 1951 saw the unveiling and dedication of this attractive monument to honor the 148 local men who served their country in World War I and the 356 local men and women who served in World War II. Since then, the men and women who served in the Korean War and the Vietnam War have been added.

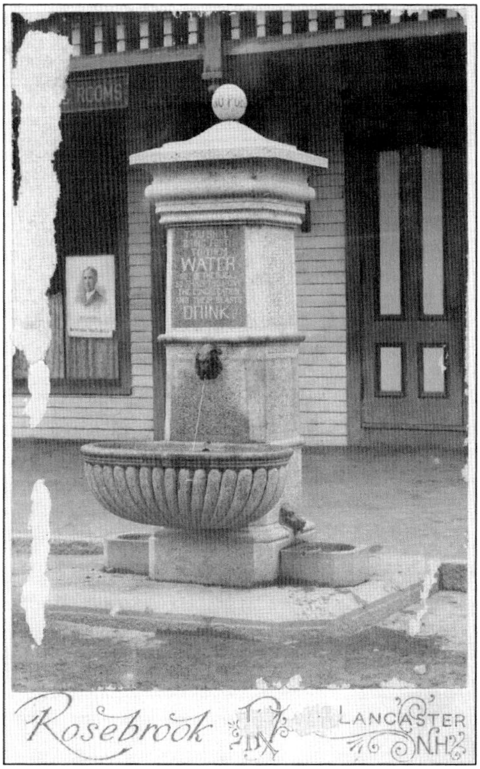

Standing in front of the town hall is the Benton Fountain, donated by Louisa Dow Benton to honor her husband, Jacob Benton, a lifelong resident of Lancaster and a well-known and successful lawyer, businessman, and politician. This fountain not only provided fresh drinking water for humans and larger animals but also for dogs and other smaller animals. It remains on the corner of Main and Mechanic Streets today.

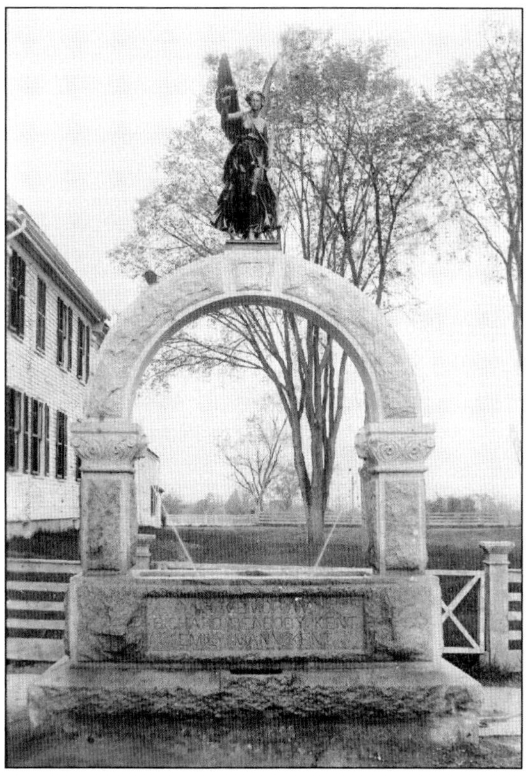

In 1892, the sons of Richard P. Kent had this fountain built and donated to the town in memory of their parents, who had been instrumental in the business and social interests of Lancaster. It was designed to provide drinking water to "man and beasts" and to be an ornament to the town. The top was graced by a bronzed Victory.

Two

DOWNTOWN

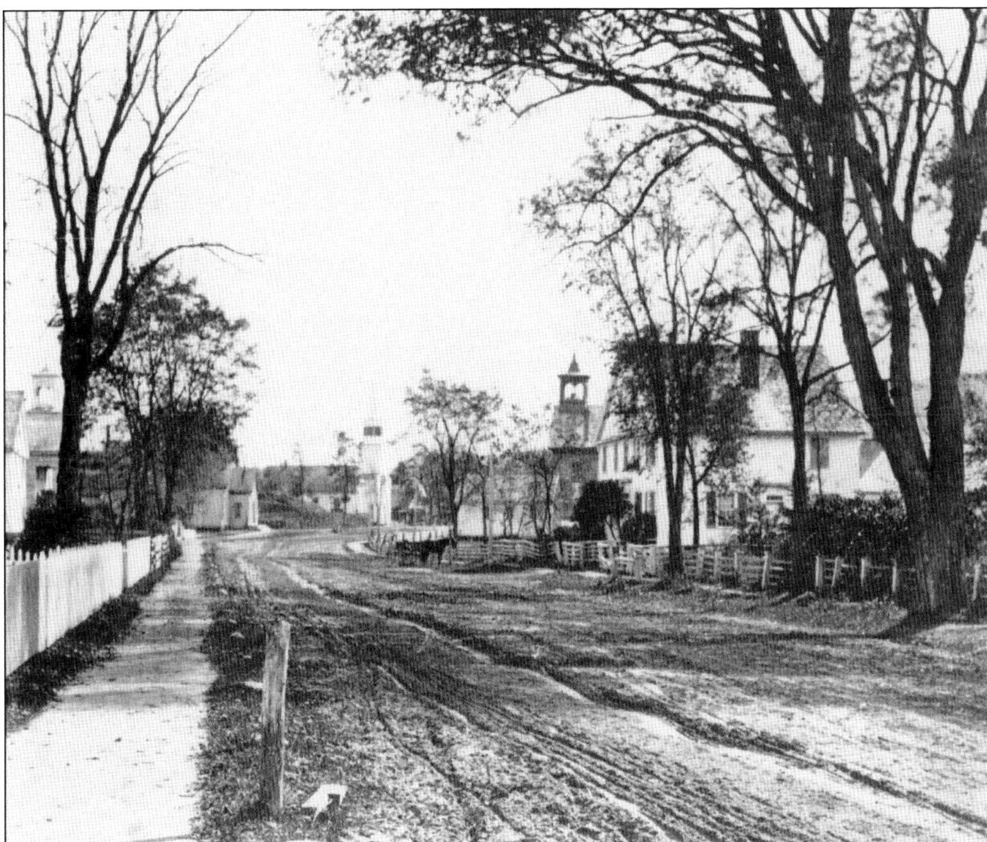

This very early view of Main Street, taken in 1868, looks south from above the courthouse.

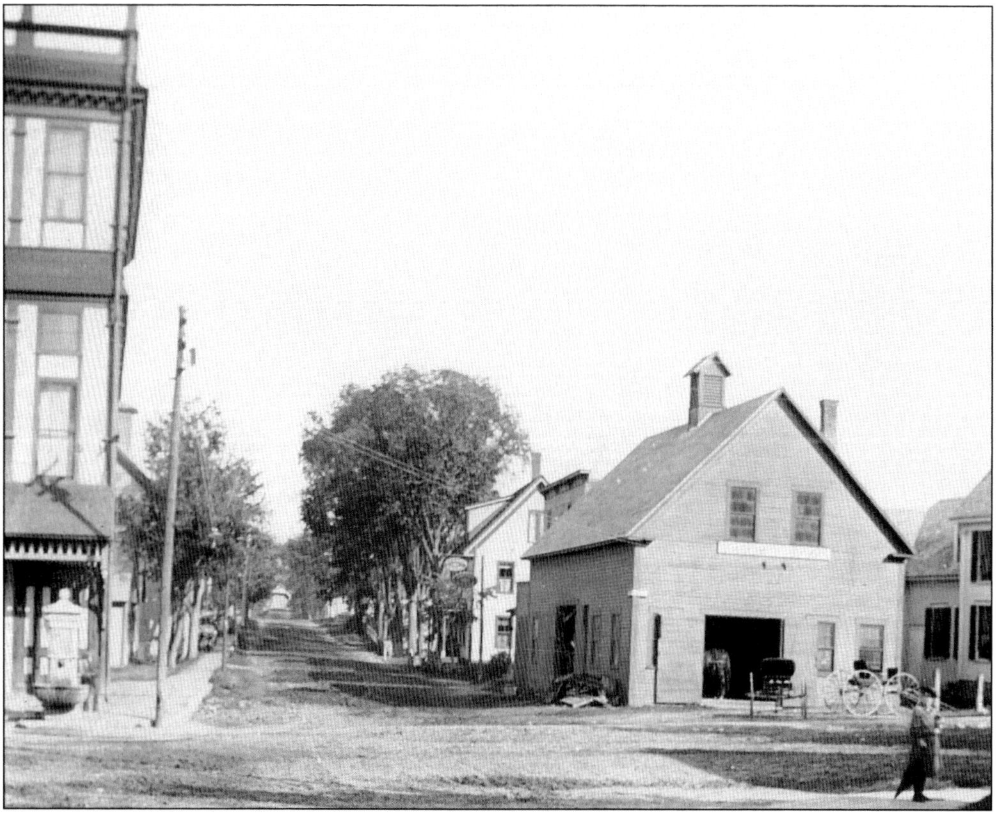

The view looking up Mechanic Street in the 1890s includes the old town hall, Benton Fountain, and a blacksmith shop.

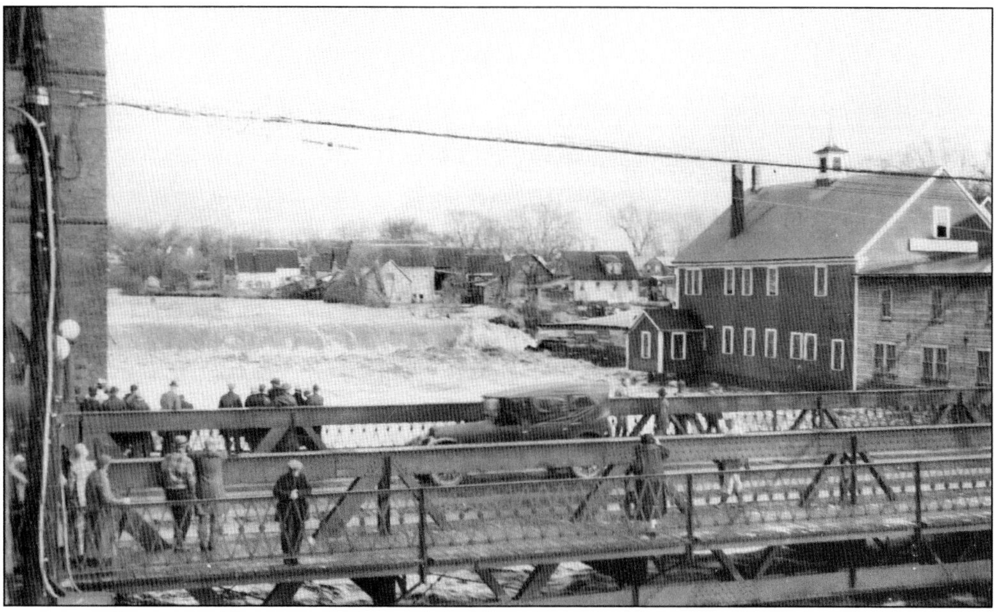

Spectators begin to fill the second iron bridge to view the raging Israel's River going over the upper dam during the New England Flood of November 1927.

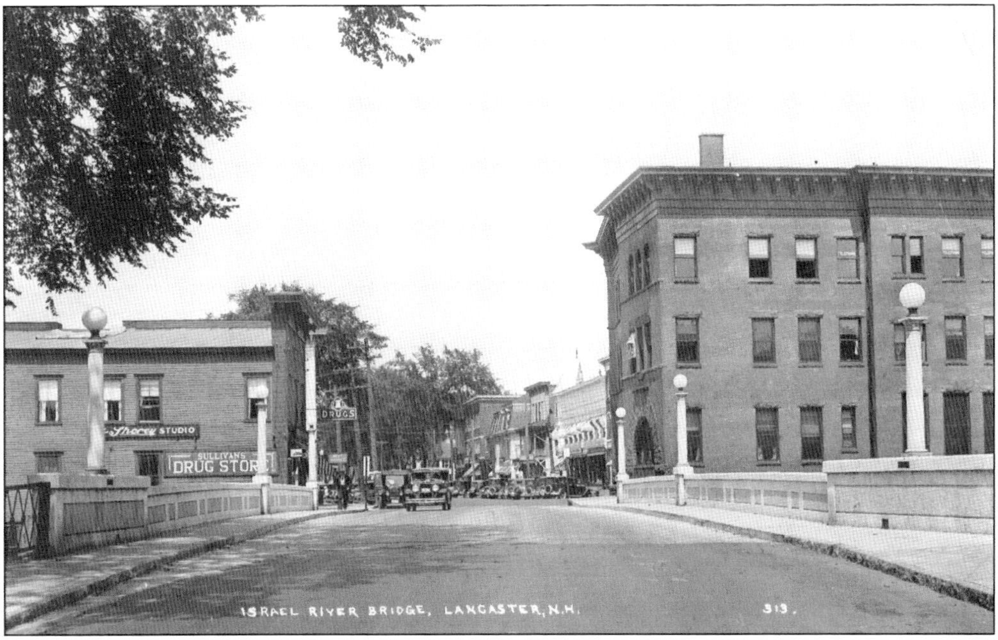

Ready for the next 60 years, the new bridge over Israel's River opened in 1929.

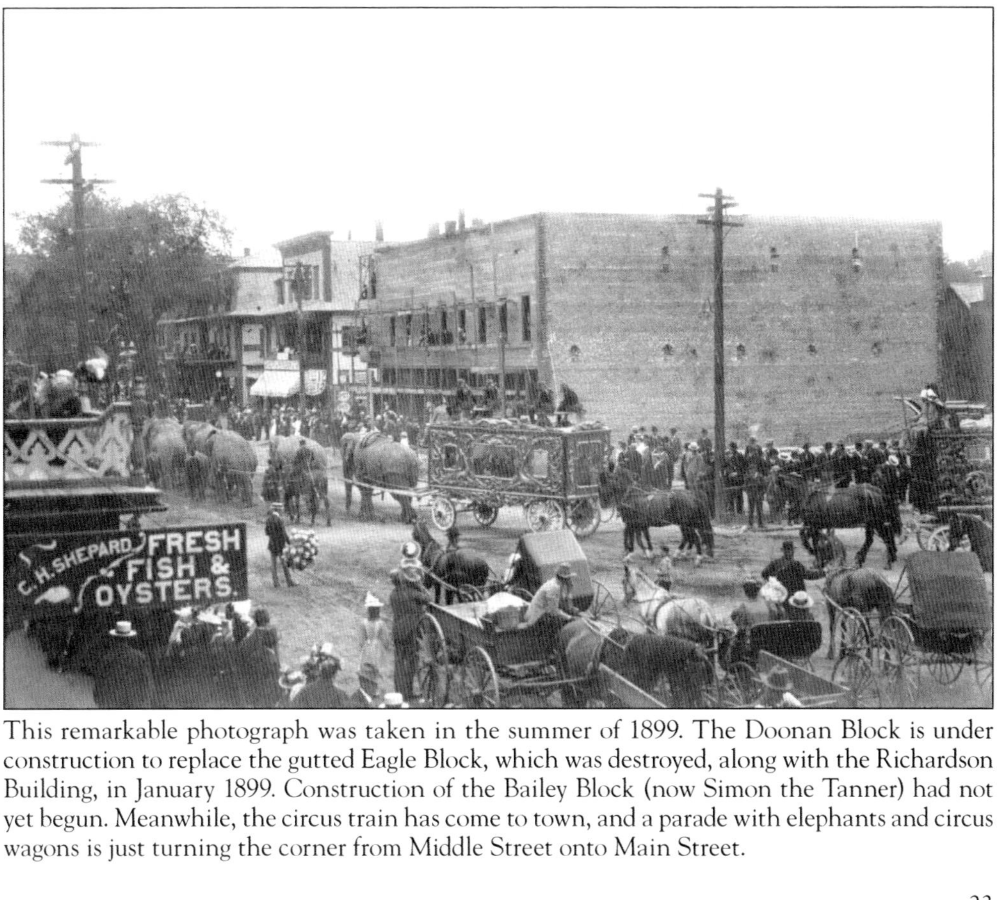

This remarkable photograph was taken in the summer of 1899. The Doonan Block is under construction to replace the gutted Eagle Block, which was destroyed, along with the Richardson Building, in January 1899. Construction of the Bailey Block (now Simon the Tanner) had not yet begun. Meanwhile, the circus train has come to town, and a parade with elephants and circus wagons is just turning the corner from Middle Street onto Main Street.

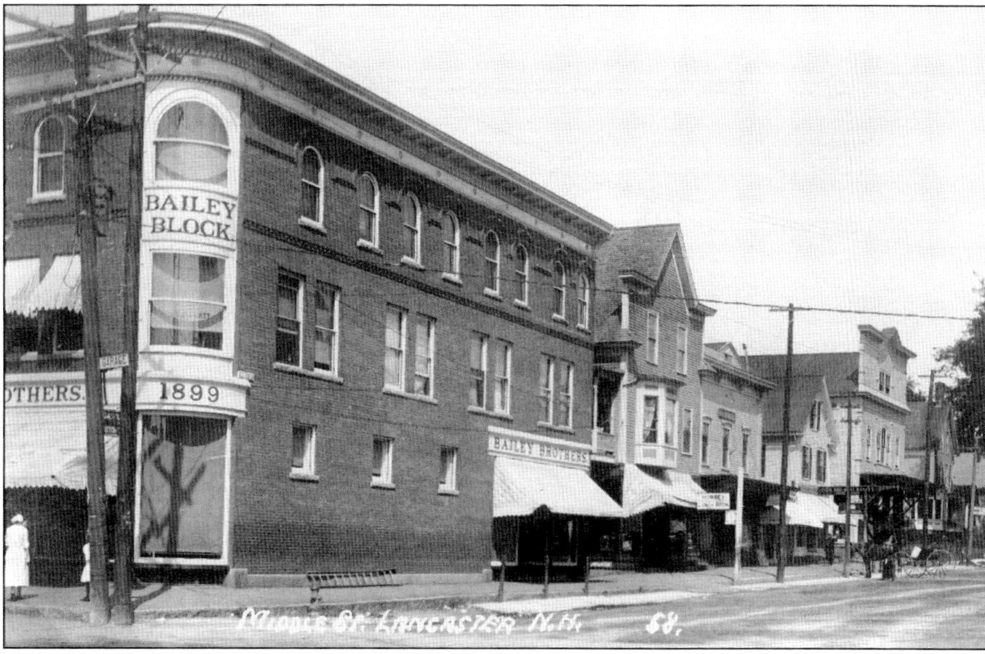

Pictured is the corner of Main and Middle Streets in 1900 and the new Baily block, which replaced the Richardson building after it was destroyed by fire (see the bottom photograph on page 23).

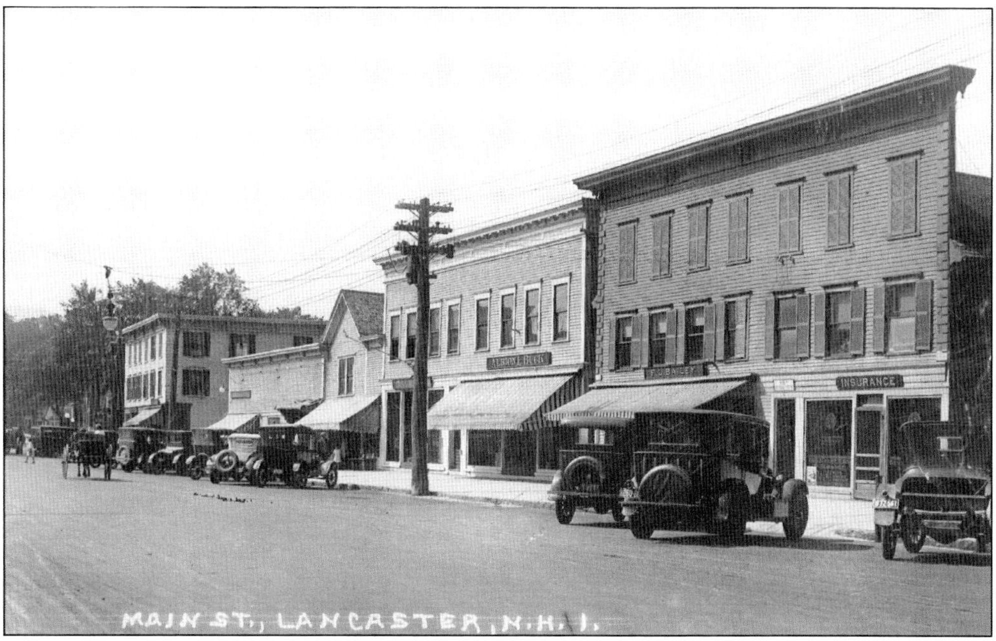

The west side of Main Street is seen here in the early 1920s. This view remained pretty much the same until 1996, when a fire destroyed the buildings in the center.

The east side of Main Street is seen in this photograph looking south from Bunker Hill Street in 1878, before the first of many fires that would devastate this side of the street.

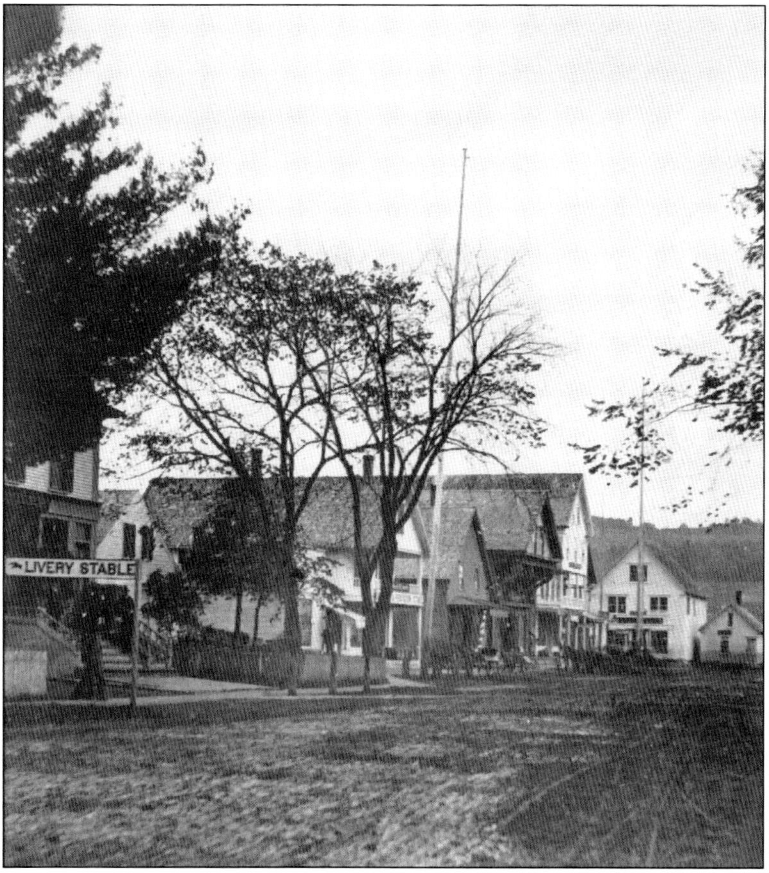

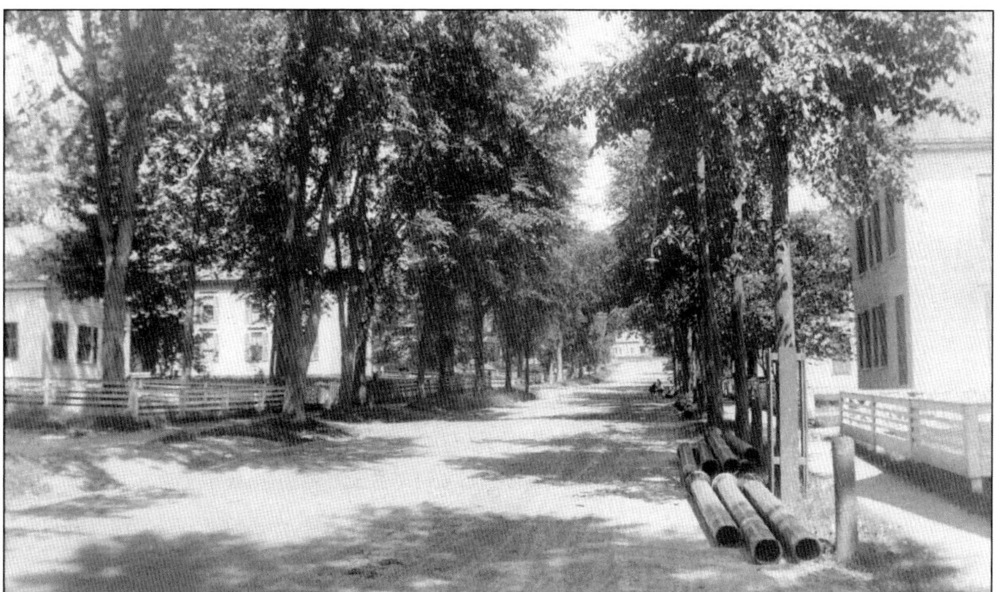

This photograph looks from Main Street up Middle Street as far as Wesson Street in the early 1890s. It appears that construction of water mains is underway.

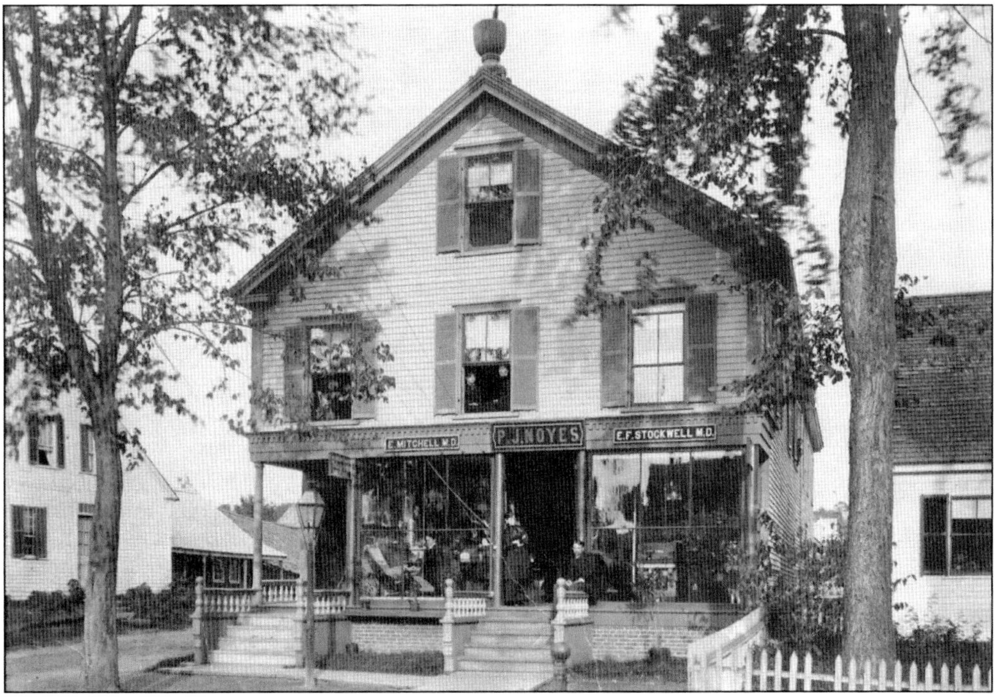

Pharmacist Parker J., or P.J., Noyes came to Lancaster in 1868 and developed a thriving business that employed 15 people by 1888. He developed the process by which a sugar coating could be put on the outside of pills and had the Thompson Manufacturing Company produce the equipment. The P.J. Noyes Company continues to produce pharmaceuticals in Lancaster to this day, now in a modern facility. Noyes's Main Street building is seen here in the 1880s. Dr. Ezra Mitchell and Dr. Emmans Stockwell had their offices above the store.

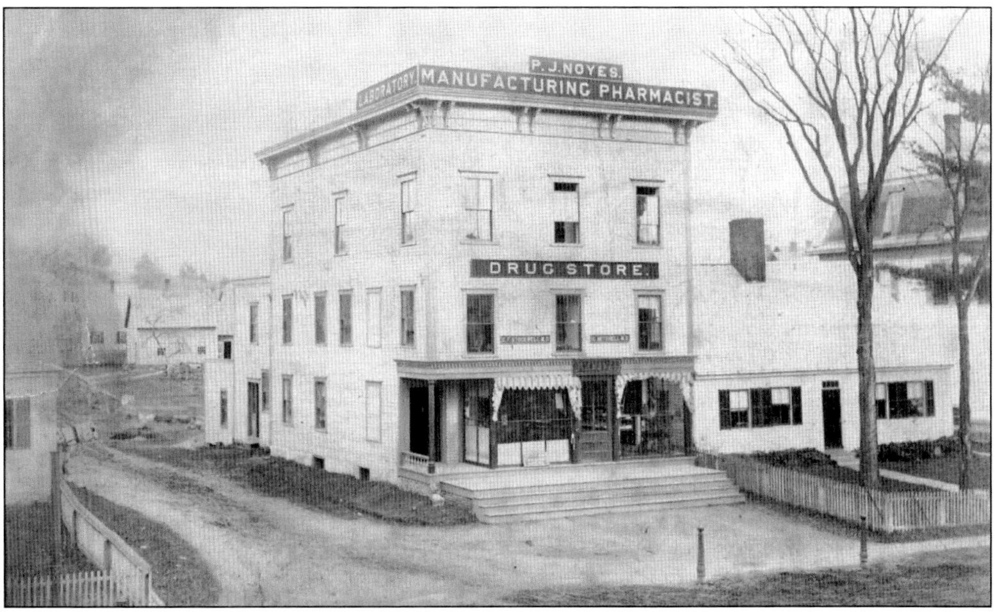

The P.J. Noyes Building, on the corner of Main and Bunker Hill Streets, is seen here after the addition of a third story but before the addition of the ell.

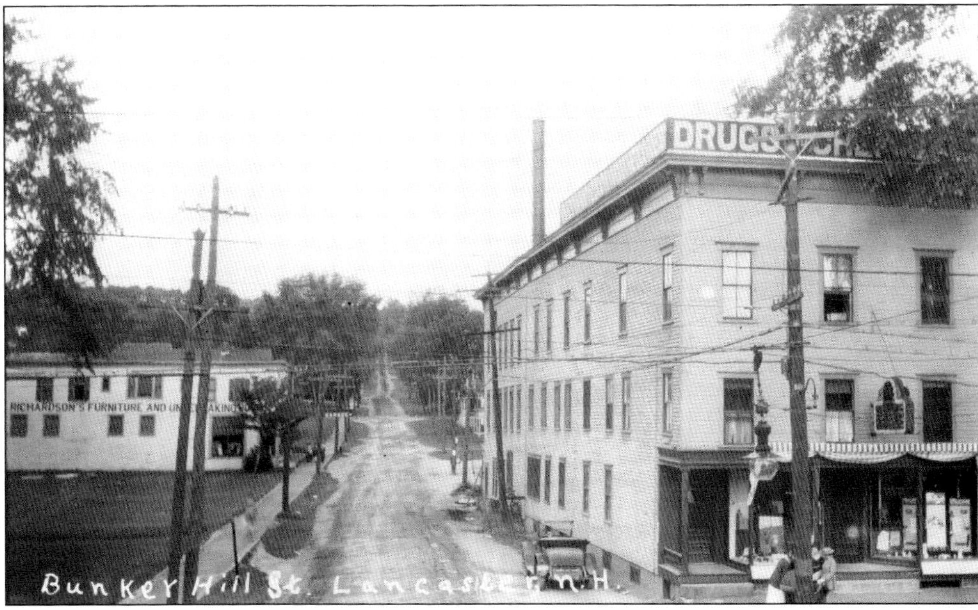

Bunker Hill Street is seen here from Main Street around 1920. In the lower right corner, behind the power pole, a group of women are gathered around a baby in a carriage.

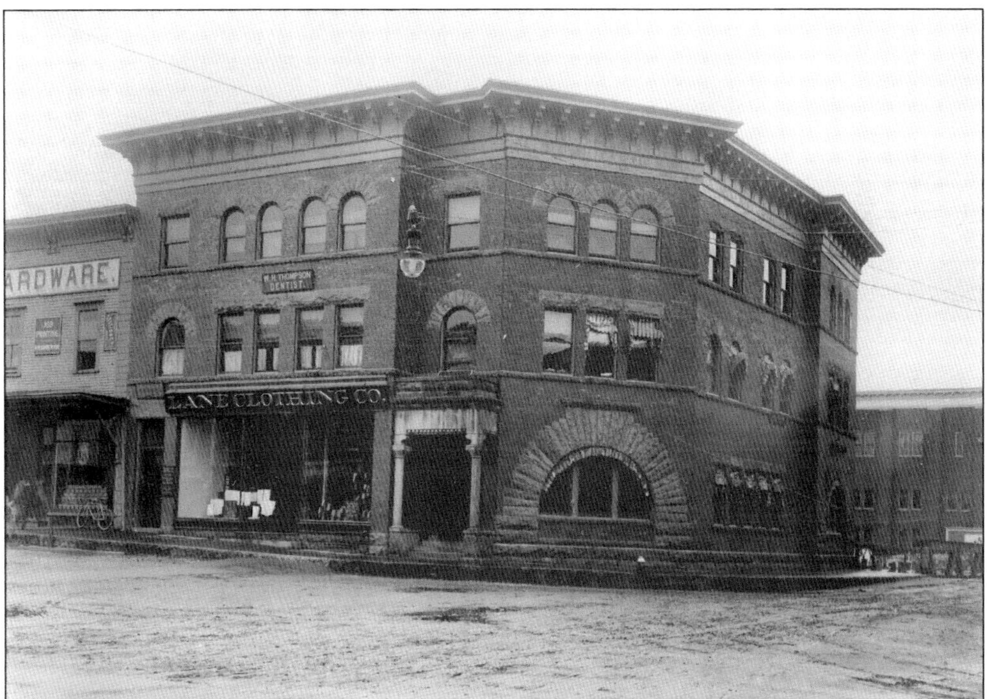

The Lancaster National Bank building, at Main and Middle Streets, is seen here during mud season in 1910.

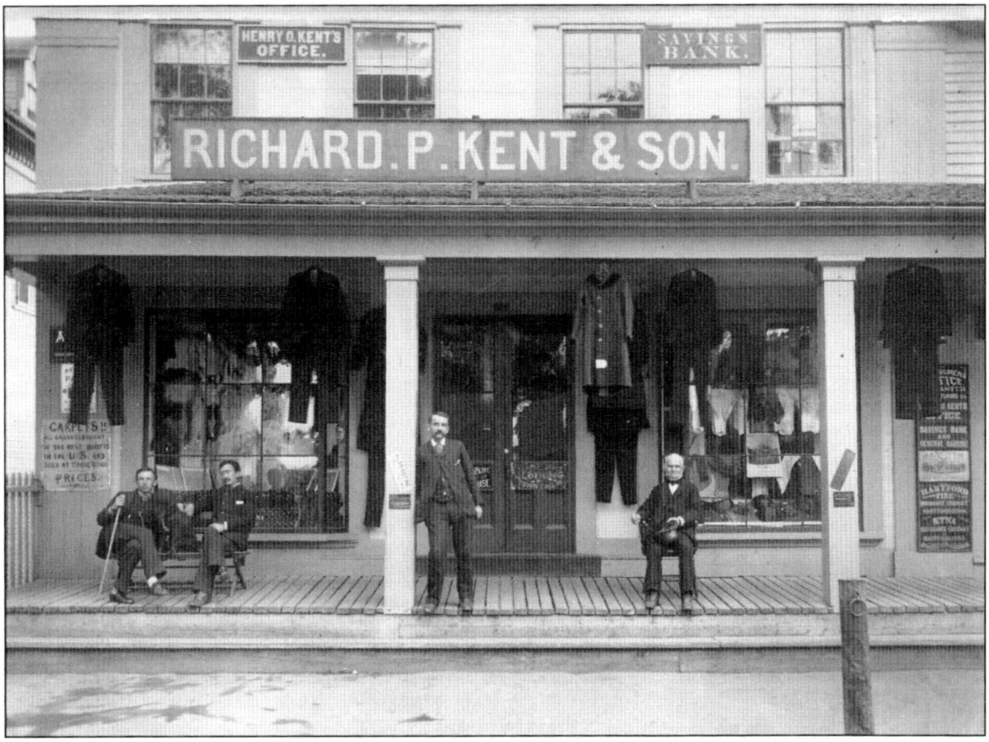

The Richard P. Kent & Son general store is seen here in the 1880s. In front of the store are, from left to right, Fielding Smith, Fred Streeter, Edward R. Kent, and Richard P. Kent.

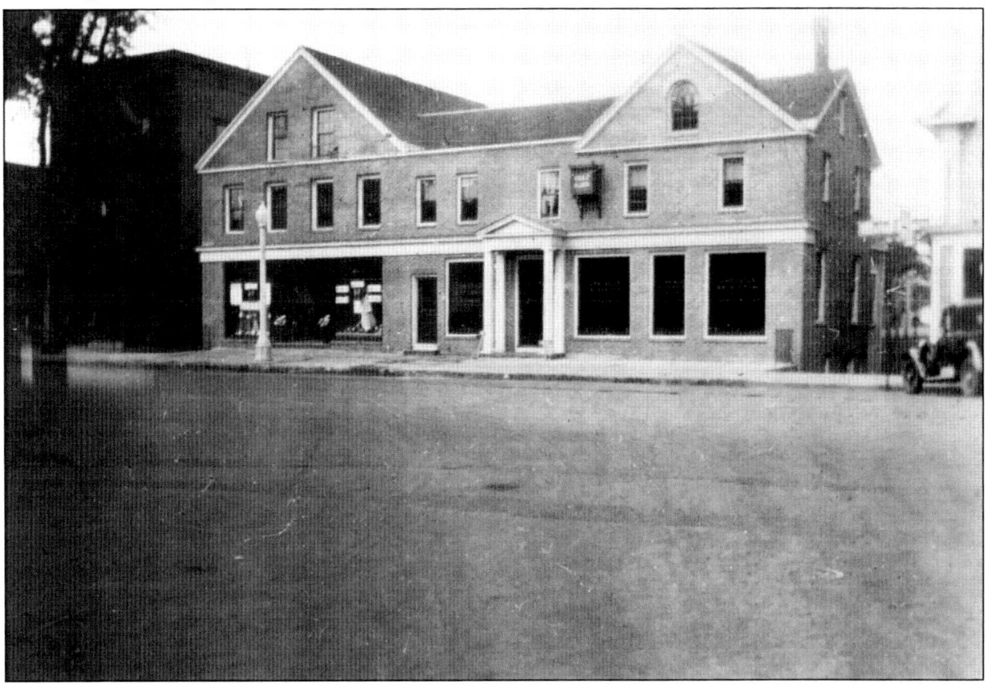
The Kent Building is seen here, newly faced with brick in the 1920s. A savings bank is still on the second floor. This building was destroyed by fire on February 9, 1941.

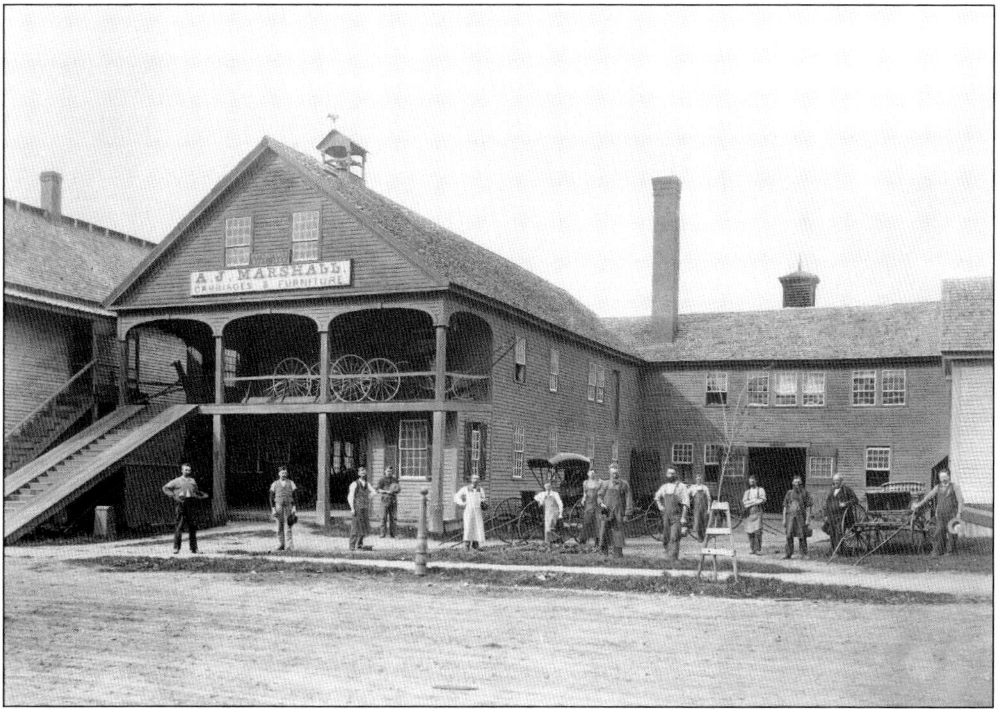

Beginning in 1848 when Anderson J. Marshall (1819–1883) established a carriage shop on Middle Street, this building was the place to buy a new wagon or sleigh or have a carriage painted. After a fire in 1852, business continued in rebuilt quarters, seen here in the 1870s. The following advertisement was in the *Coös Republican* on May 10, 1859: "A.J. Marshall is building wagons of all descriptions, as well as sofas, chairs, secretaries, tables, bedsteads, bureaus, chamber sets, also coffins readymade."

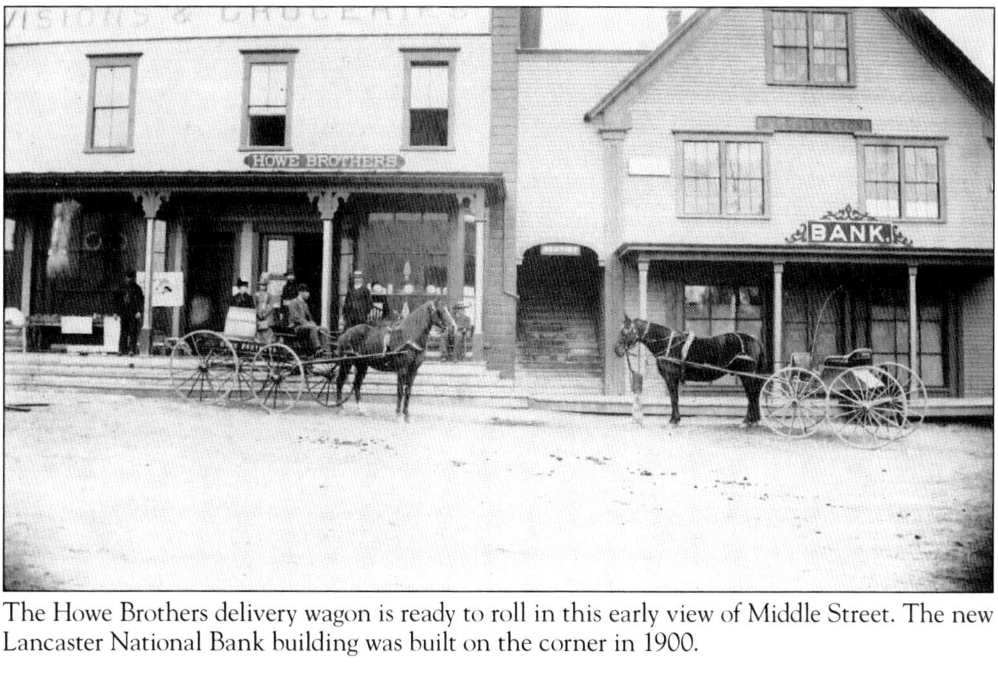

The Howe Brothers delivery wagon is ready to roll in this early view of Middle Street. The new Lancaster National Bank building was built on the corner in 1900.

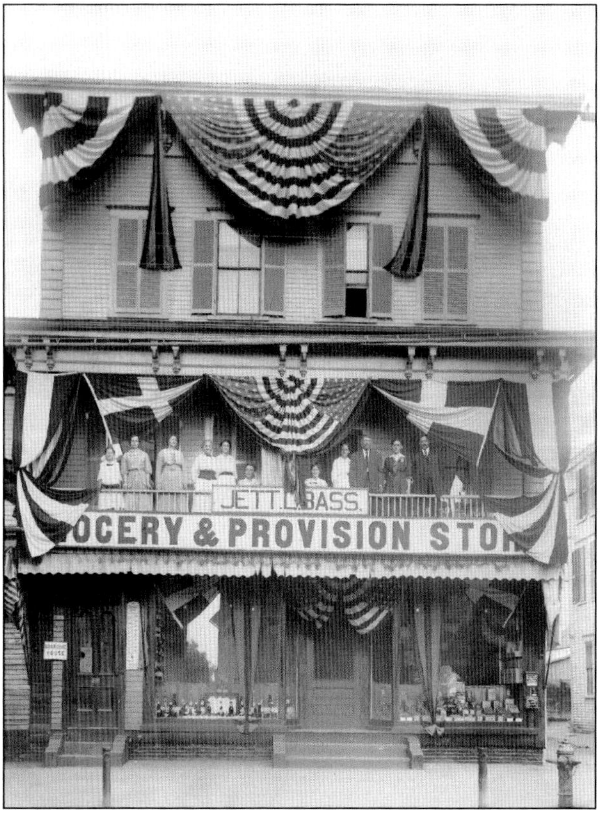

Spectators above the Jett L. Bass grocery await the parade during the 150th anniversary of Lancaster, on July 12, 1914.

Though the surrounding buildings are now gone, the versatile building below still remains on the west side of Main Street. In the 1890s, it housed Bailey Brothers, Rosebrook Photography Studio, and Hatch Jewelry. More recently, it has been home to Old Susannah's, the Double SS Restaurant, and the Moonbeam Café.

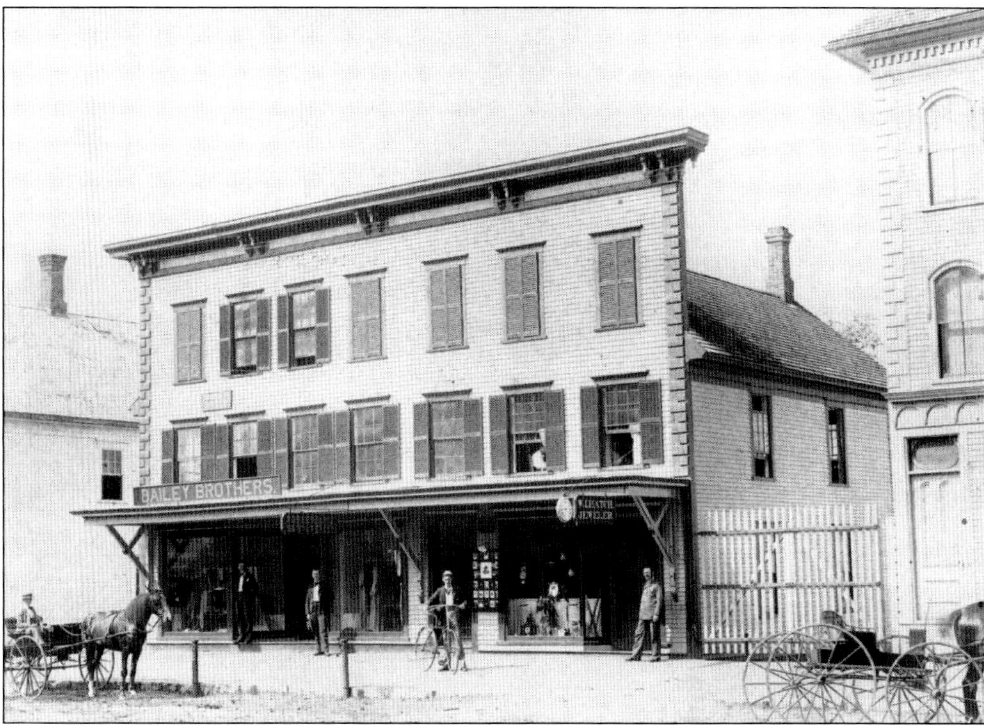

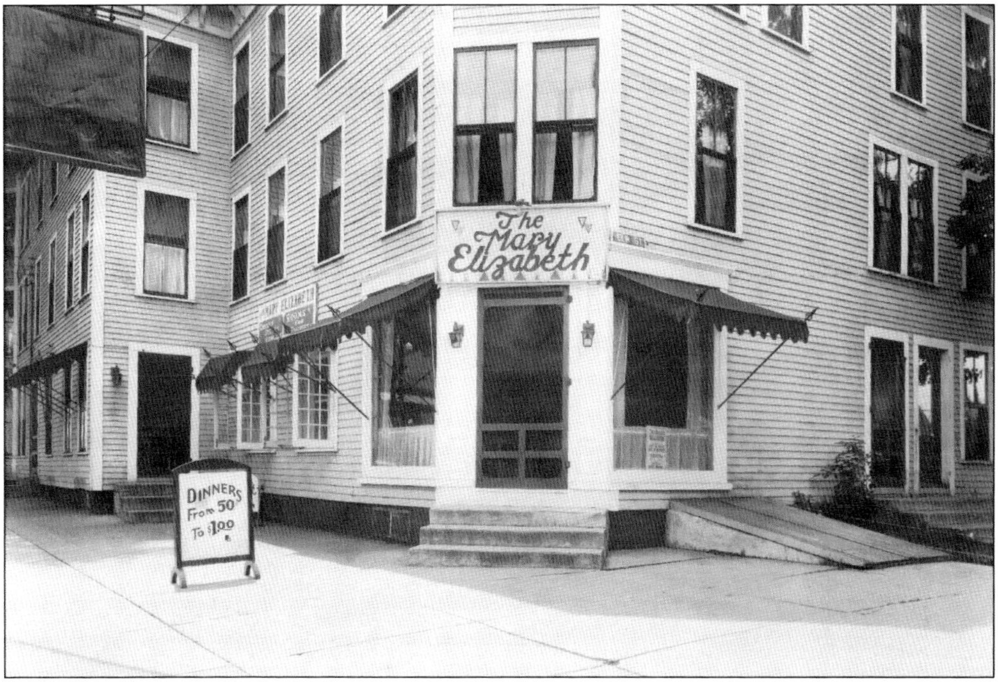

The Mary Elizabeth Tea Room, opened in 1927 and run by sisters Alice and Maude Monahan, was at the corner of Main and Elm Streets in the building now referred to as the Monahan Block.

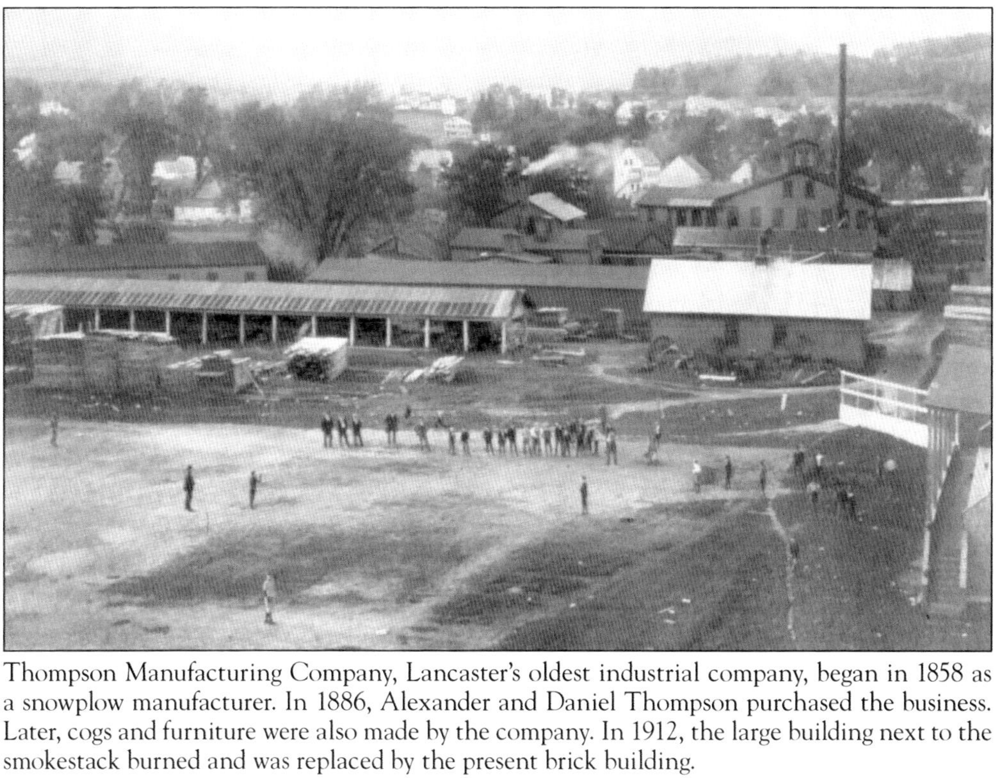

Thompson Manufacturing Company, Lancaster's oldest industrial company, began in 1858 as a snowplow manufacturer. In 1886, Alexander and Daniel Thompson purchased the business. Later, cogs and furniture were also made by the company. In 1912, the large building next to the smokestack burned and was replaced by the present brick building.

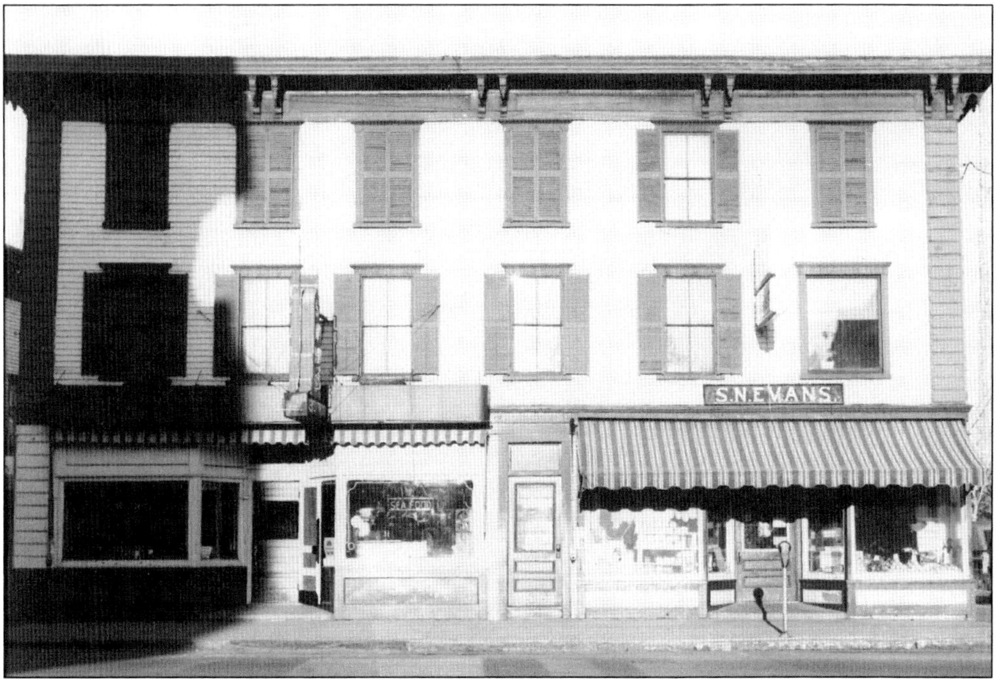

The S.N. Evans store, with its penny candy counter, was a popular stop for generations of local schoolchildren. (Courtesy of Lawrence "Gomer" Powell.)

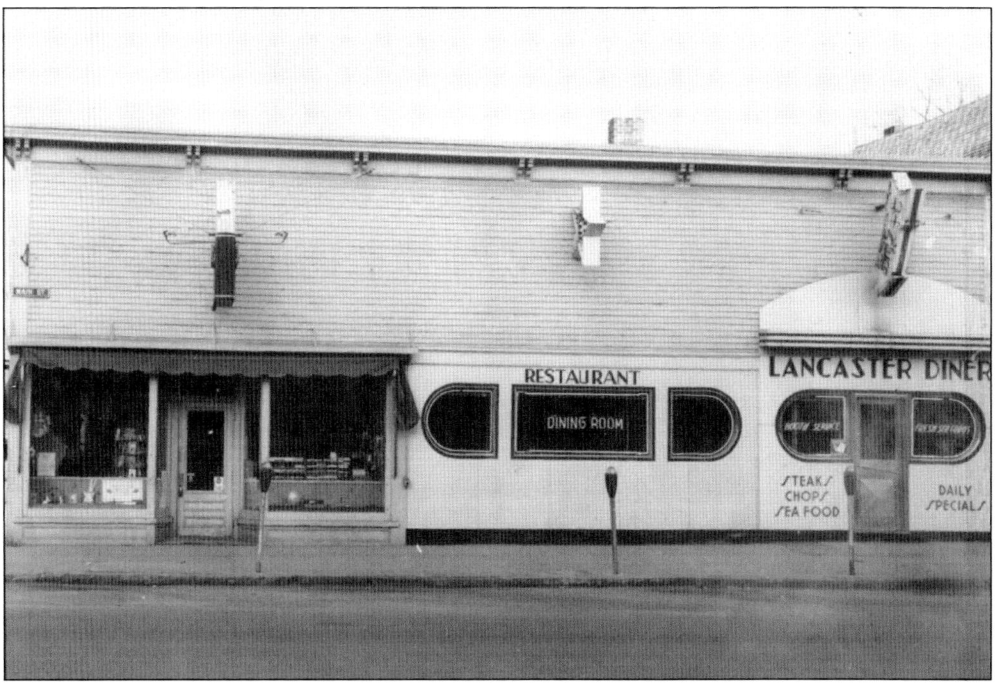

The Lancaster Diner, in the heart of the business district on Main Street, became a popular gathering place for friends, who would gather there over a cup of coffee or a delicious meal until it burned down in the June 10, 1996, fire. It remains today merely as a fond memory among its former customers. (Courtesy of Lawrence "Gomer" Powell.)

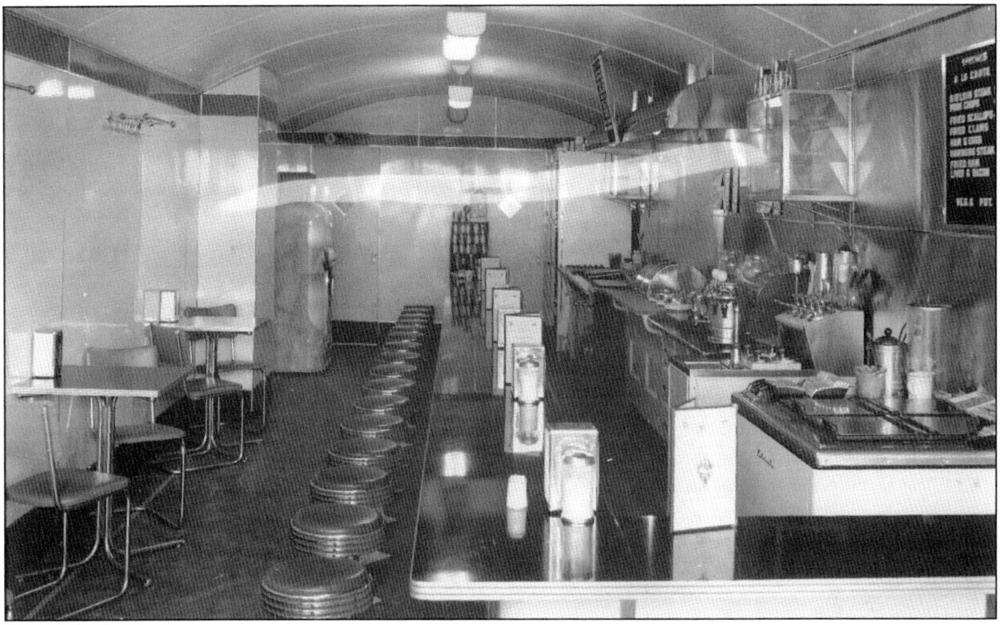

Walter Snell and Harvey Hicks built the Lancaster Diner in the mid-1940s between Eddie Dumont's barbershop and Mauro Busi's Lancaster Fruit Company. Soon, after Dumont moved his barbershop to a new building, a dining room was added to the diner. It is seen here just before opening for the day.

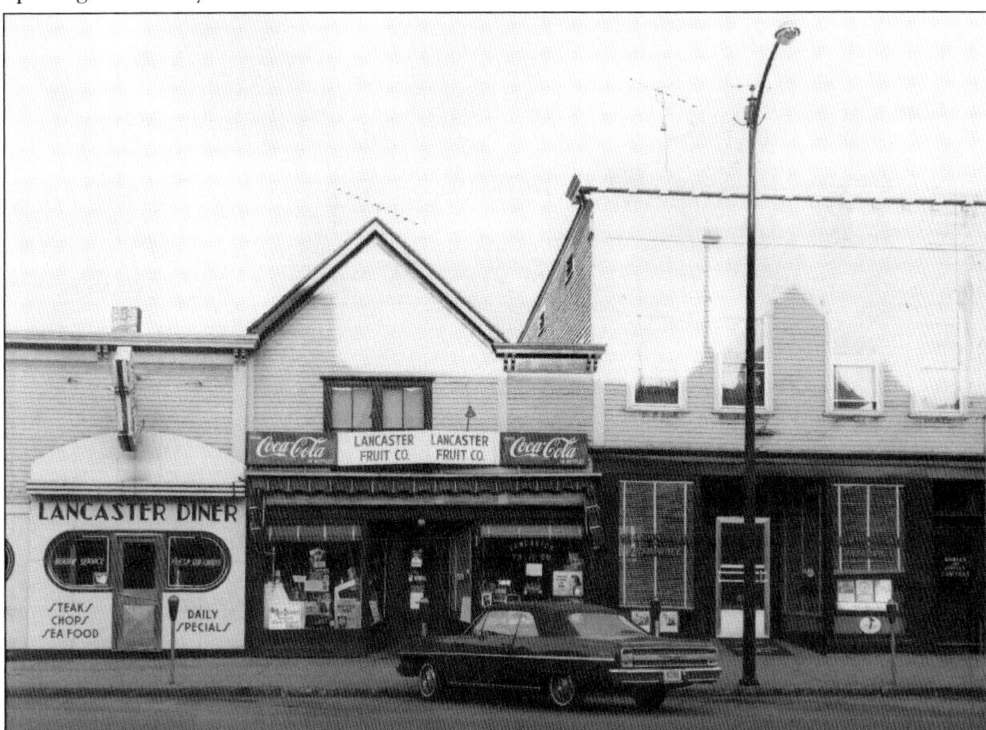

Gone but not forgotten, the Lancaster Diner and Mauro Busi's Lancaster Fruit Company were fixtures on Main Street for decades. (Courtesy of Lawrence "Gomer" Powell.)

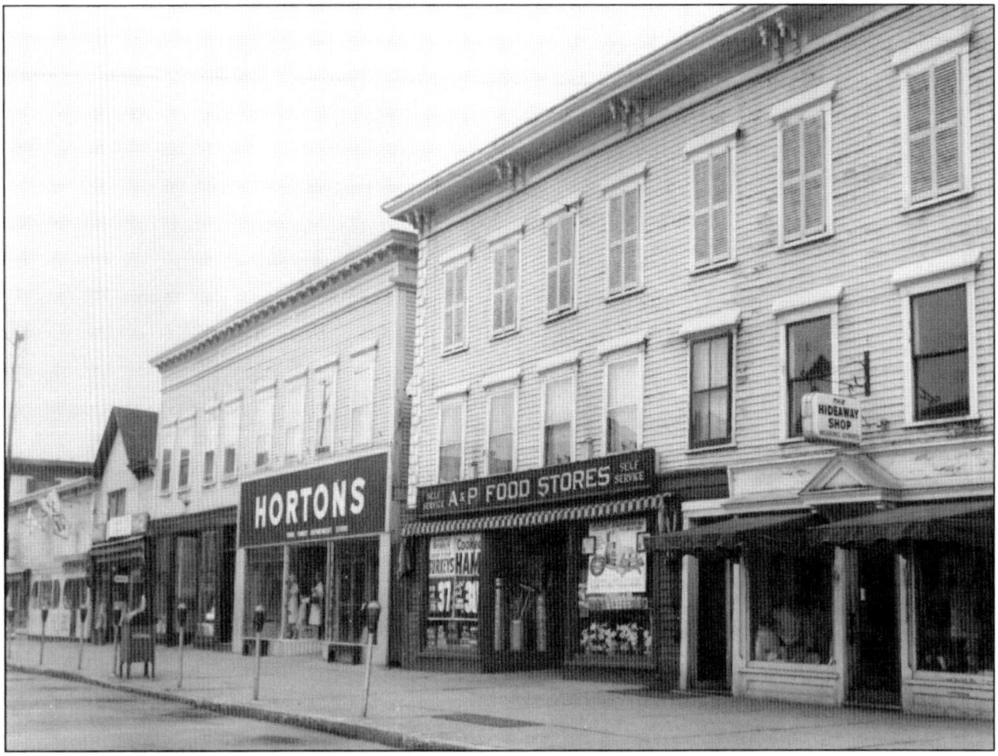

The west side of Main Street, above the Lancaster Diner, is seen here in the 1960s. (Courtesy of Lawrence "Gomer" Powell.)

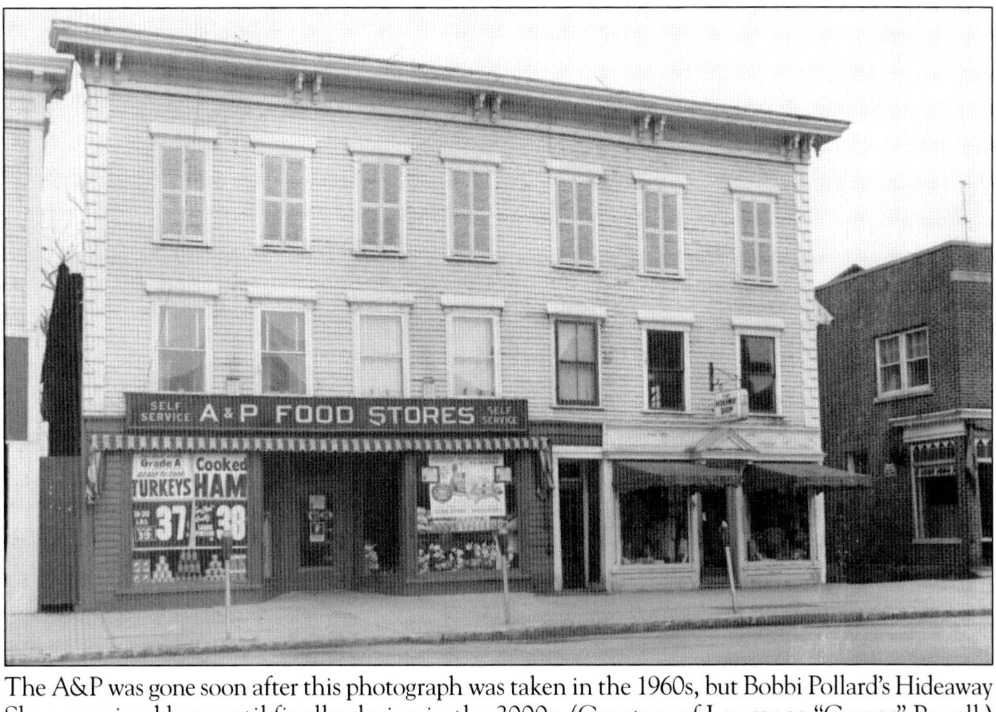

The A&P was gone soon after this photograph was taken in the 1960s, but Bobbi Pollard's Hideaway Shop remained here until finally closing in the 2000s. (Courtesy of Lawrence "Gomer" Powell.)

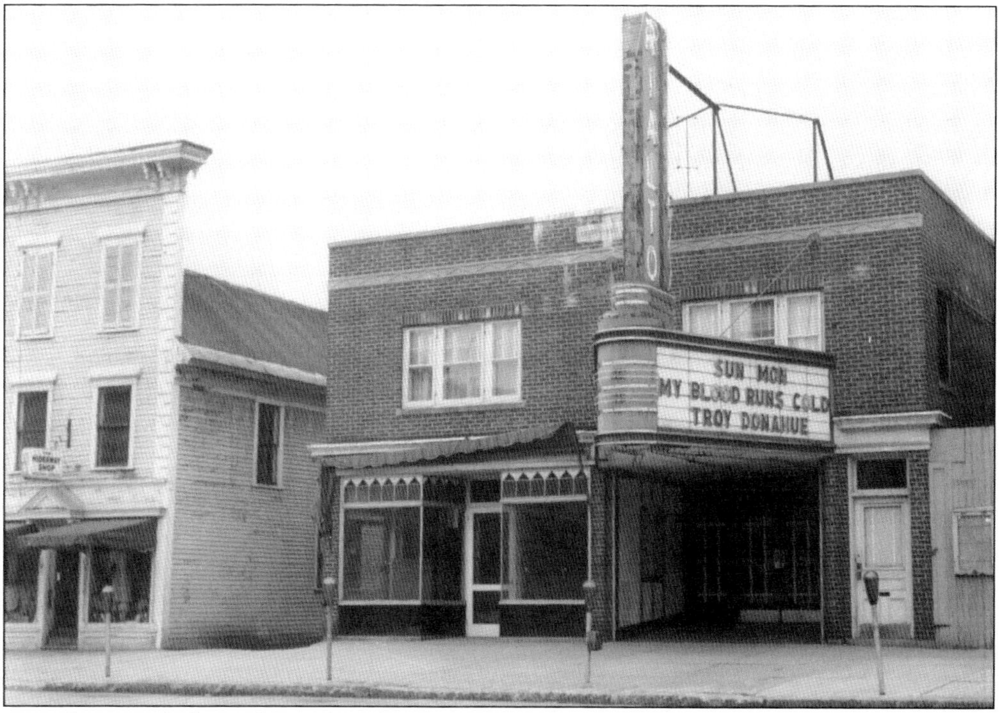

This photograph shows the Rialto Theater, on Main Street, when it was showing *My Blood Runs Cold*, starring Troy Donahue. (Courtesy of Lawrence "Gomer" Powell.)

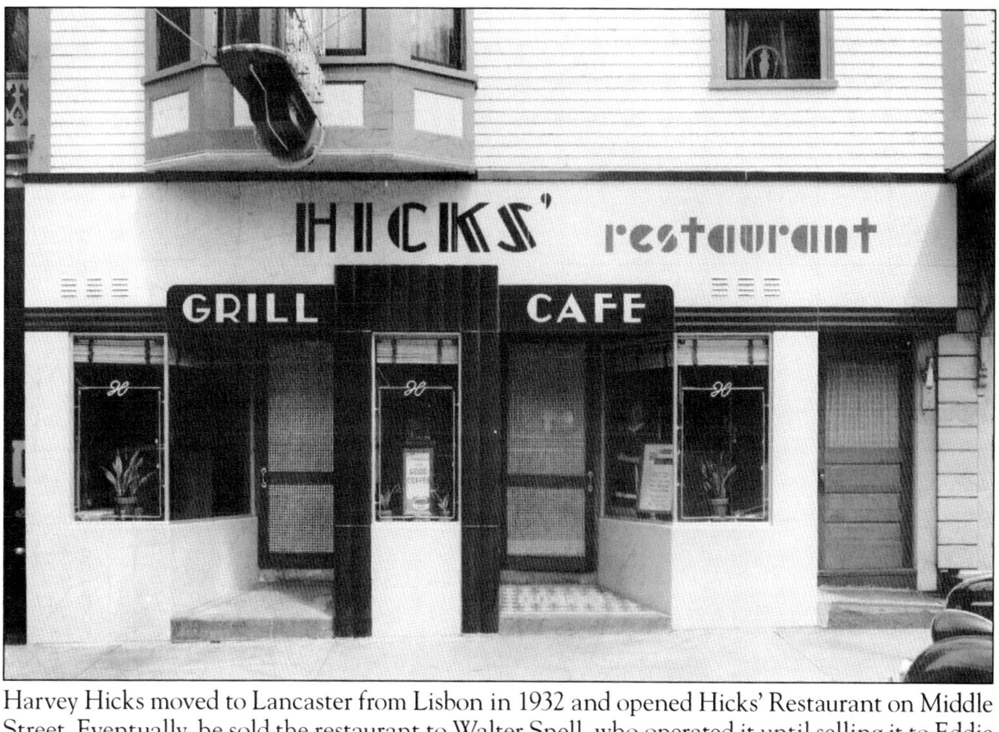

Harvey Hicks moved to Lancaster from Lisbon in 1932 and opened Hicks' Restaurant on Middle Street. Eventually, he sold the restaurant to Walter Snell, who operated it until selling it to Eddie Dorr and friends in 1946.

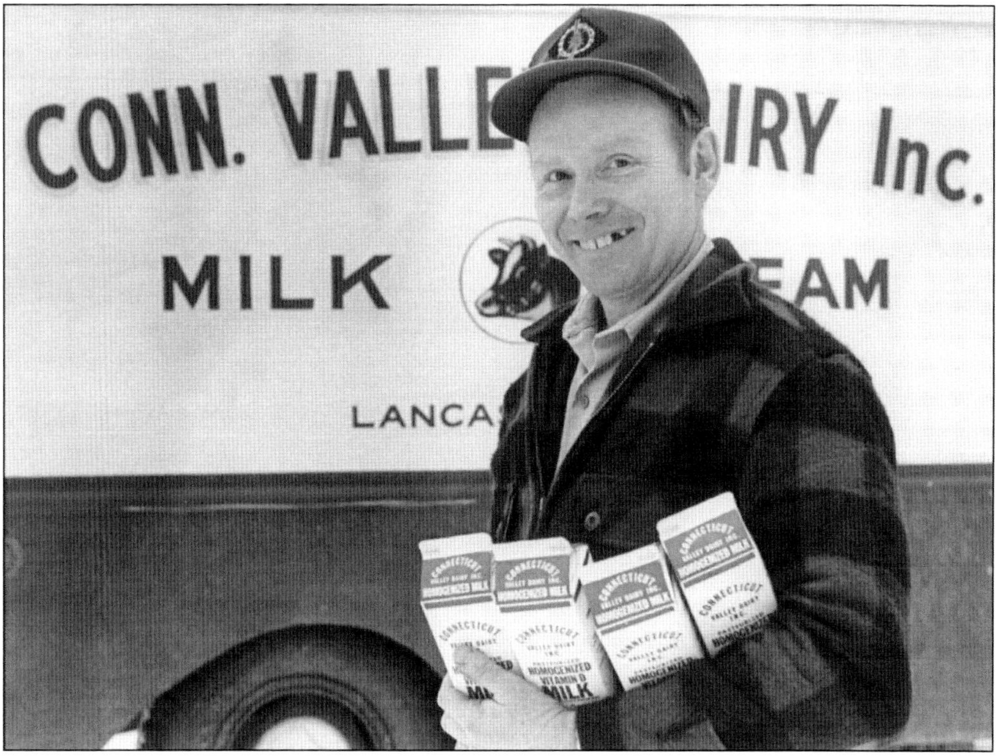

Who could resist Connecticut Valley Dairy's smiling milkman? The company had a creamery where the Rite Aid is today. (Courtesy of Lawrence "Gomer" Powell.)

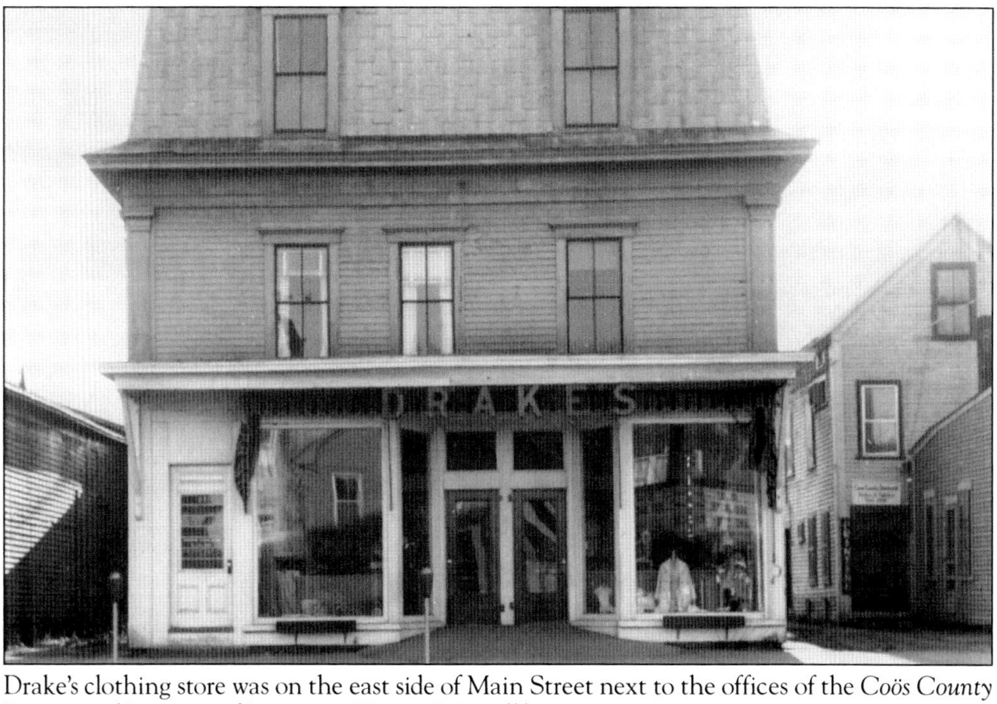

Drake's clothing store was on the east side of Main Street next to the offices of the *Coös County Democrat*. (Courtesy of Lawrence "Gomer" Powell.)

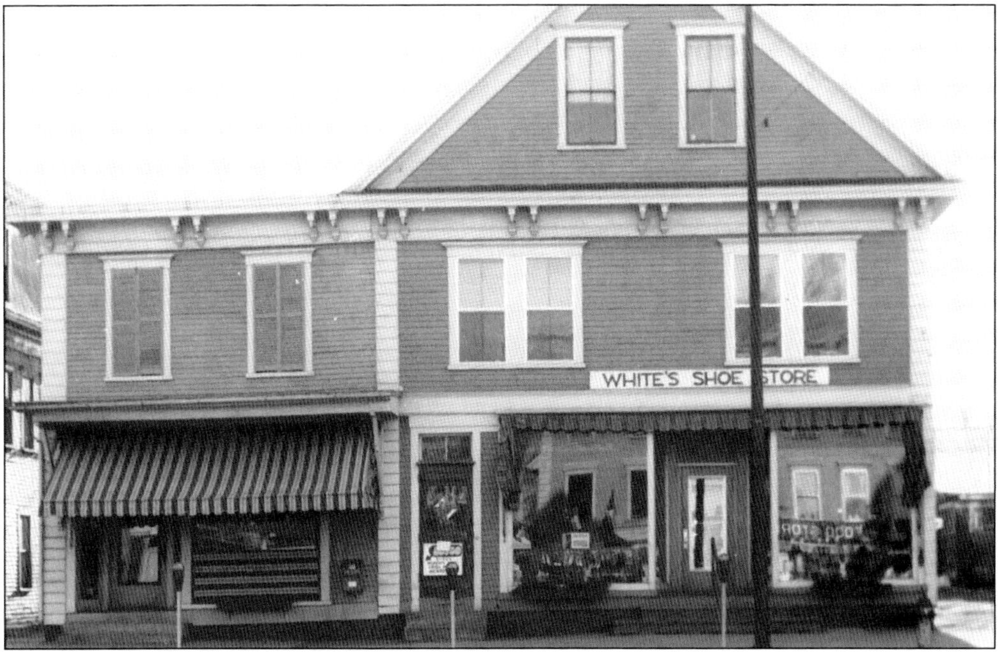

Recently damaged by fire, this building, which housed Vail's Jewelry and White's Shoe Store in the 1960s, was last home to Tri-County Cap and Heart, Hearth and Home. It will soon get a new lease on life. (Courtesy of Lawrence "Gomer" Powell.)

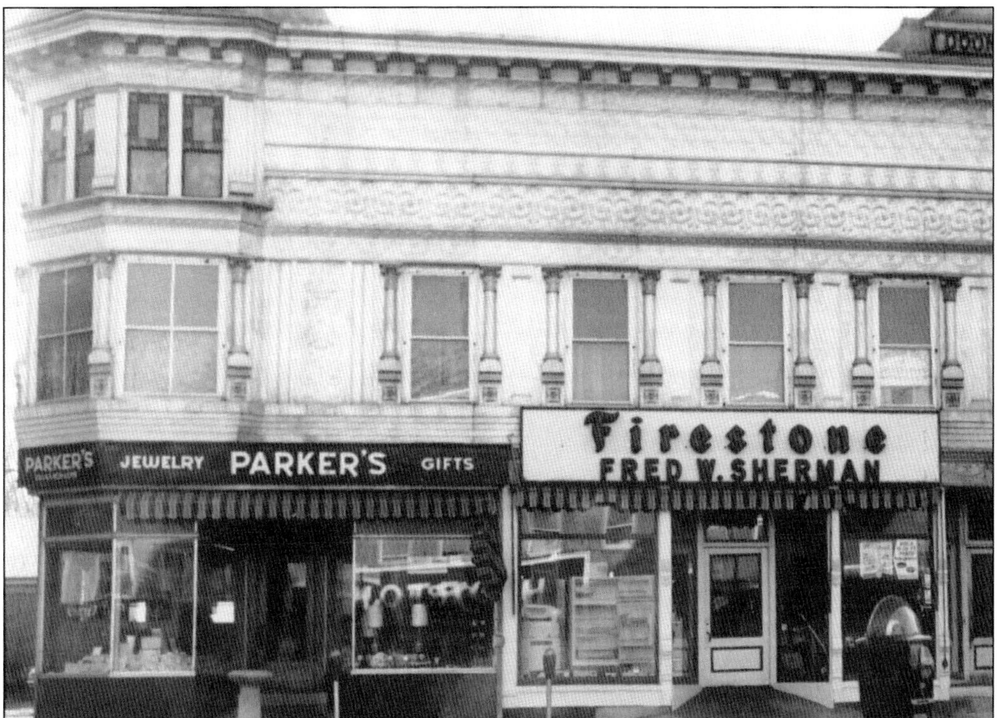

Surviving until 2013, Parker's Jewelry filled a special niche both in this location and in the former P.J. Noyes Building. (Courtesy of Lawrence "Gomer" Powell.)

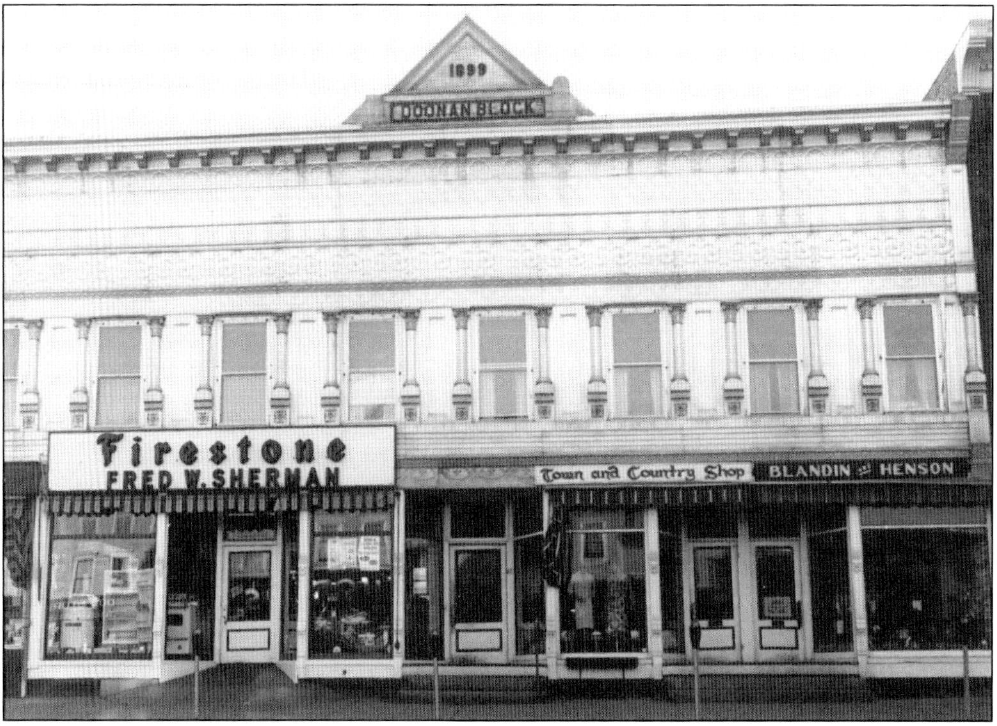

Built to replace the Eagle Block, which was gutted in the fire of 1899, the Doonan Block still stands today. It is seen here in the early 1960s. (Courtesy of Lawrence "Gomer" Powell.)

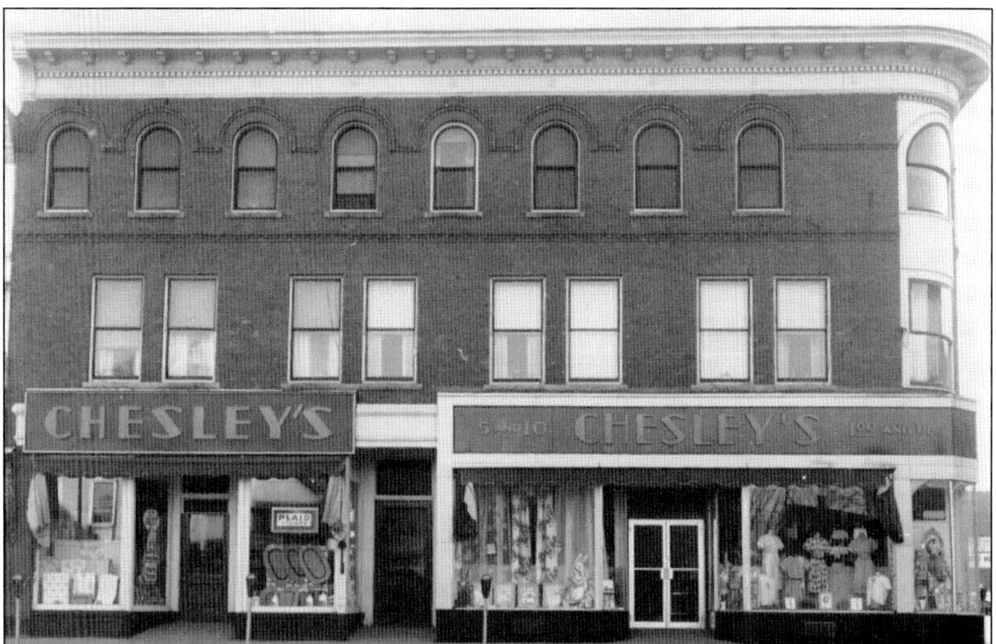

Built in 1899 after the destruction of the Richardson Building, the Bailey Block was built in 1899. Through the years, it has been home to Piche's, Chesley's, and, now, Simon the Tanner. (Courtesy of Lawrence "Gomer" Powell.)

Three

Lodging and Entertainment

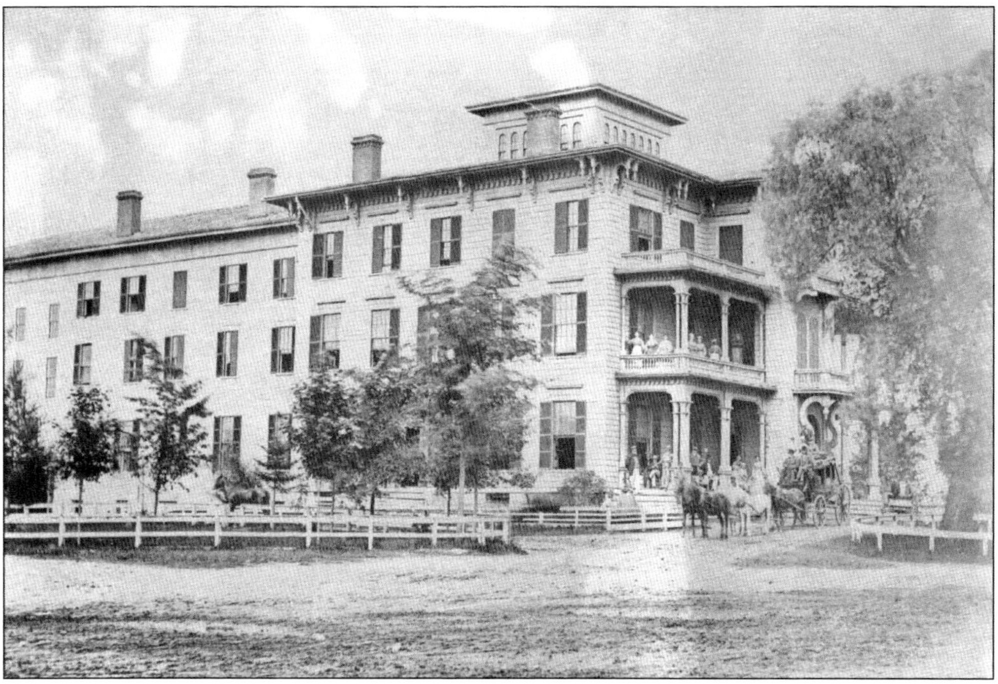

On August 4, 1858, the first Lancaster House was opened for guests. It was built with funds paid to the town by the Atlantic & St. Lawrence Railroad after its failure to build a railroad through Lancaster, in accordance with an agreement to that effect. This building burned on September 28, 1878, with damages to the building and furniture totaling around $30,000. Unfortunately, it only had $2,500 in insurance.

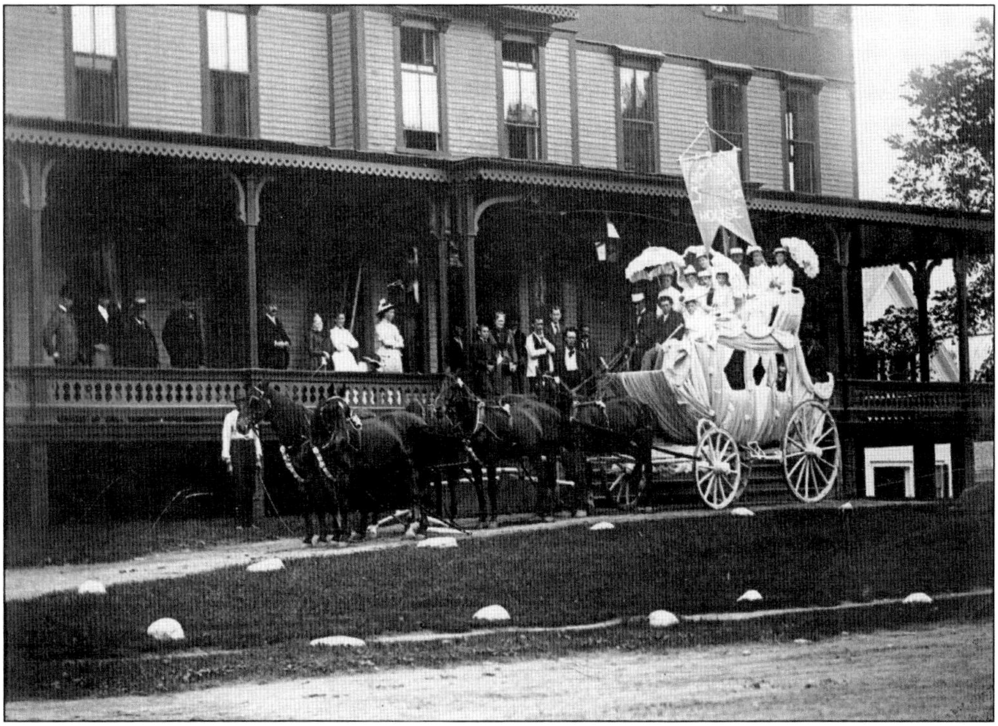

Pausing in front of the second Lancaster House and drawn by six horses, the Lancaster House coach is ready for the 1896 coaching parade.

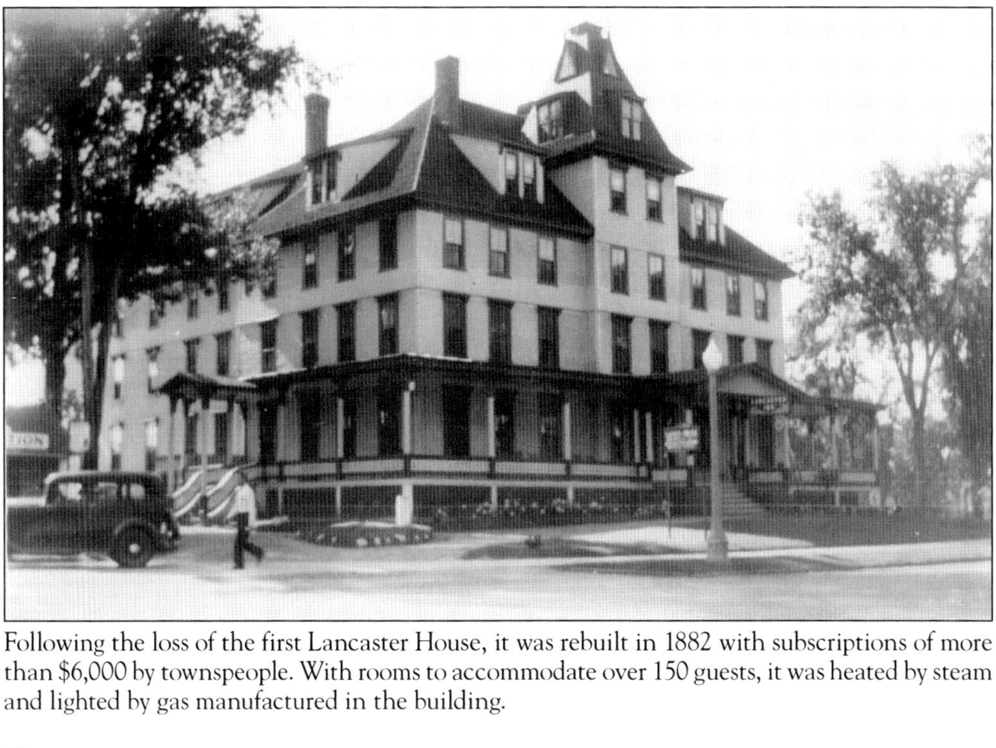

Following the loss of the first Lancaster House, it was rebuilt in 1882 with subscriptions of more than $6,000 by townspeople. With rooms to accommodate over 150 guests, it was heated by steam and lighted by gas manufactured in the building.

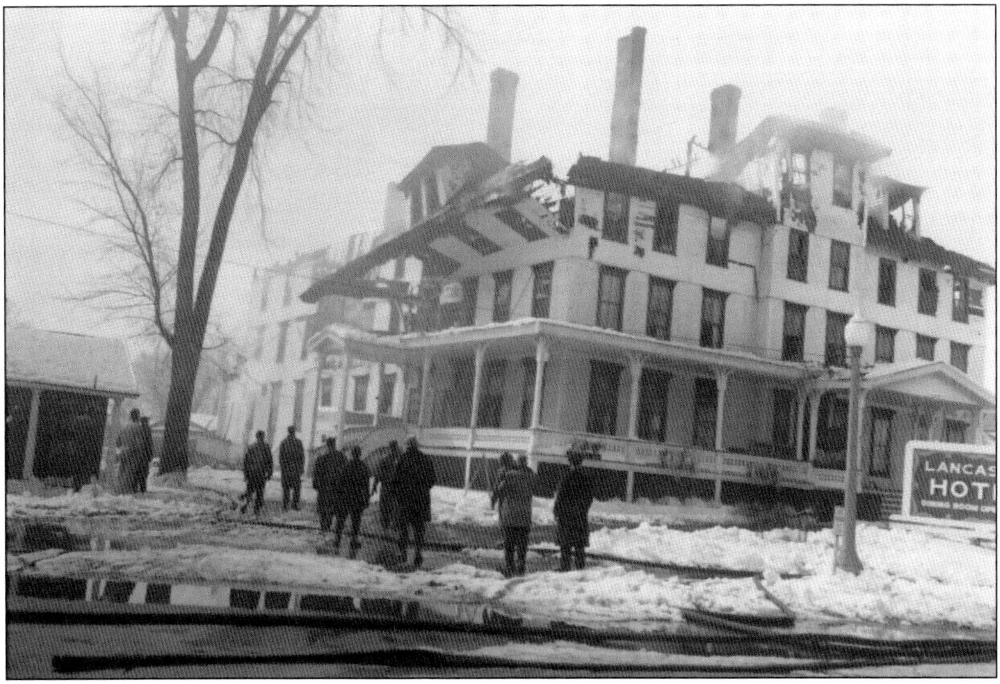

The second Lancaster House burned in a fatal fire on March 31, 1954. Maurice Doucet, a leather salesman from Bedford, New Hampshire, died of smoke inhalation. Owner Fred Pahud was able to get 27 guests to safety in temperatures of 10 degrees below zero. He reported an $80,000 loss, and he only had $37,000 in insurance. The site was later purchased by the McLaughlin family of Lunenburg, Vermont, who built the Lancaster Motor Inn, which still stands there today.

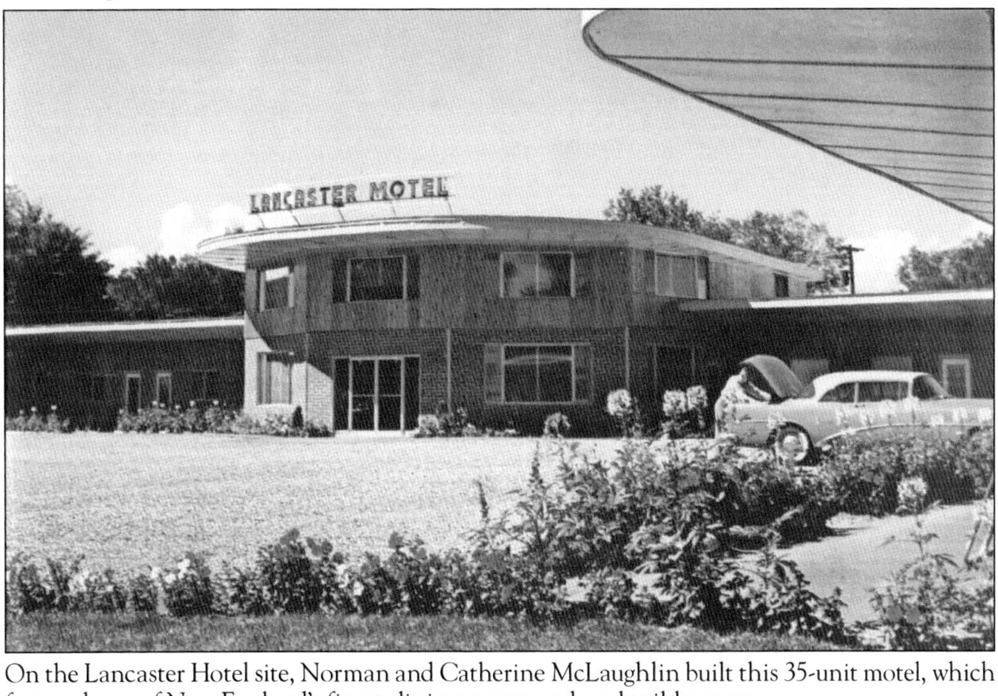

On the Lancaster Hotel site, Norman and Catherine McLaughlin built this 35-unit motel, which featured one of New England's finest dining rooms and cocktail lounges.

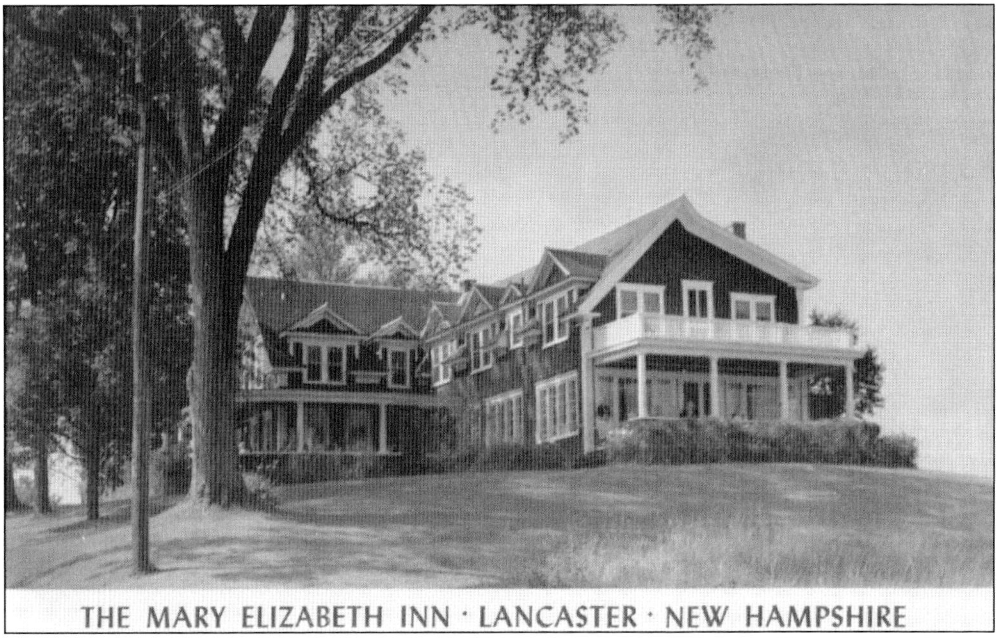

Adelaide Monahan operated the Mary Elizabeth Inn on Prospect Street for 65 years. The business eventually grew to include nine cabins, a motel, and a full restaurant in the inn itself. Her family home for 100 years, it was torn down, as stipulated in her will, in 1992.

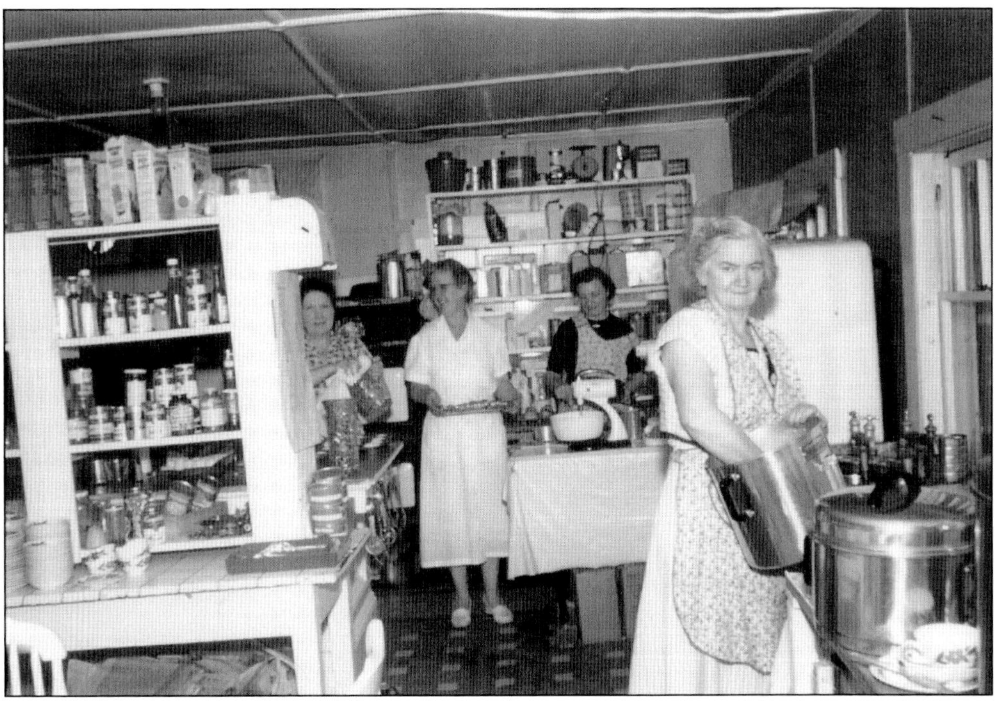

Adelaide Monahan (far left) and some of her staff pose in the kitchen of the Mary Elizabeth Inn in the late 1940s. In 1938, a complete roast chicken dinner cost $1, including dessert. A piece of apple or blueberry pie, gingerbread, or chocolate bread pudding was 15¢.

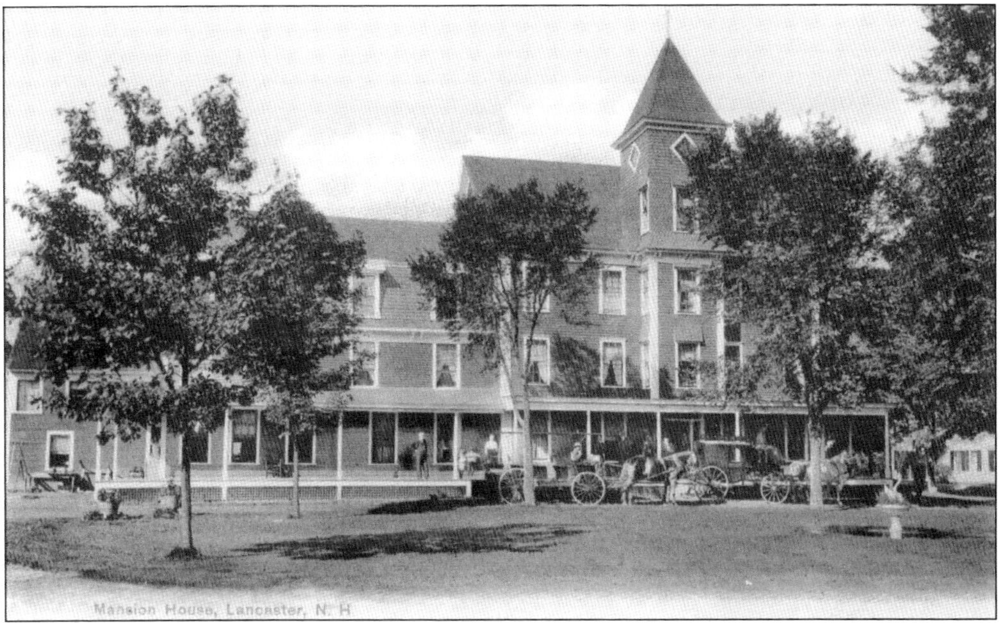

In the spring of 1872, John M. Hopkins bought the former residence of Gov. Jared Williams, on Elm Street, and fitted it up as a hotel by adding an ell to it. In 1889, the main building was raised up one story. The main portion of the building was built by Governor Williams in 1847. For many years, it was home to the Elms, a popular bar and restaurant. It was demolished in 2011.

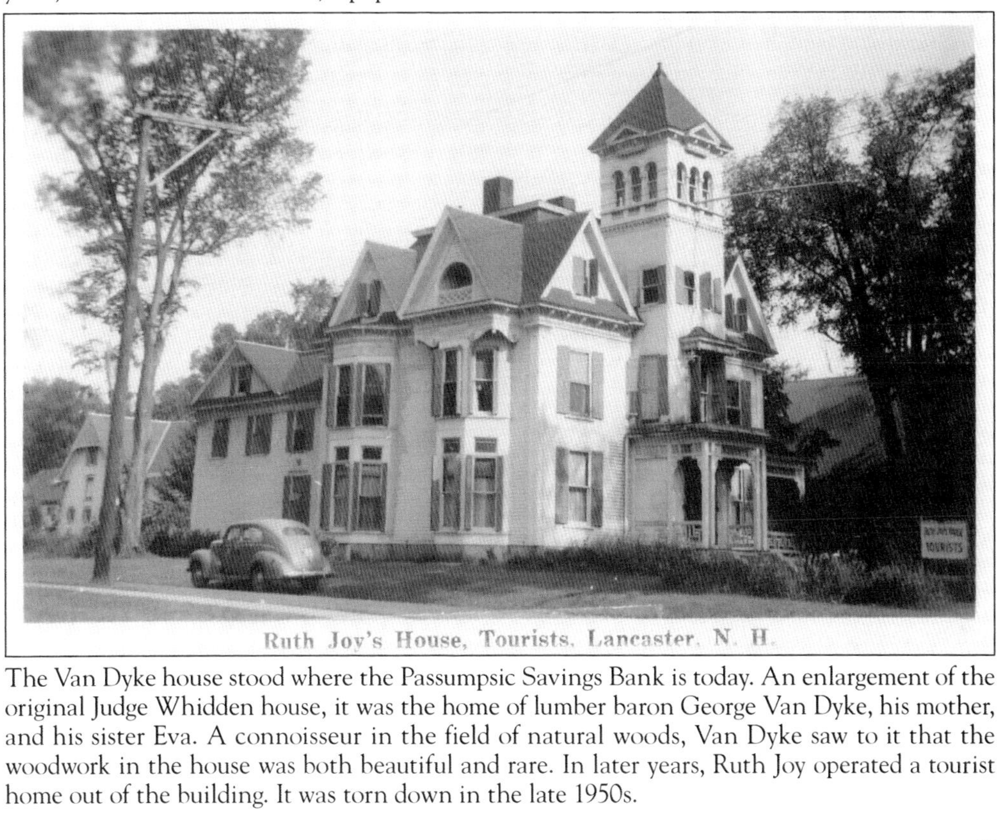

The Van Dyke house stood where the Passumpsic Savings Bank is today. An enlargement of the original Judge Whidden house, it was the home of lumber baron George Van Dyke, his mother, and his sister Eva. A connoisseur in the field of natural woods, Van Dyke saw to it that the woodwork in the house was both beautiful and rare. In later years, Ruth Joy operated a tourist home out of the building. It was torn down in the late 1950s.

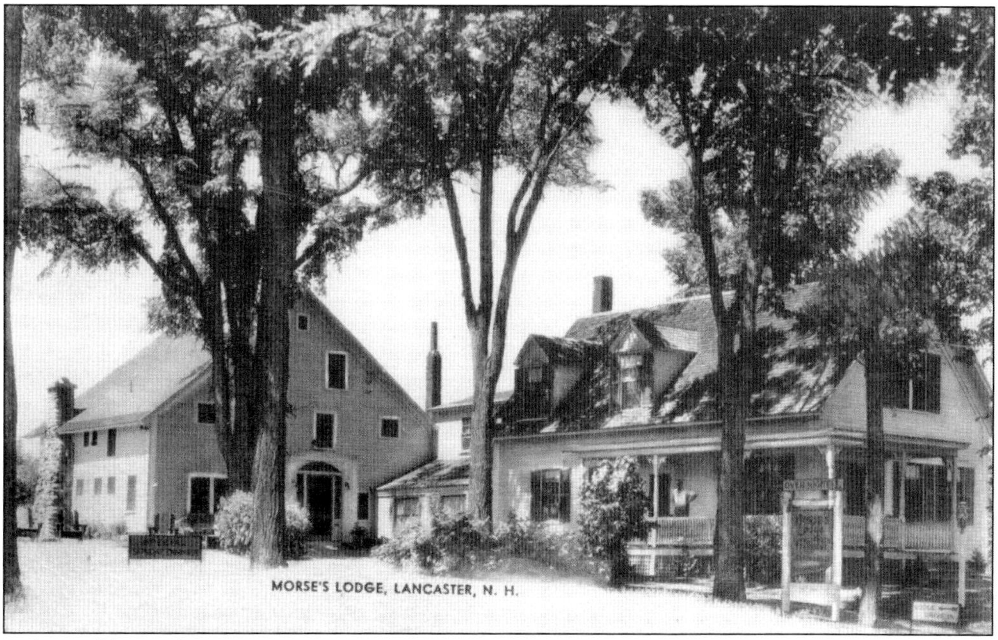

Fashioned from a barn in 1932, Morse's Lodge had comfortable rooms and wholesome entertainment in a completely informal atmosphere. They served excellent home-cooked food prepared by the genial hosts and their staff. Charles "Pop" Morse could humble the best bridge or cribbage player, trounce everyone on the croquet court, catch the most trout, and pick the most wild berries.

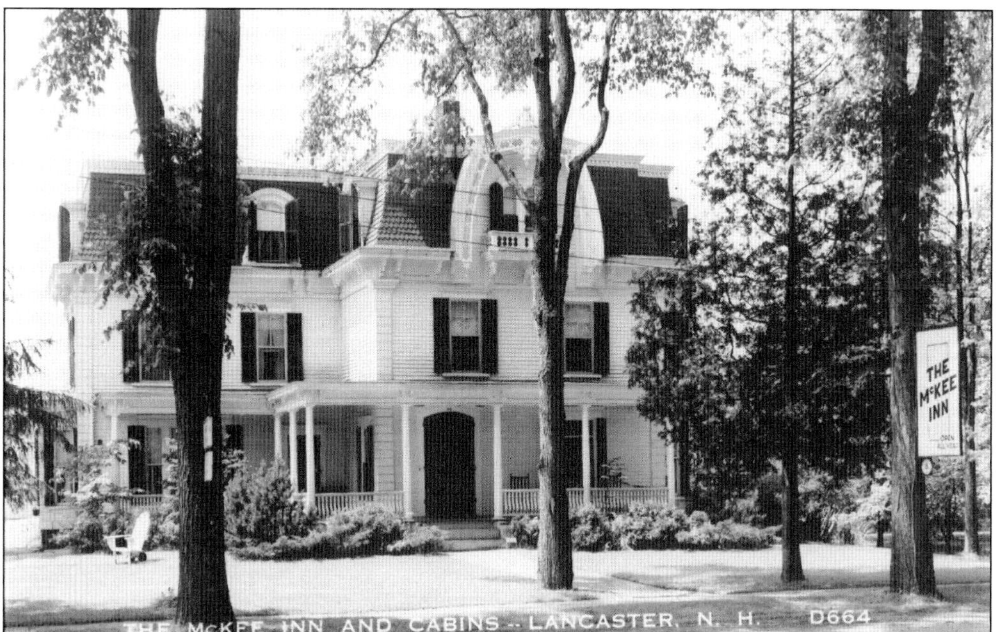

The McKee Inn and Cabins accommodated tourists on Main Street for many years. It is now used as apartments for seniors.

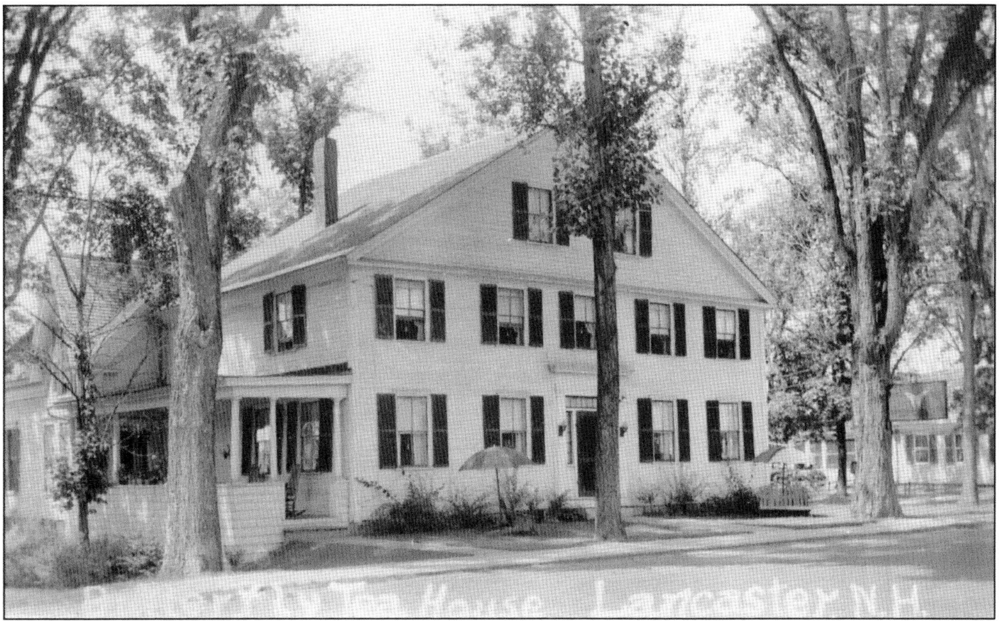

Identified as the Butterfly Teahouse, this tourist home stood opposite Depot Street and the Boston & Maine railroad station. It was built by John Haven, who died in 1813, for his daughter Sally Boardman. Later, it was owned by Ethan Crawford, a descendant of Ethan Allen Crawford of Crawford Notch. It was demolished in 2012.

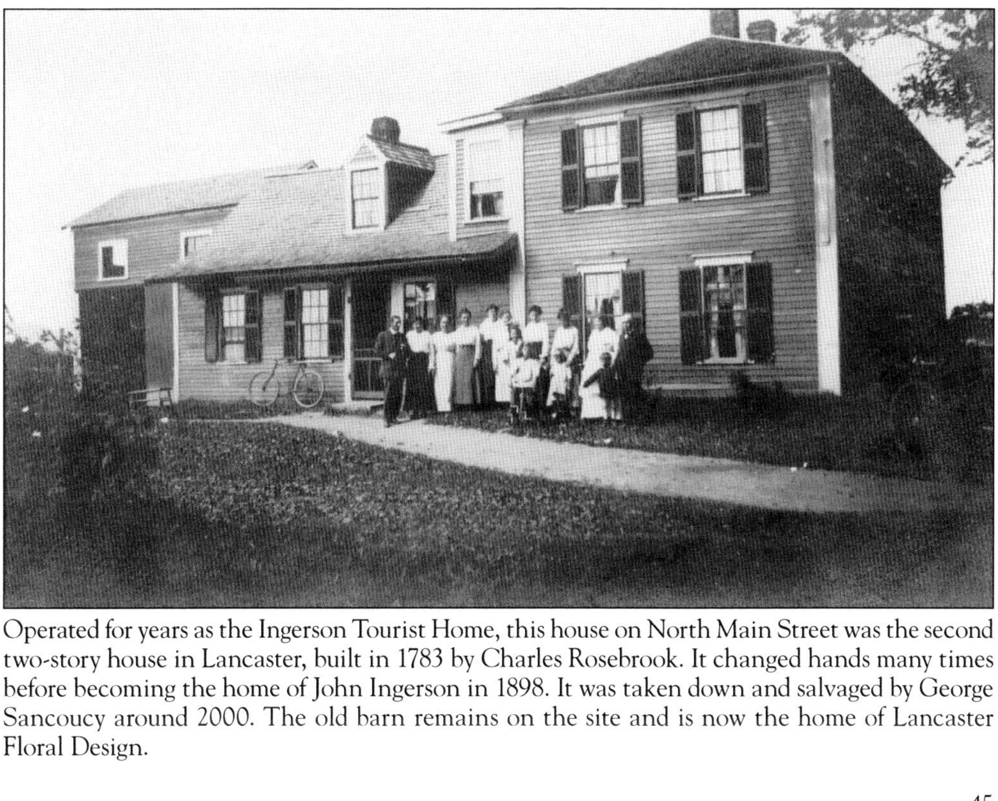

Operated for years as the Ingerson Tourist Home, this house on North Main Street was the second two-story house in Lancaster, built in 1783 by Charles Rosebrook. It changed hands many times before becoming the home of John Ingerson in 1898. It was taken down and salvaged by George Sancoucy around 2000. The old barn remains on the site and is now the home of Lancaster Floral Design.

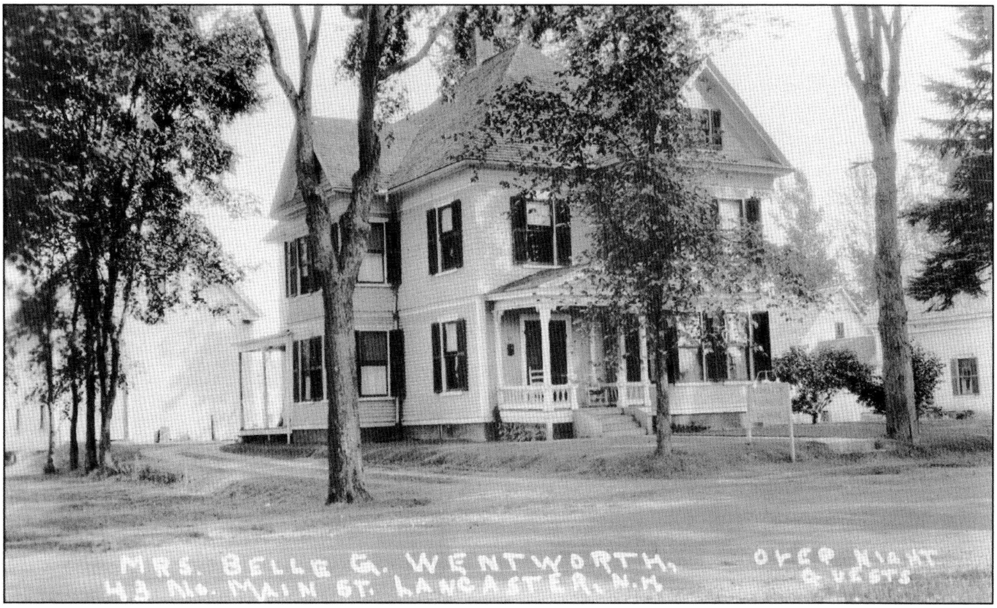

The guest home of Belle G. Wentworth, at 43 North Main Street, is seen here around 1935. A graceful Queen Anne Victorian, it has three porches, natural woodwork throughout, and brass chandeliers in each first-floor room.

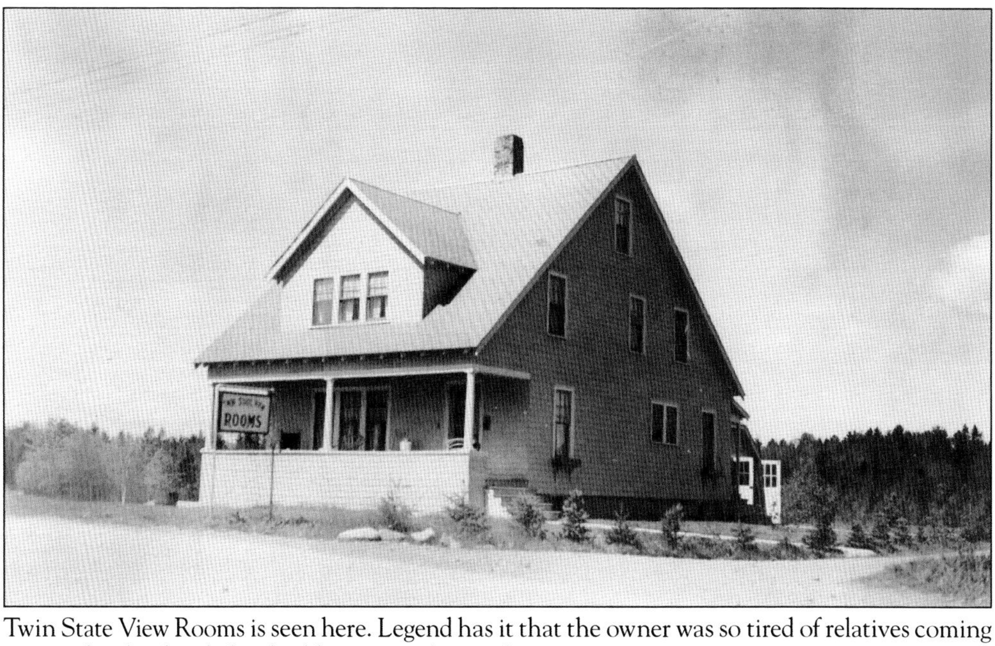

Twin State View Rooms is seen here. Legend has it that the owner was so tired of relatives coming to stay that he decided to build a guest cabin and put up a sign.

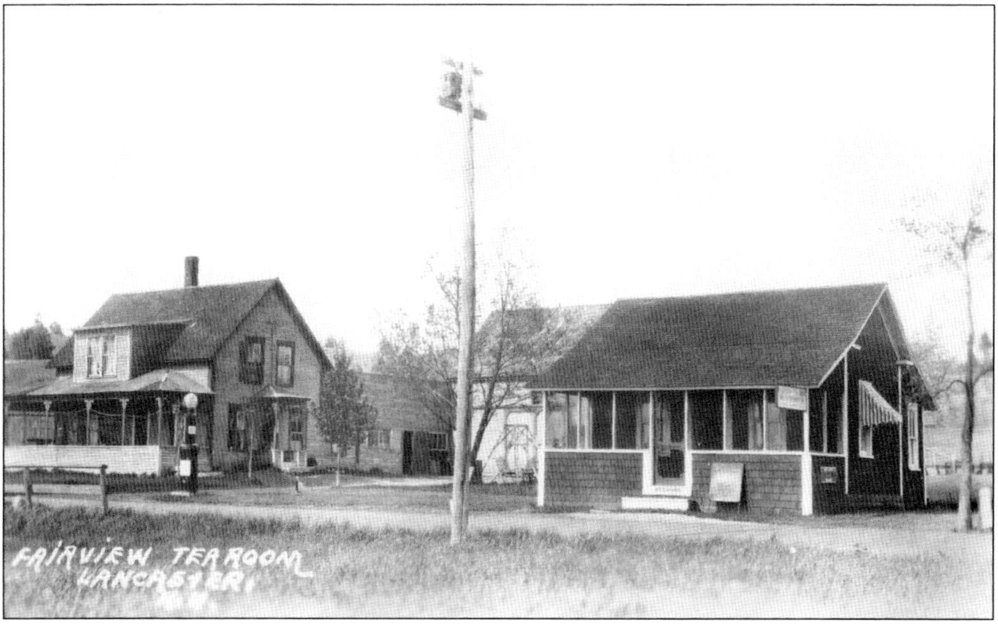

Located on North Main Street, the Fairview Tea Room is seen above awaiting customers in the 1920s.

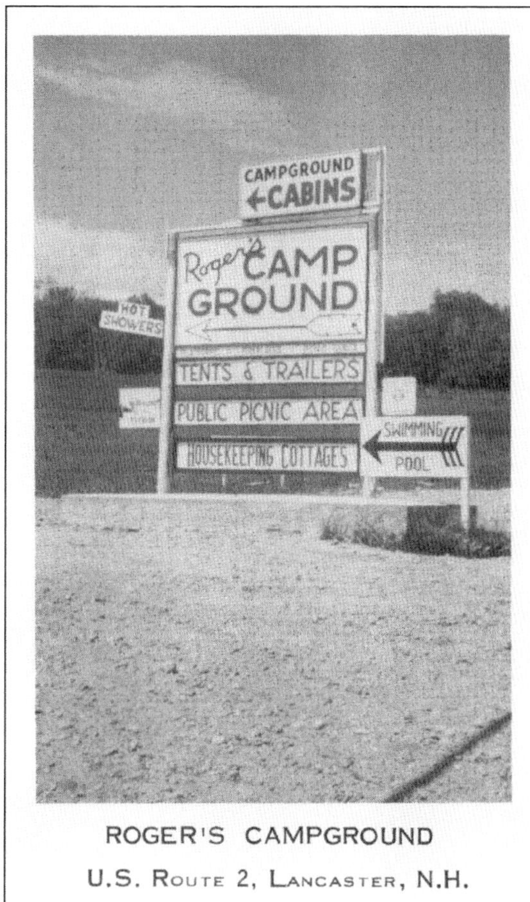

Started by the Choquette family, Roger's Campground continues to draw campers and tourists to the Great North Woods today.

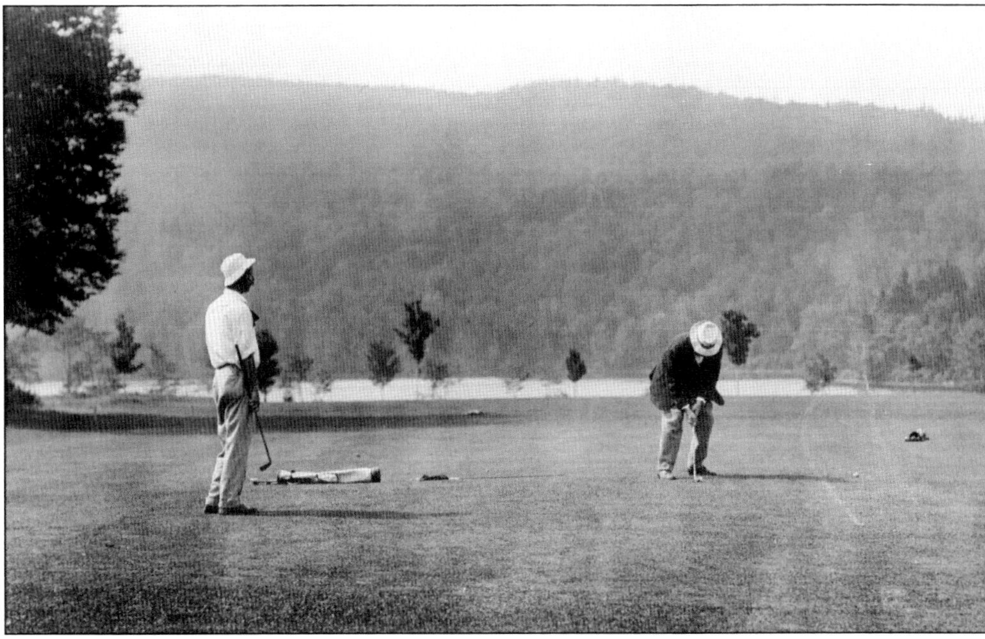

In the late 1920s, a nine-hole golf course was built by Fr. John Casey, the priest at All Saints Church, and James L. Dow, the owner of the P.J. Noyes Drug Company, in the area of Grove Street and its surrounding fields. It was a picturesque and tricky course that some professional golfers called "the Wonder Course."

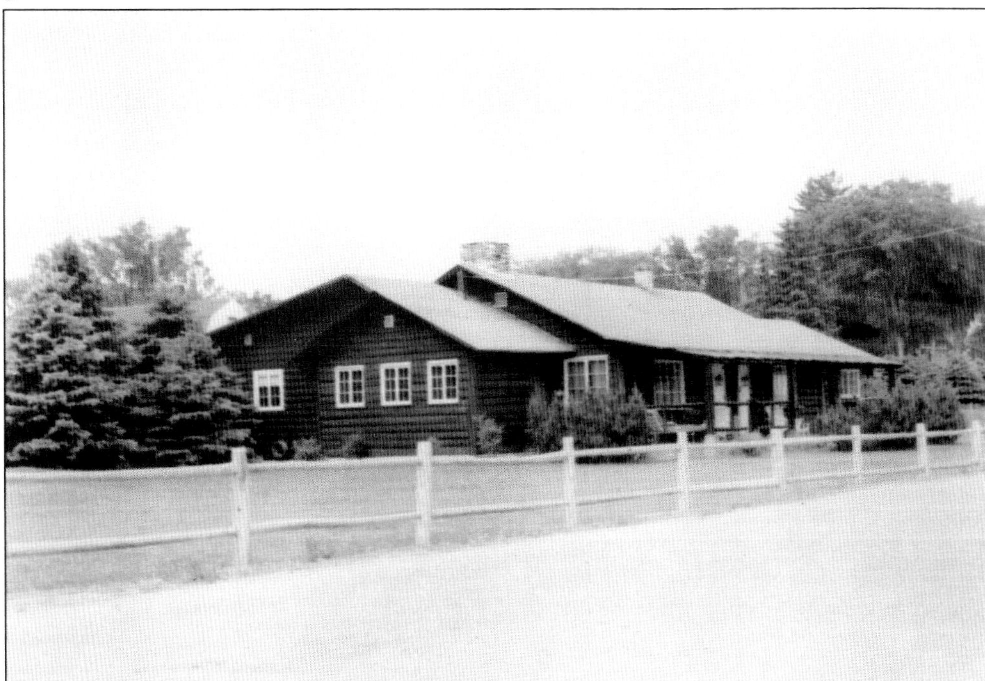

The golf course clubhouse was part of the log house now owned by Erling "Butch" Roberts. The course closed down during World War II due to lack of interest and was reopened only briefly after the war. It closed for good in 1947 because it was too expensive to keep in good shape.

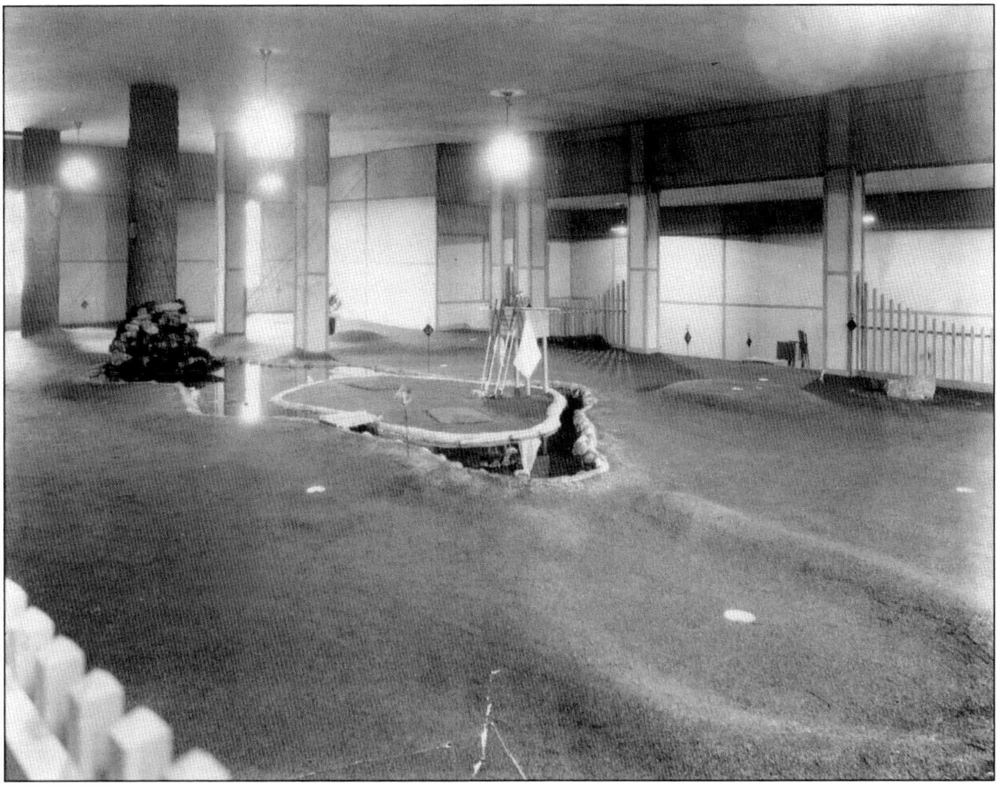

This indoor golf course was located on the second floor above Frank Smith & Company. It was conceived by Reynold Finnegan and operated unsuccessfully in the early 1930s.

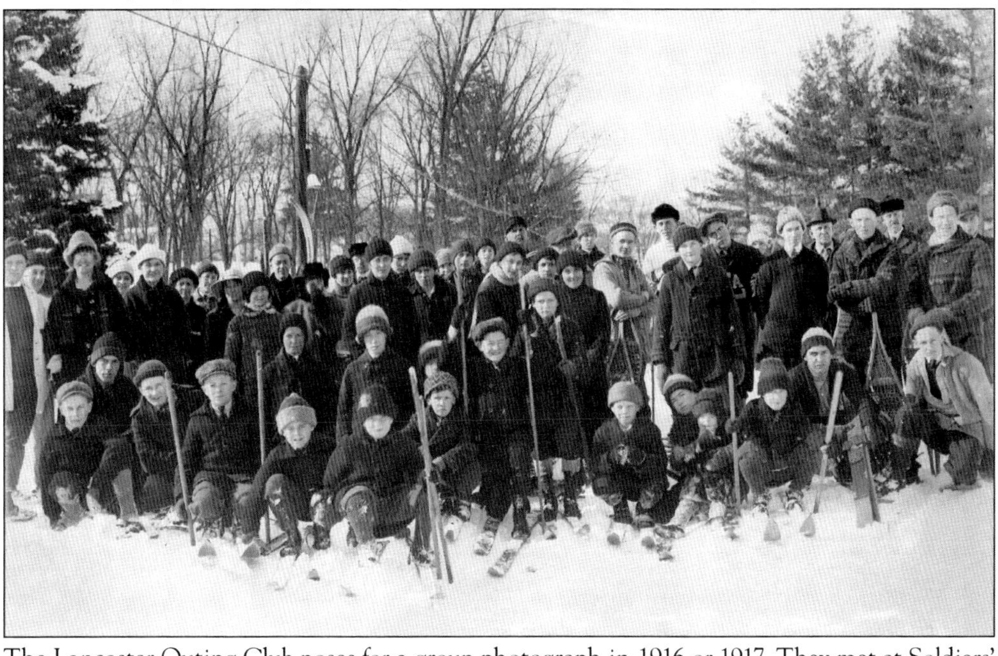

The Lancaster Outing Club poses for a group photograph in 1916 or 1917. They met at Soldiers' Park and cross-country skied over Holton Hill to a farm on Reed Road.

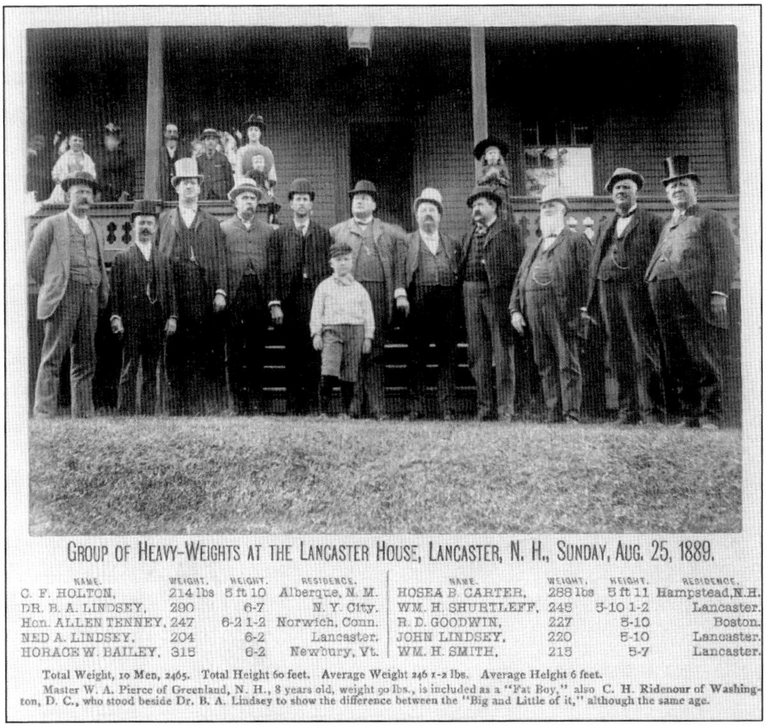

This group of heavyweights poses for a photograph at the Lancaster House on Sunday, August 25, 1889. The total weight of the 10 men was 2,465 pounds.

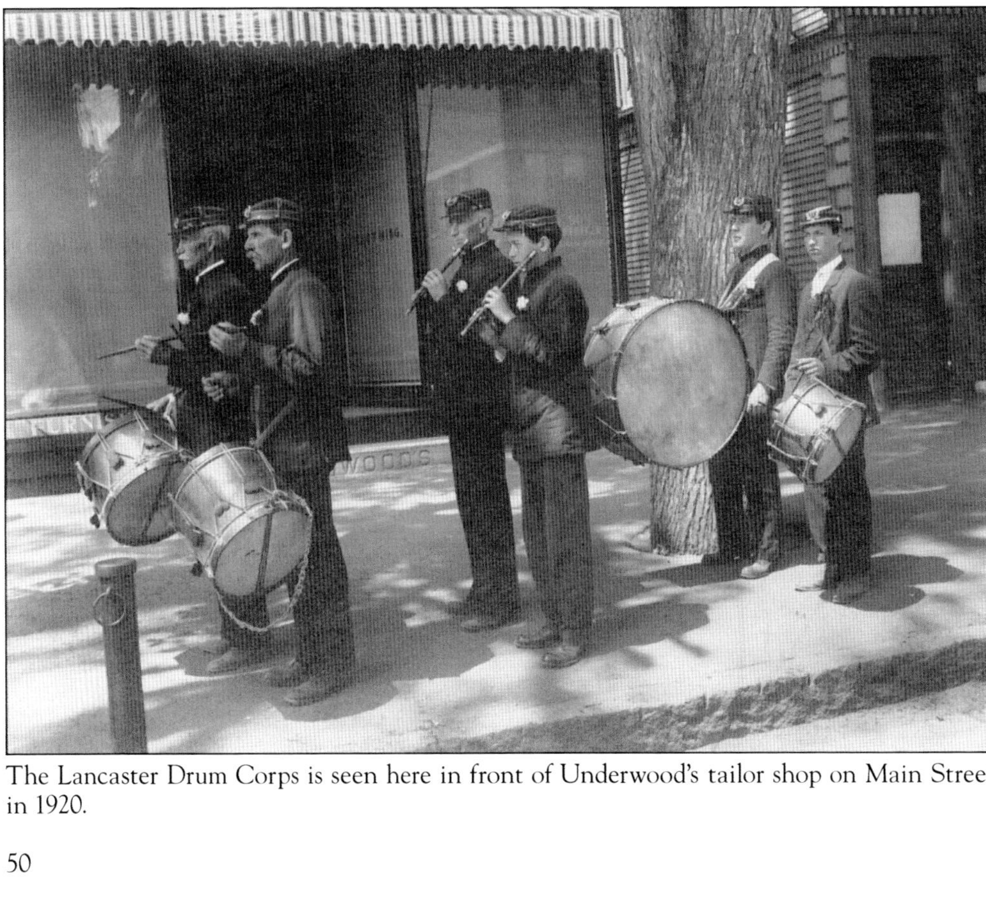

The Lancaster Drum Corps is seen here in front of Underwood's tailor shop on Main Street in 1920.

Movies were first shown in Lancaster at the Lyric Theater, located in the opera house at the town hall. When this photograph was taken, the theater was showing *Less Than the Dust*, the 1916 silent classic starring Mary Pickford.

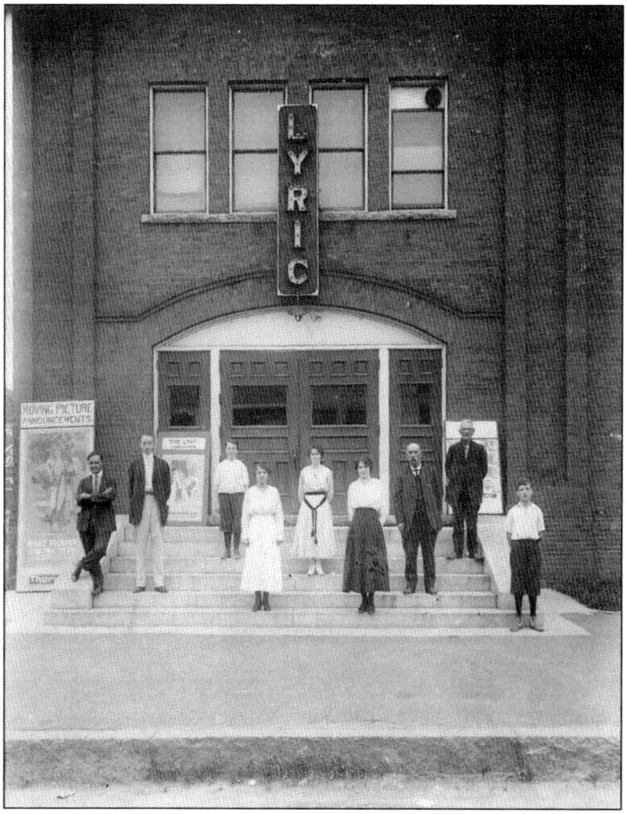

Below, a string band made up of local talent prepares to perform in the new town hall, built in 1901.

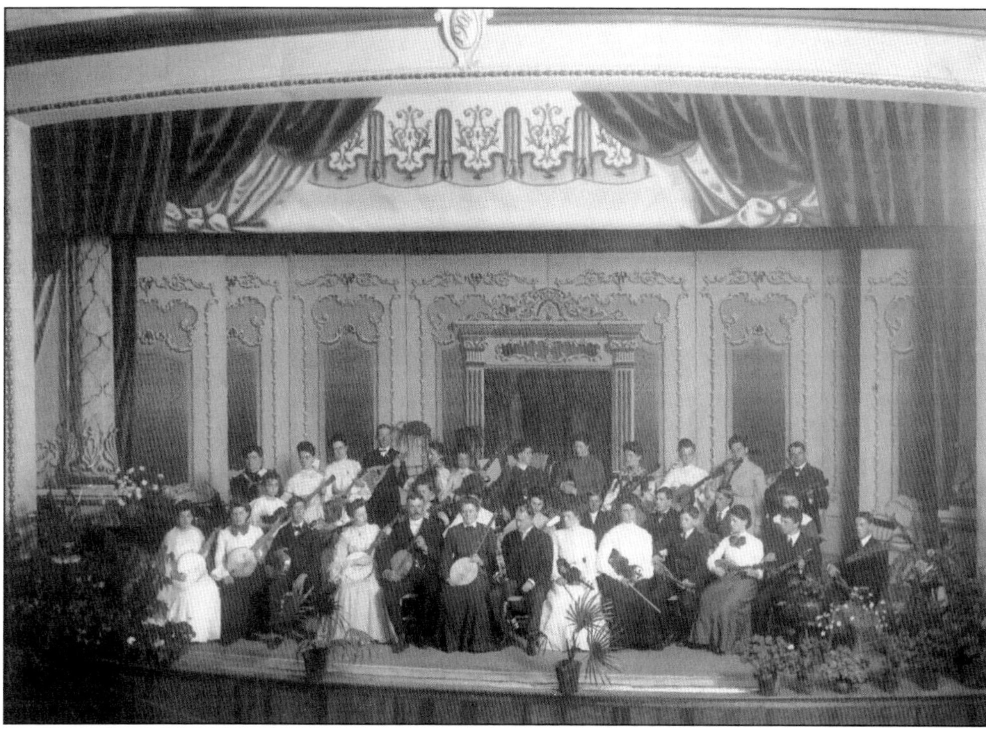

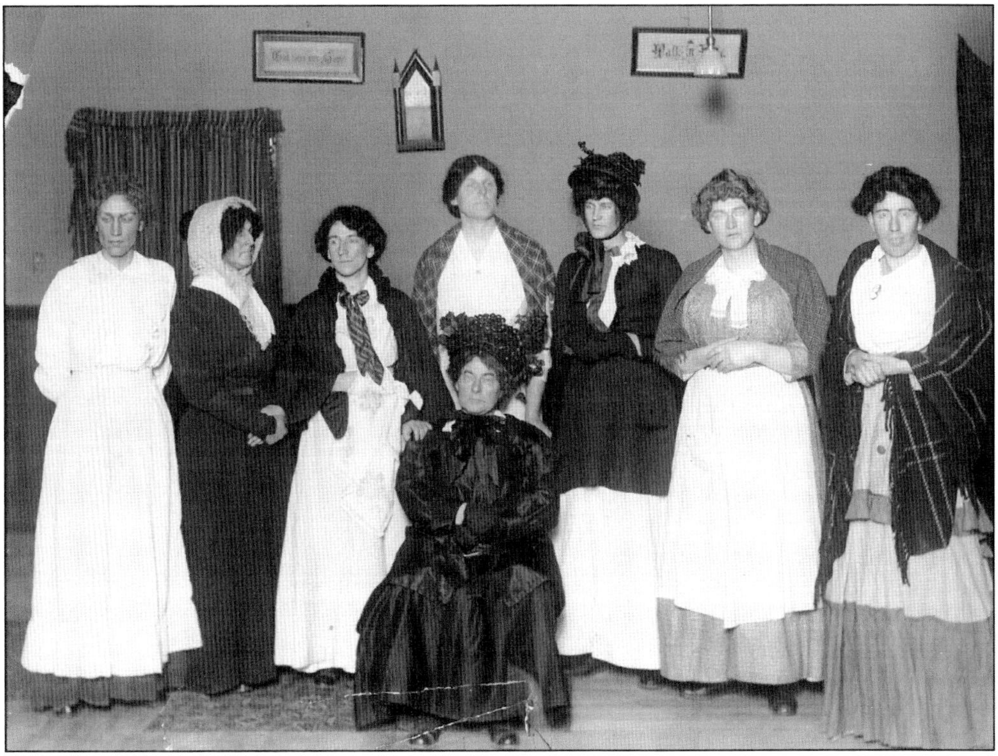

Tom Wallace, Elwin Damon, Fred Congdon, Neil Twitchell, and other gentlemen of the town prepare to entertain while dressed as their grandmothers in this comedy sketch staged in the early 1900s.

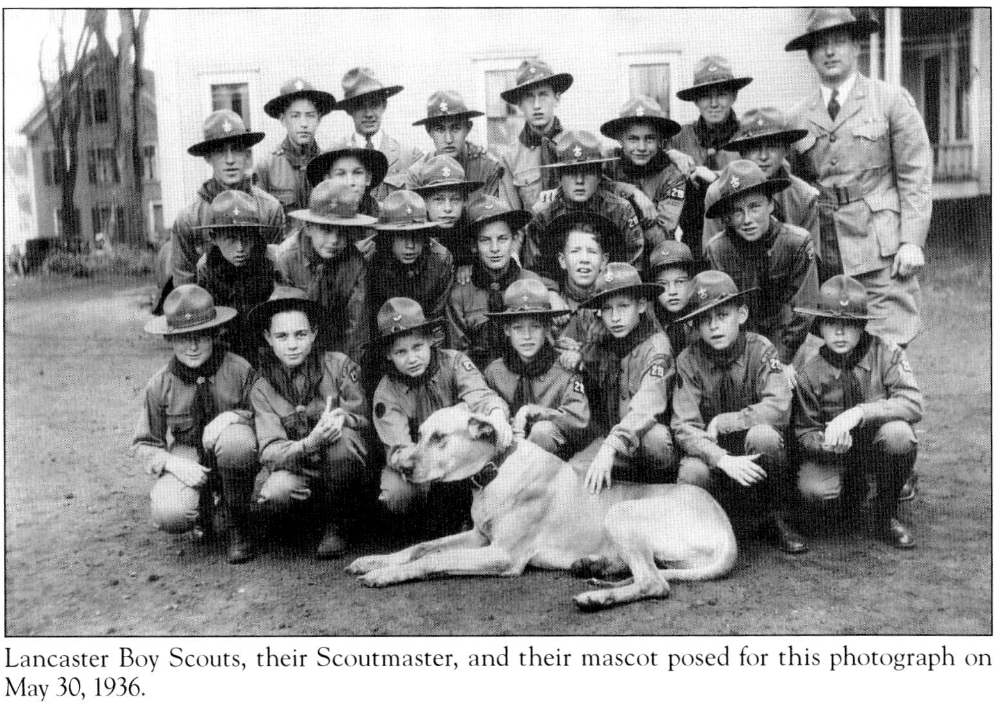

Lancaster Boy Scouts, their Scoutmaster, and their mascot posed for this photograph on May 30, 1936.

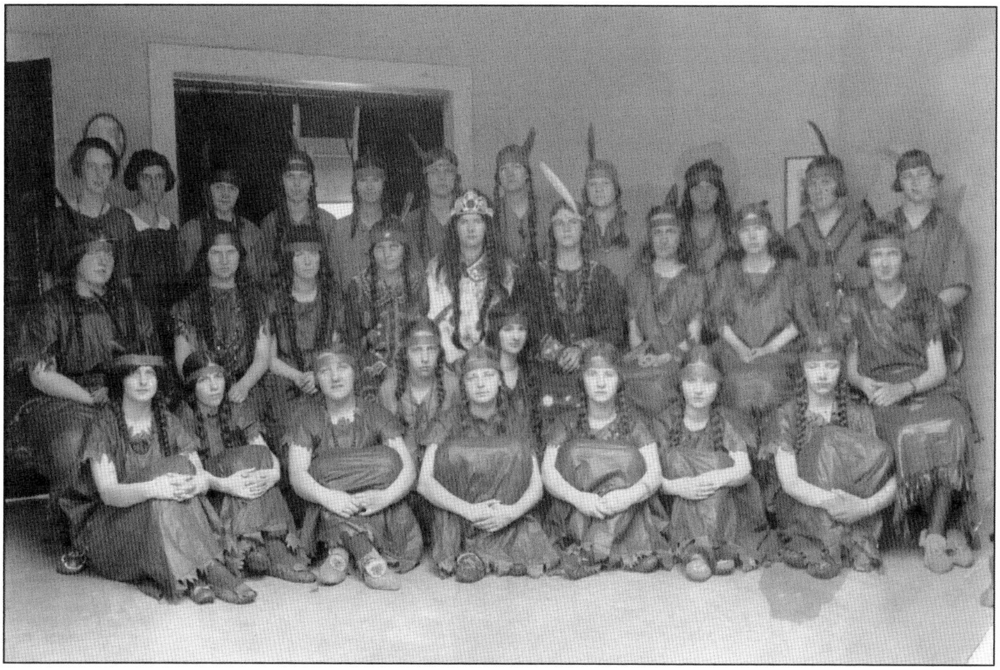
The local Campfire Girls chapter is seen here in the 1920s. During the summer, they often camped out at the Colonial Town Community Camp, Out East.

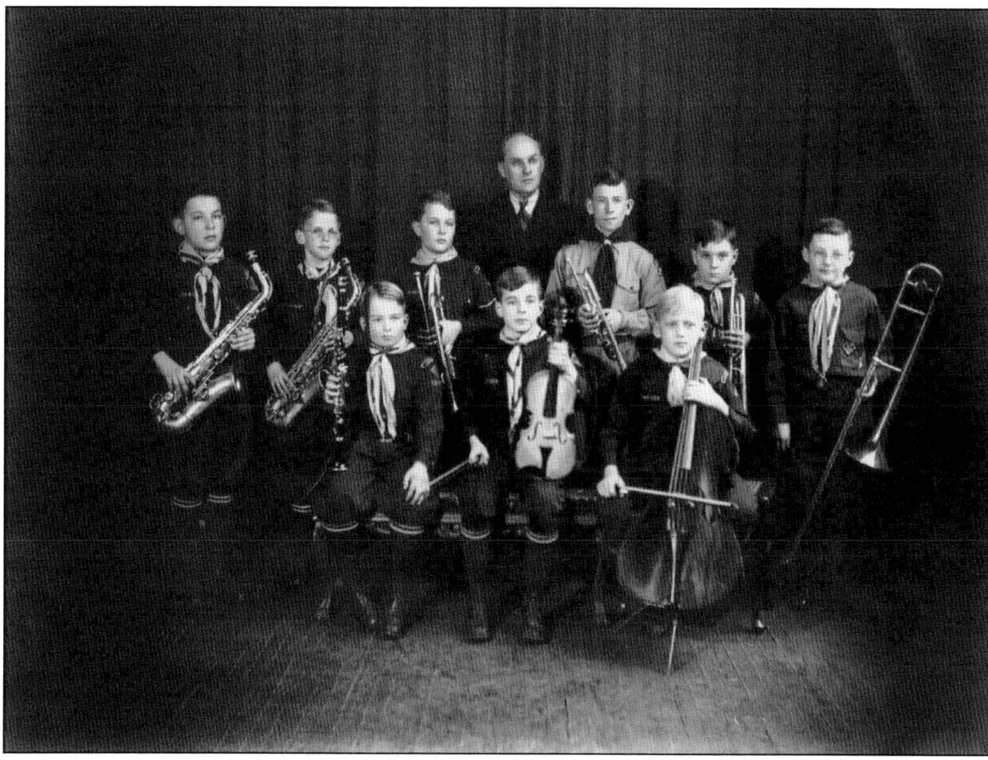
The Cub Scout Orchestra, under the direction of longtime music teacher Gardner Wentworth, performs in the 1930s.

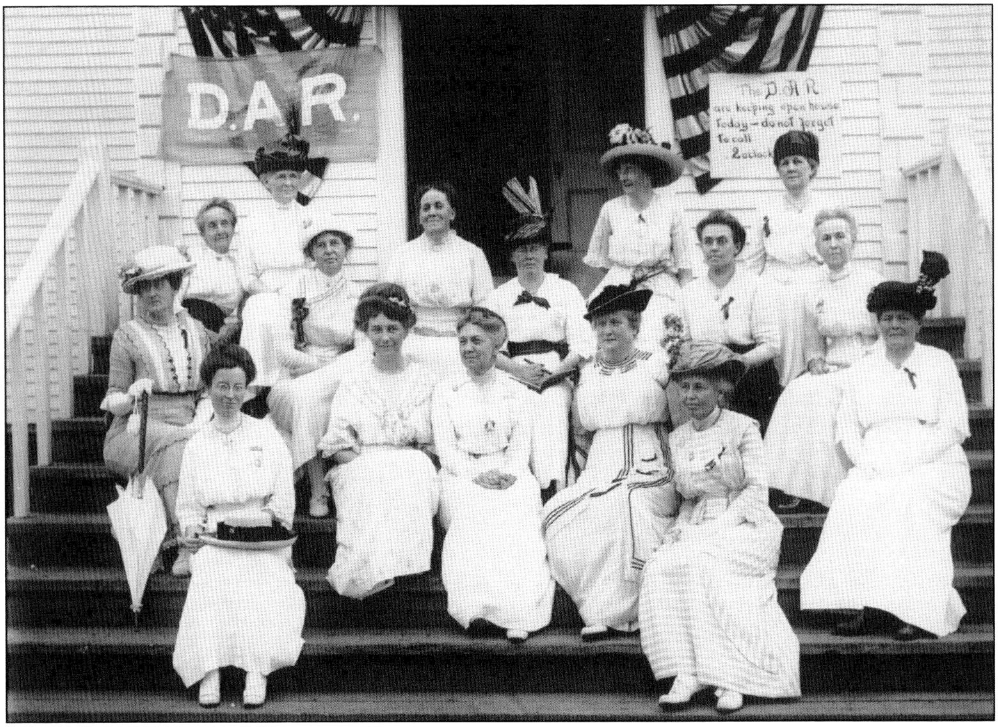

The ladies of the local Daughters of the American Revolution (DAR) chapter pose during their open house in the old courthouse building during the town's 150th anniversary celebration in 1914. This building moved at least three times and was also used as a school, a library, an armory, and a church.

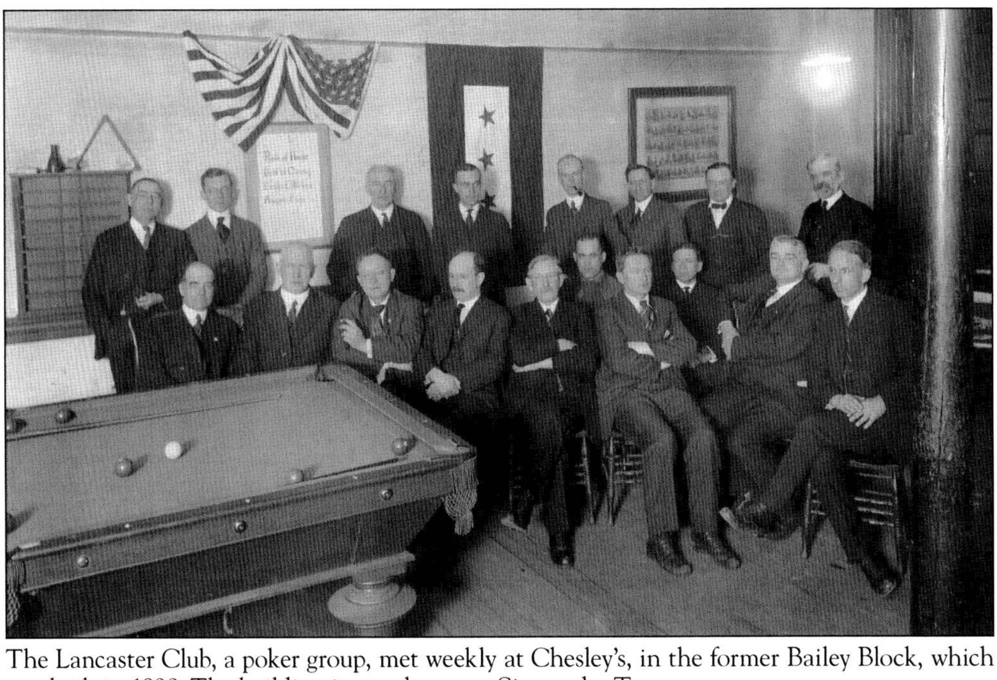

The Lancaster Club, a poker group, met weekly at Chesley's, in the former Bailey Block, which was built in 1899. The building is now home to Simon the Tanner.

Four

CELEBRATIONS

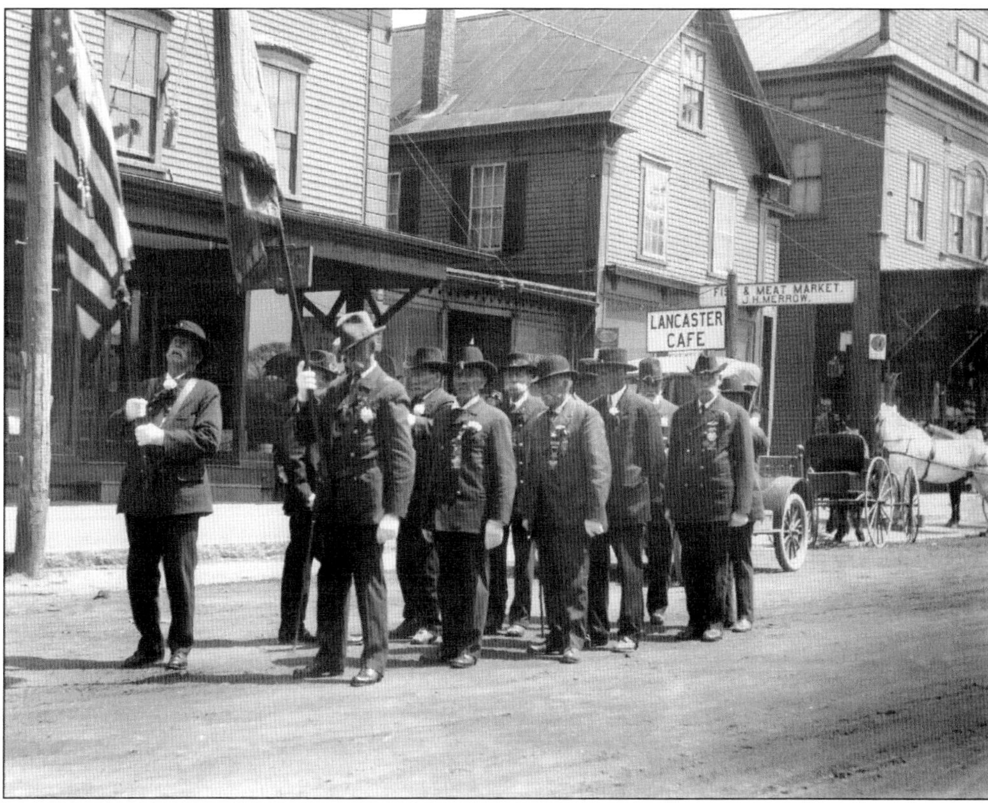

Surviving members of the Edward E. Cross Post of the Grand Army of the Republic prepare to march in what may have been their last formal Memorial Day parade, around 1920.

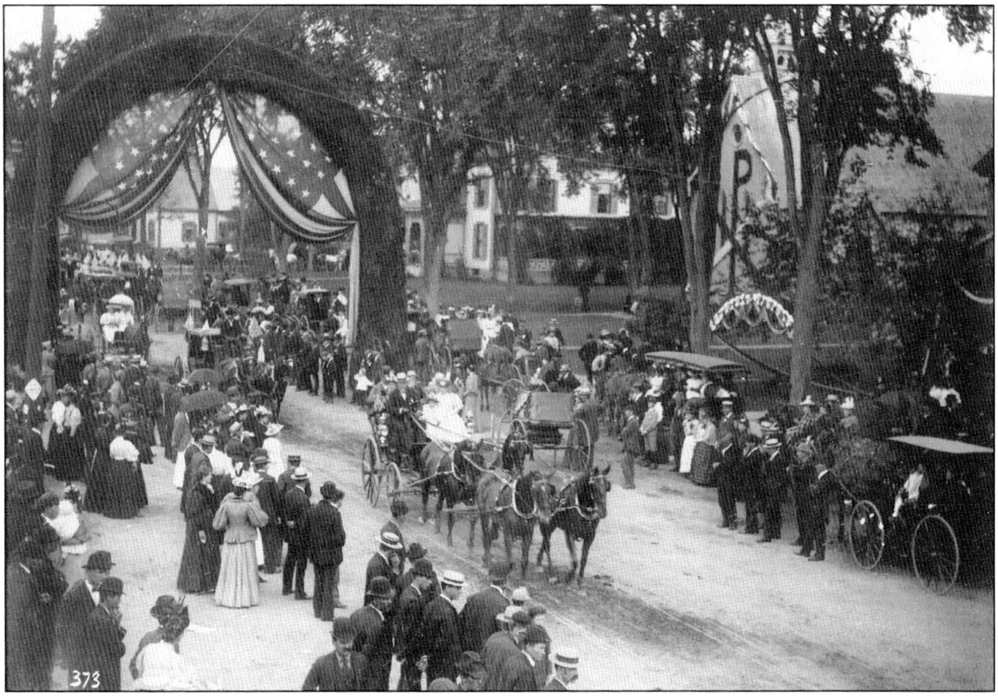

The coaching parade of 1896 was a grand affair, judging by the immense, flag-draped arch in front of the Episcopal church on Main Street.

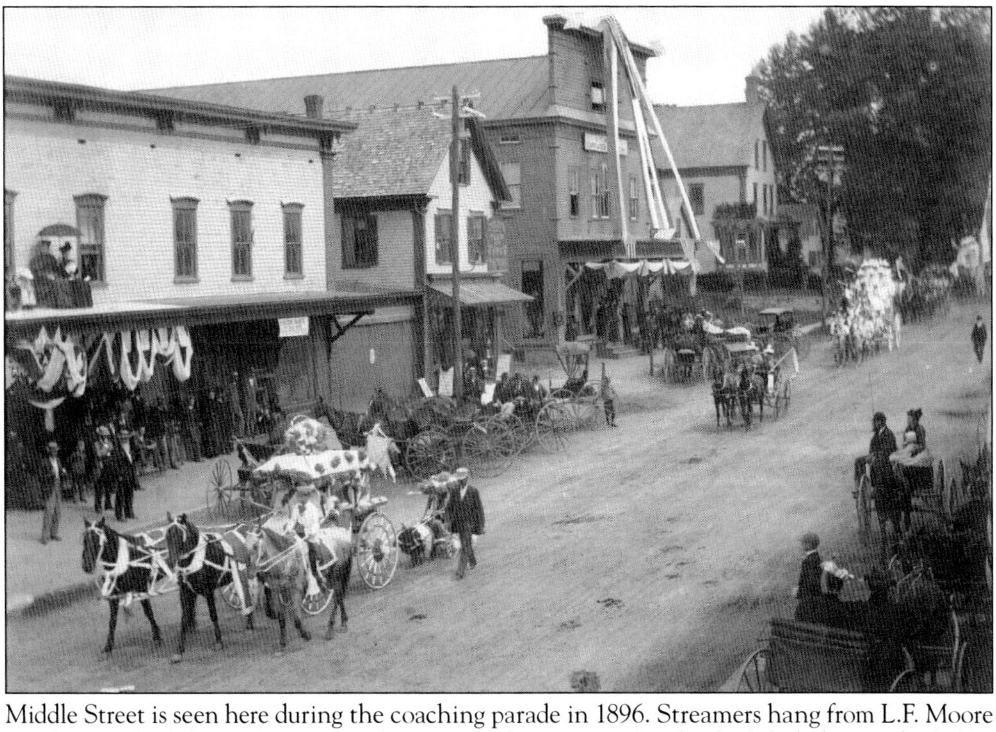

Middle Street is seen here during the coaching parade in 1896. Streamers hang from L.F. Moore Hardware, which burned in a great fire on March 14, 1922. On the far left, ladies sit shaded by an umbrella on the second floor of another building that was destroyed by fire, in 1899.

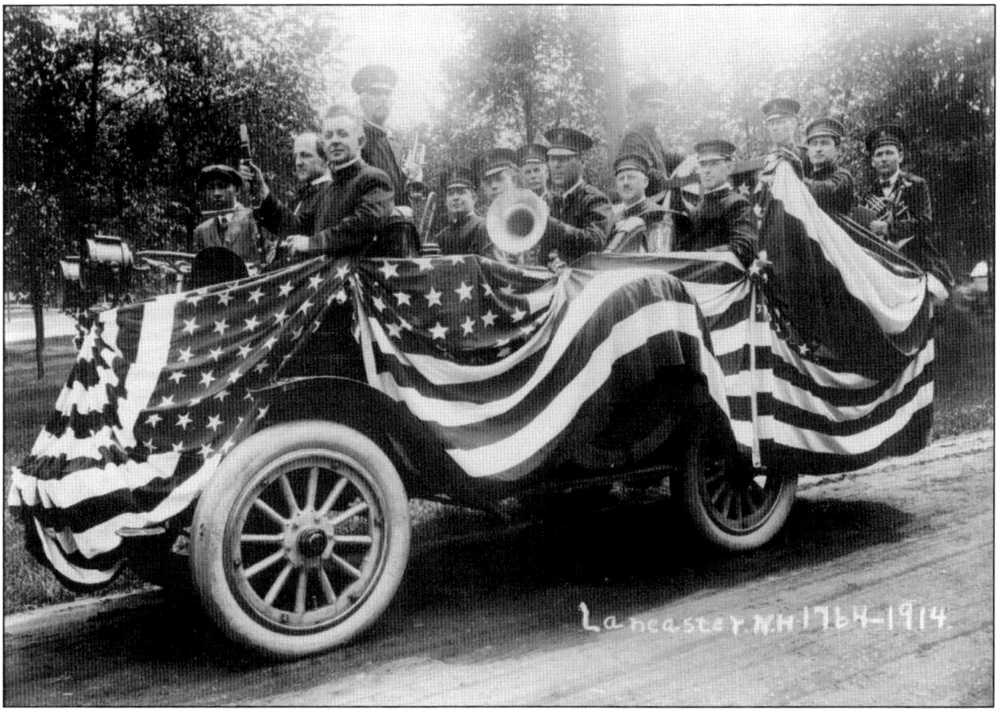

Founded during the Civil War as part of the 3rd New Hampshire Regiment, Never's Band, from Concord, delighted 150th anniversary guests both in concert and during the automobile parade.

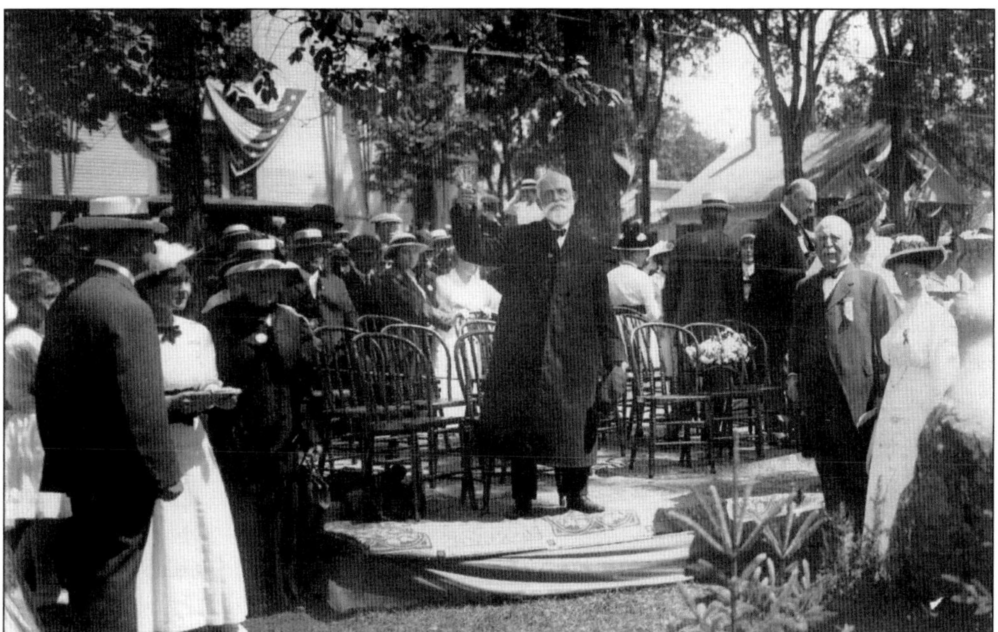

Emmons Selden Freeman, a grandson of Lancaster's first settler, Emmons Stockwell, dedicates the Fox Memorial to the early settlers on August 12, 1914. John W. Weeks stands in the right foreground.

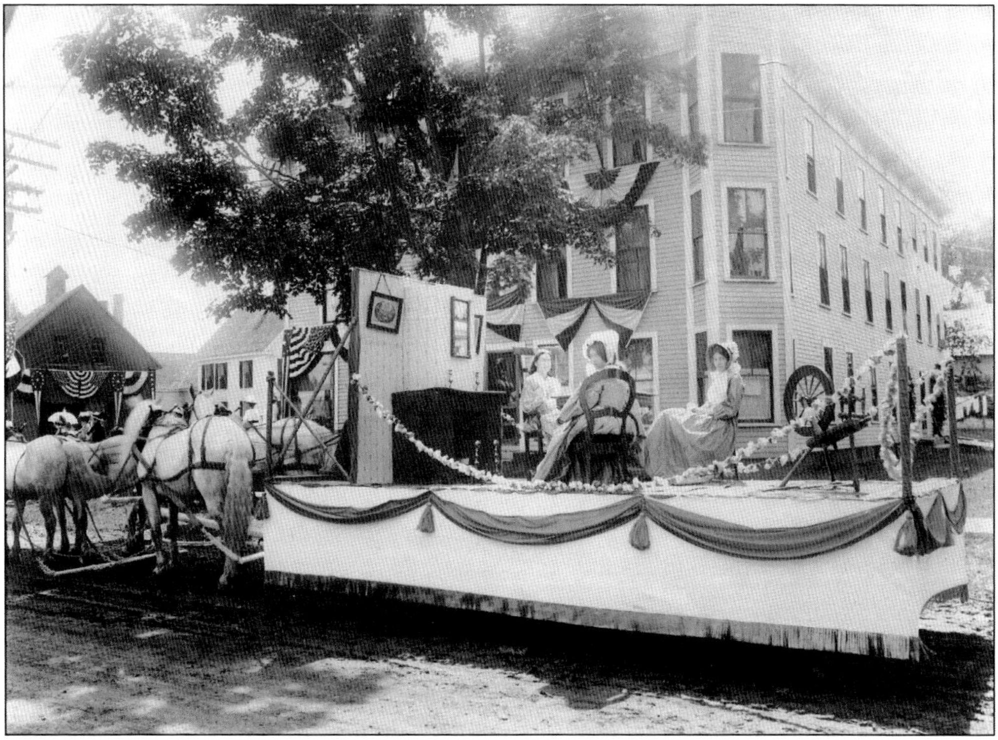

The L.G. Bailey float in the 150th anniversary parade represented an old-fashioned tearoom, with a fireplace, a flax wheel, and antique rugs. From left to right, Helen Bailey, Lillian Paul, and Bessie Johnson, chat over their tea in Colonial costumes.

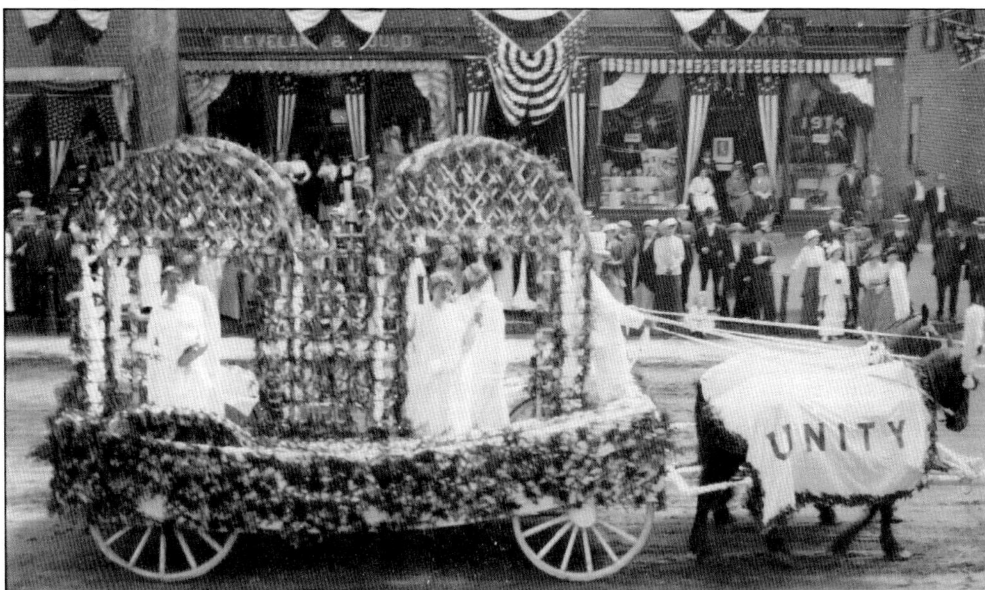

Best known for raising the funds to purchase the Fox Memorial, the Unity Club's float in the 150th anniversary parade symbolized art, history, music, and sculpture, the four departments of the club's work.

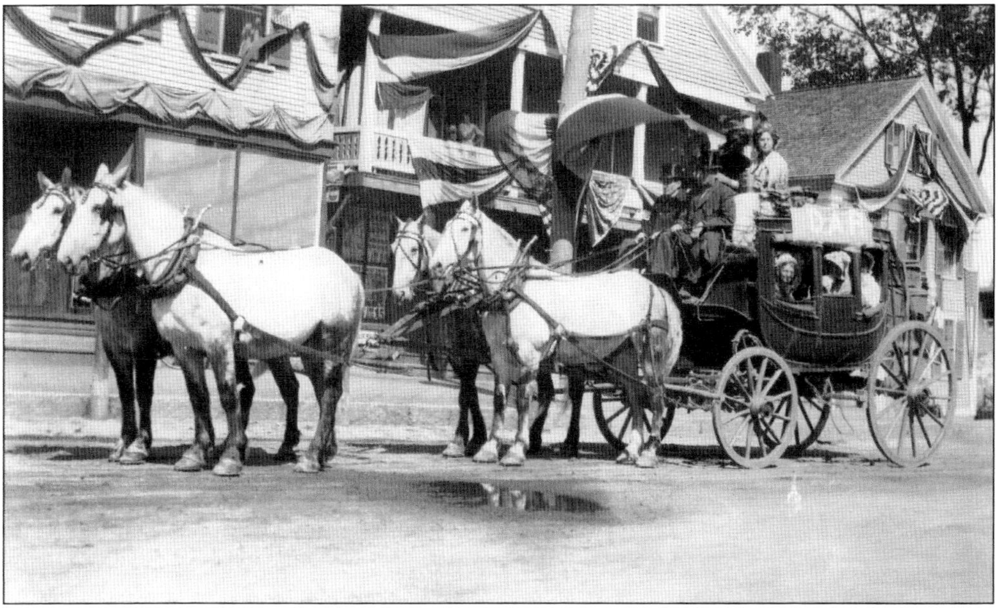

The Ruth Page DAR Chapter No. 31 float is seen here in the 150th anniversary parade. The old Concord coach was pulled by four dapple grays, with John Stalbird and Archie Barnett driving.

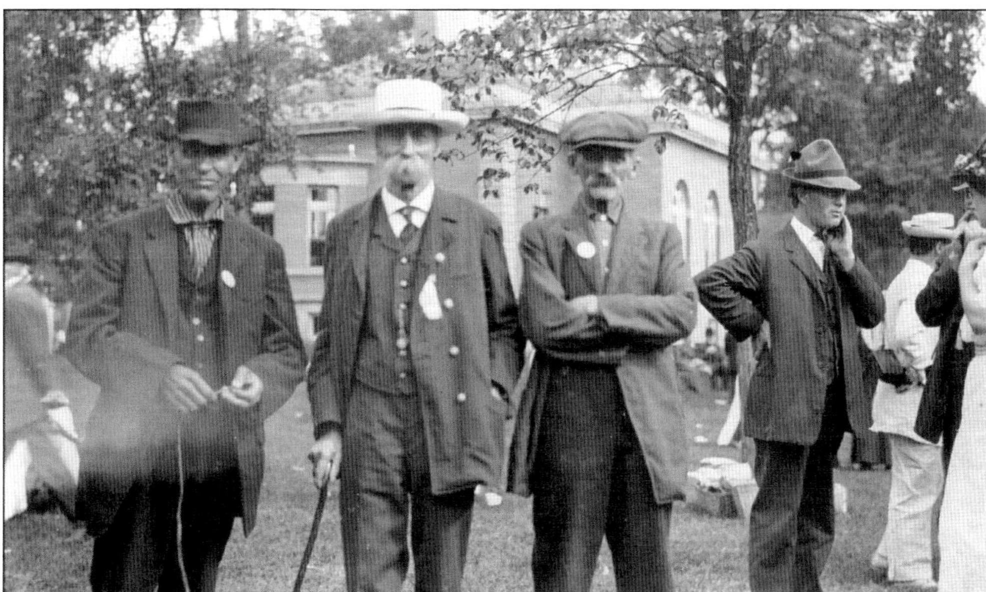

Posing near the Weeks Memorial Library, three men wear badges proclaiming that they "were here 50 years ago." Levi Parker is in the center wearing the white hat and Herman Remick is third from the left. Charly Kent is the young man in white in the right background.

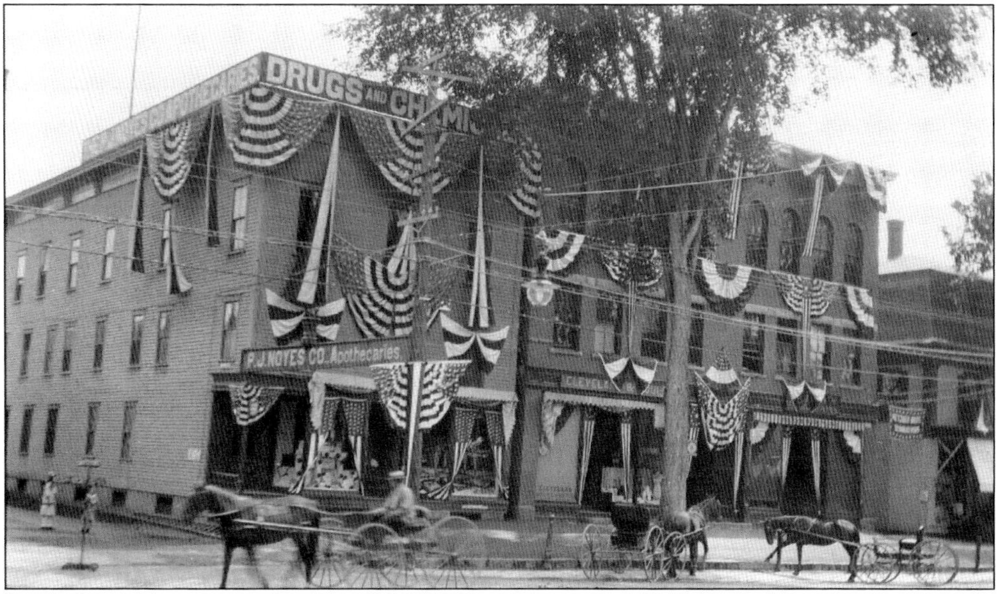

Decorated for the 150th anniversary, the east side of Main Street included the P.J. Noyes Company, Cleveland & Gould, and Bailey's Music Rooms.

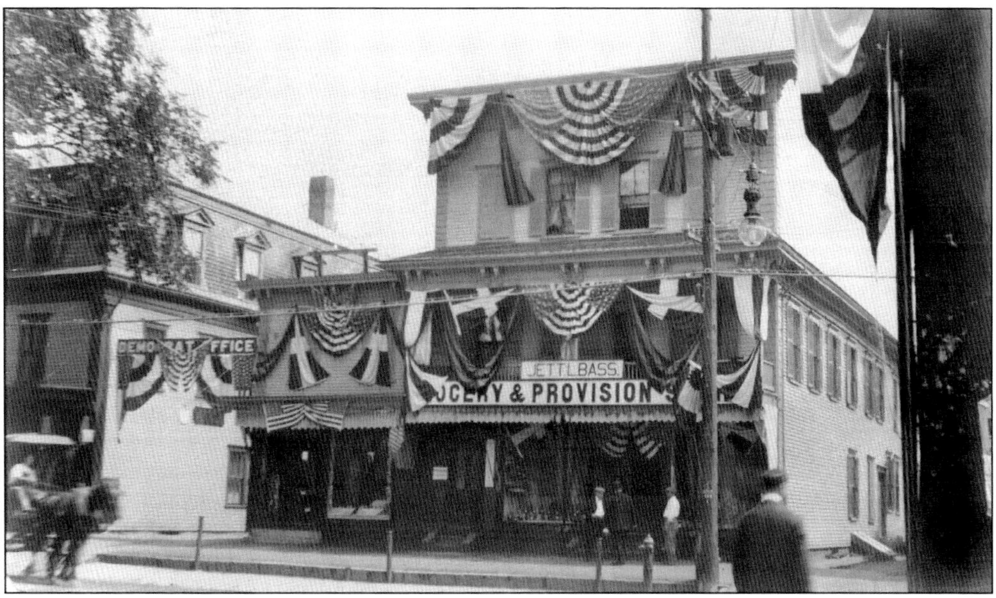

This is another view of the east side of Main Street during the 150th anniversary parade. Hatch Jewelry and the Jett L. Bass grocery are all decked out for the occasion, as is the *Democrat* sign in the alley between the buildings.

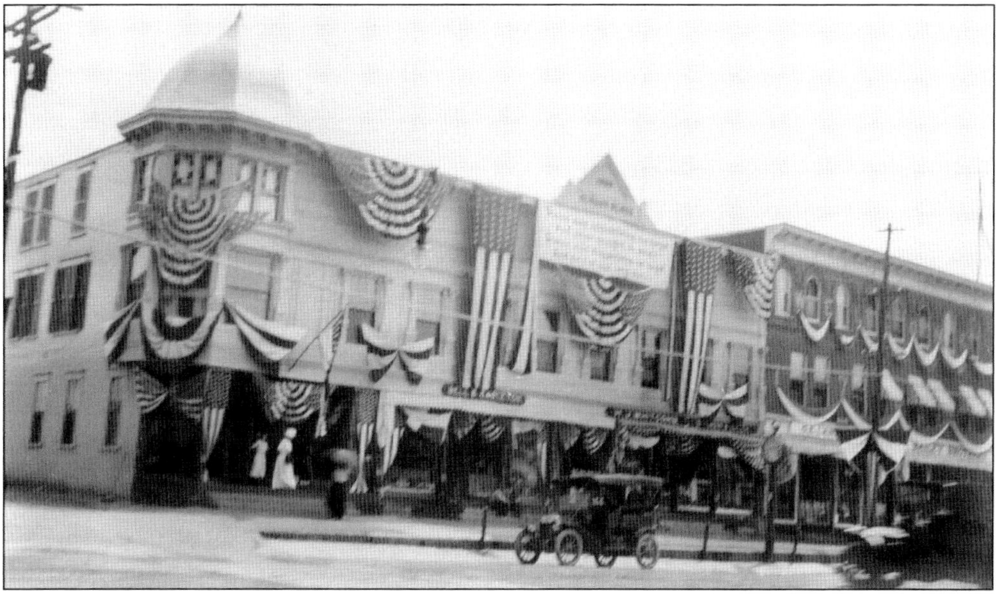

This view of the east side of Main Street during the 150th anniversary shows the Clough Block, the post office, Bell & Carlton, H.J Whitcomb, Blanding & Balch, the G.E. Lane store, and the Bailey Block.

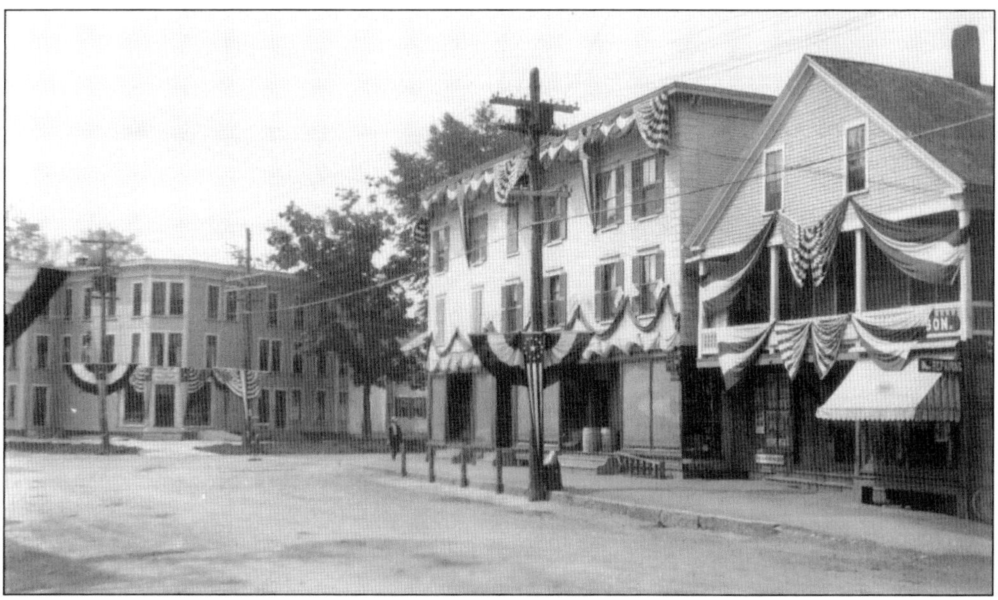

Main and Elm Streets are ready for the 150th anniversary. The Monahan and Riff Blocks remain nearly the same 100 years later, while the third building, housing a shoe repair shop, is long gone.

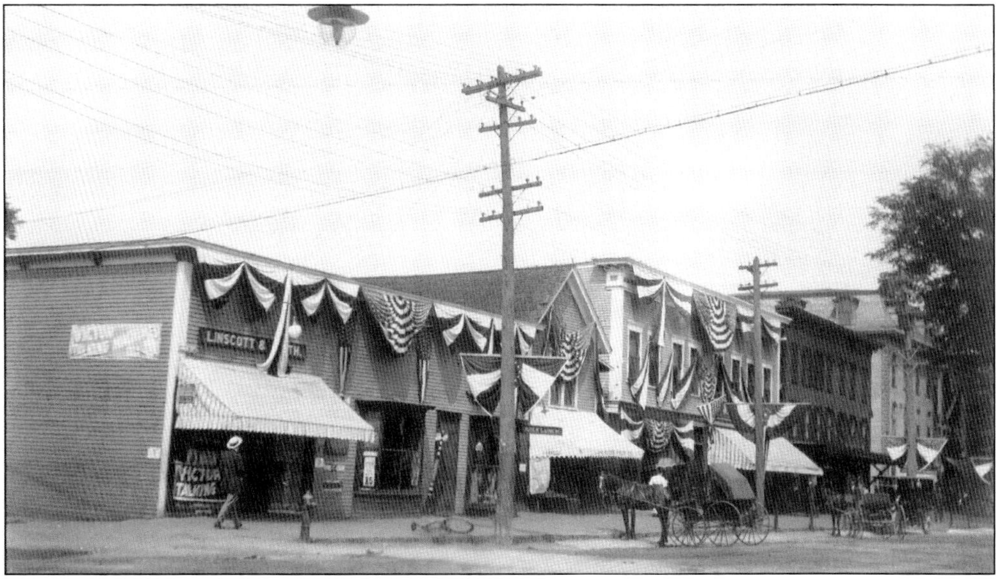

This view looking north on the west side of Main Street shows Linscott & Smith, a barbershop, Quick Lunch, the Lancaster Fruit Company, George M. Stevens Insurance, and Marshall & Sargent's during the 150th anniversary in 1914.

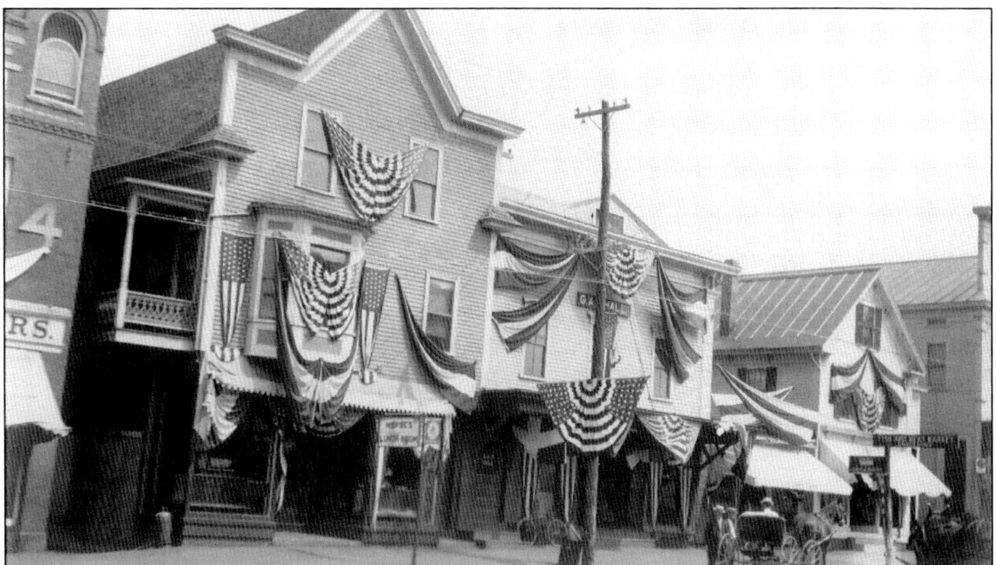

Middle Street is seen here during the 150th anniversary parade. Visible is the back corner of Main Street's Bailey Block, Morse's Lunch Room, the Grand Army of the Republic Hall, and a fish and meat market.

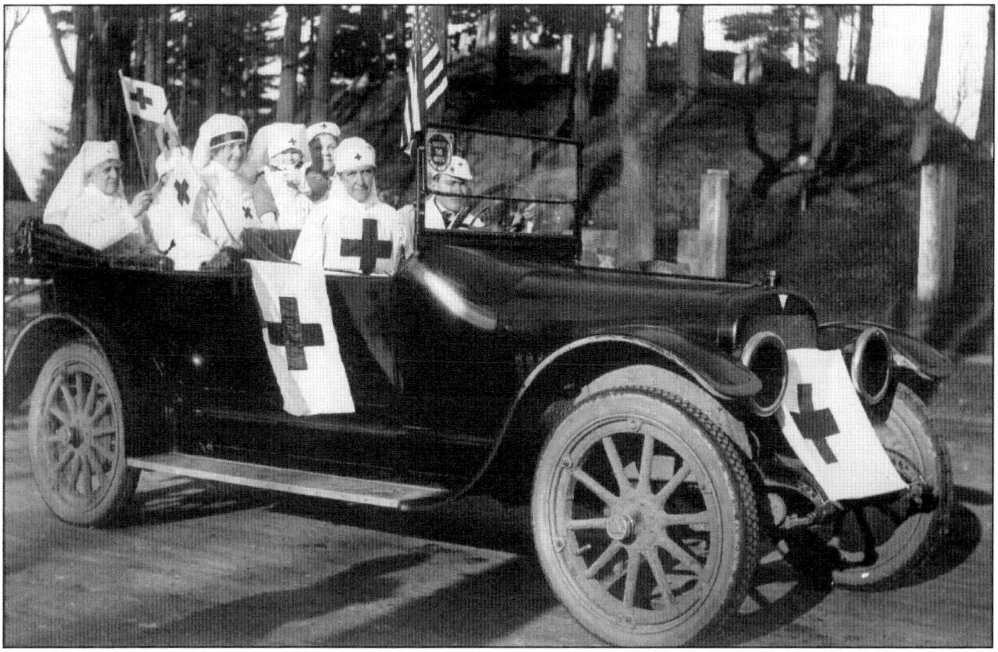

These Red Cross ladies ride past the Wilder Cemetery on Main Street during the 1918 Armistice Day parade commemorating the end of World War I.

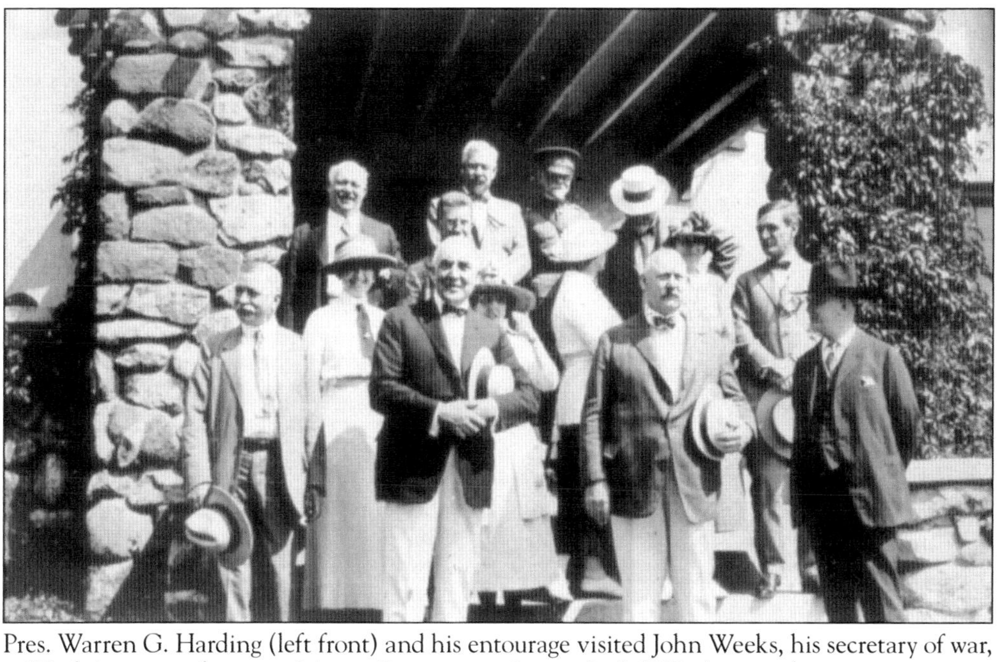

Pres. Warren G. Harding (left front) and his entourage visited John Weeks, his secretary of war, at Weeks's summer home on Mount Prospect on August 2–6, 1921. Among those accompanying the president were, in no particular order, Sen. Joseph Frelinghuyson and his wife, Emily; Sen. Lawrence C. Phipps and his wife; George Christian Jr.; Weeks's daughter Katherine Weeks Davidge, who was acting as hostess; Sen. Fredrick Hale of Maine; and Brig. Gen. Charles Sawyer.

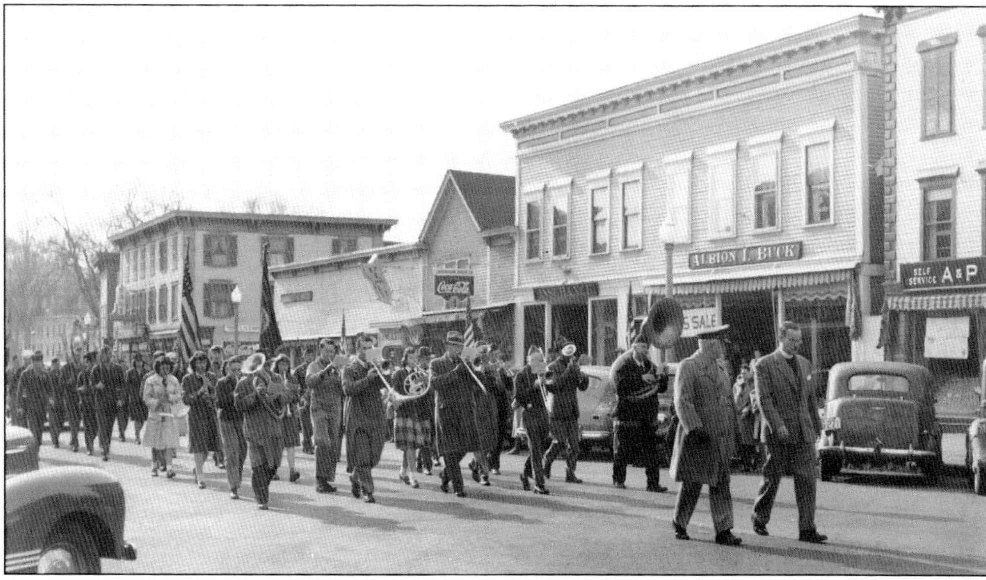

A Veterans Day parade heads down Main Street toward Centennial Park in the late 1940s.

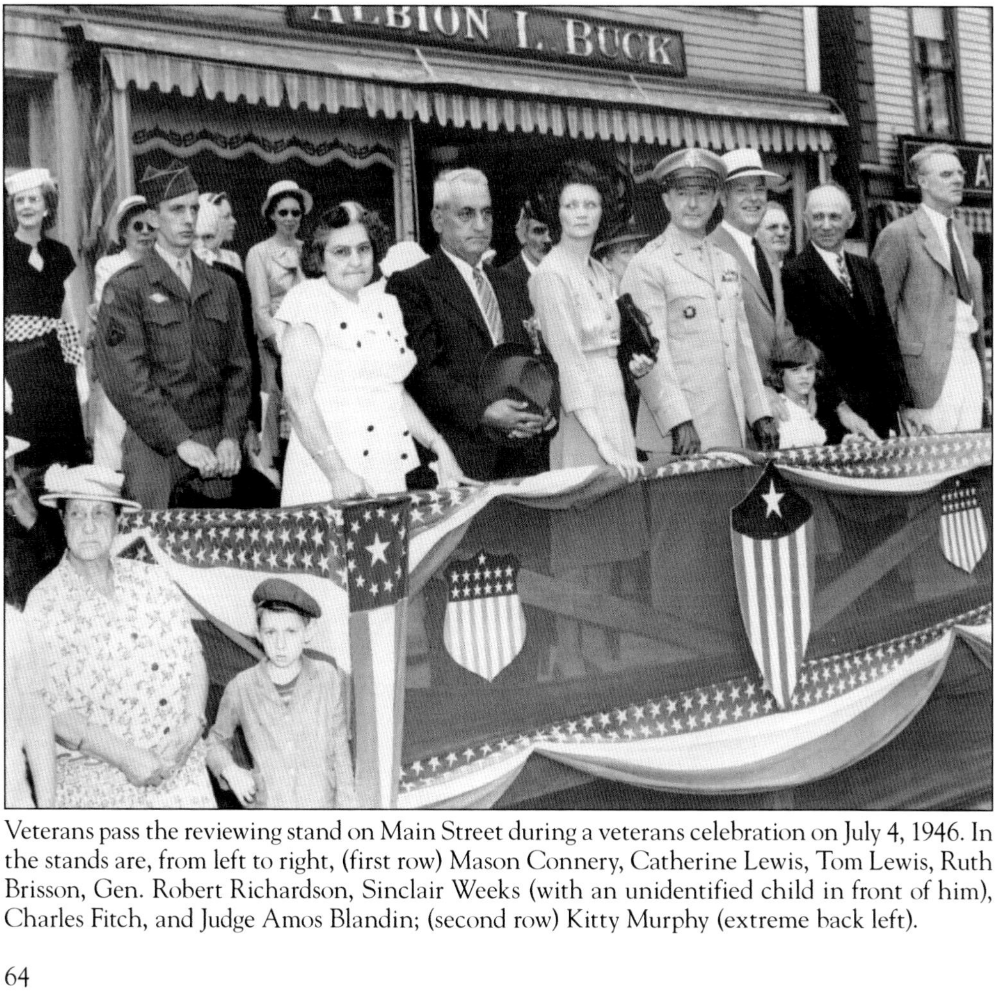

Veterans pass the reviewing stand on Main Street during a veterans celebration on July 4, 1946. In the stands are, from left to right, (first row) Mason Connery, Catherine Lewis, Tom Lewis, Ruth Brisson, Gen. Robert Richardson, Sinclair Weeks (with an unidentified child in front of him), Charles Fitch, and Judge Amos Blandin; (second row) Kitty Murphy (extreme back left).

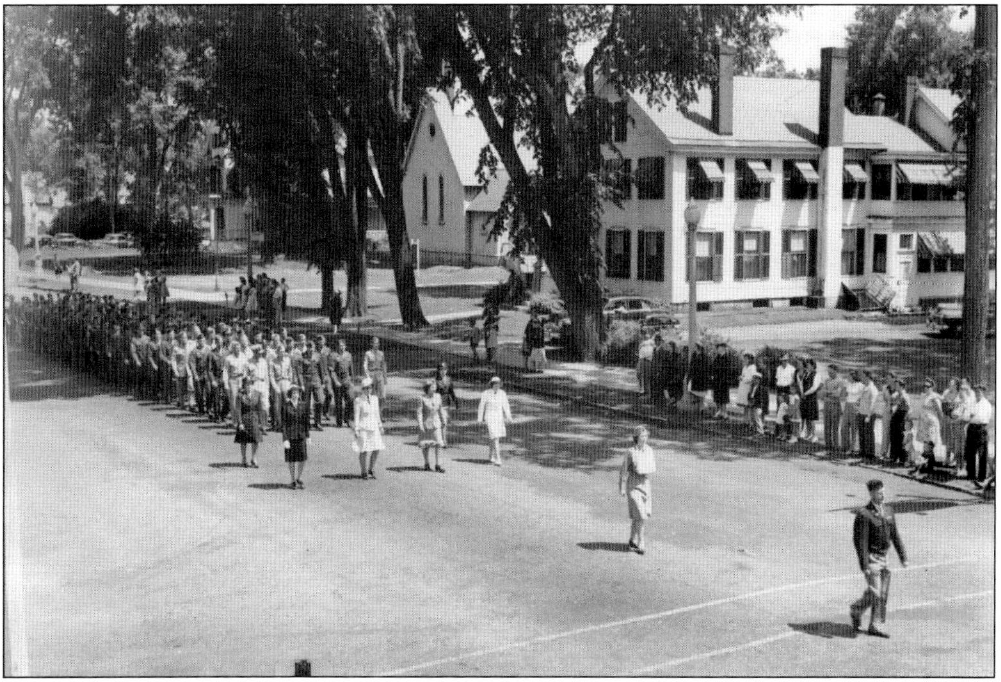

A homecoming celebration for Lancaster's veterans was prepared by the Mahoney-Brisson Post No. 36 on July 4, 1946. Thousands lined the streets to welcome home the veterans representing the several branches of the military.

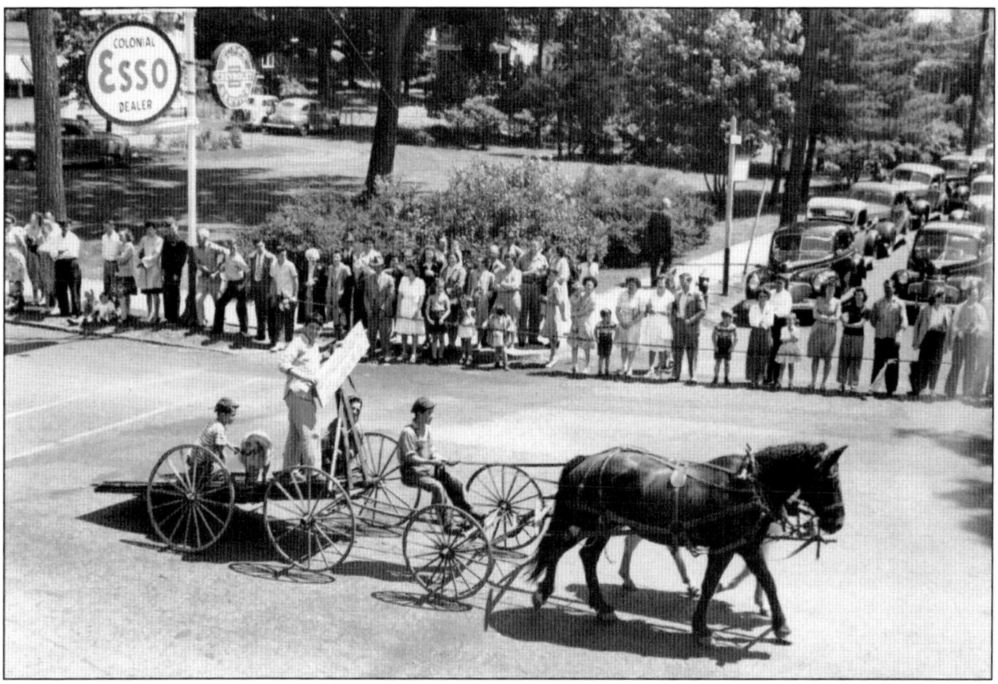

A humorous float was entered in the parade by the Lancaster Grange No. 48 called "Farming is Tough." Stanely Way, Marty Reynolds, Richard Sullivan, and Roger Sylvan rode on a dilapidated hay rack with a missing wheel. Of course, all realized this was just a joke.

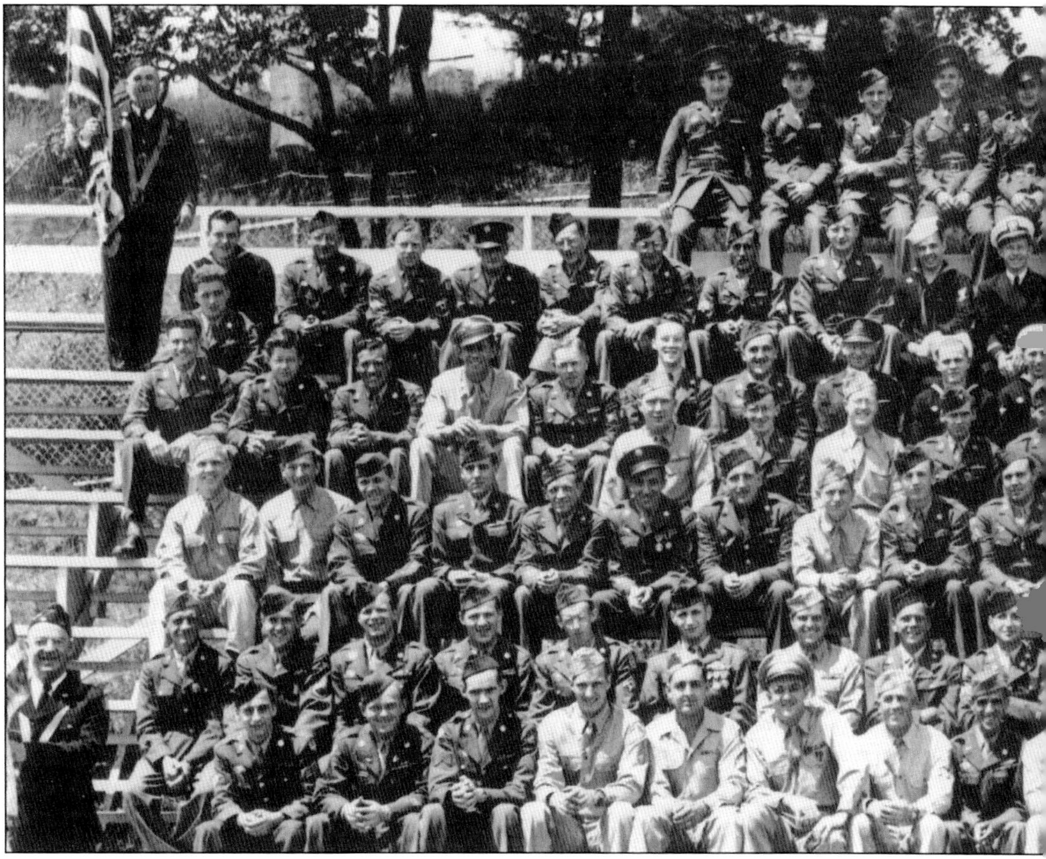

Following the parade and celebrations on July 4, 1946, many local veterans filled the Colonel Town field grandstand for a photograph in their honor. Not all of Lancaster's veterans were

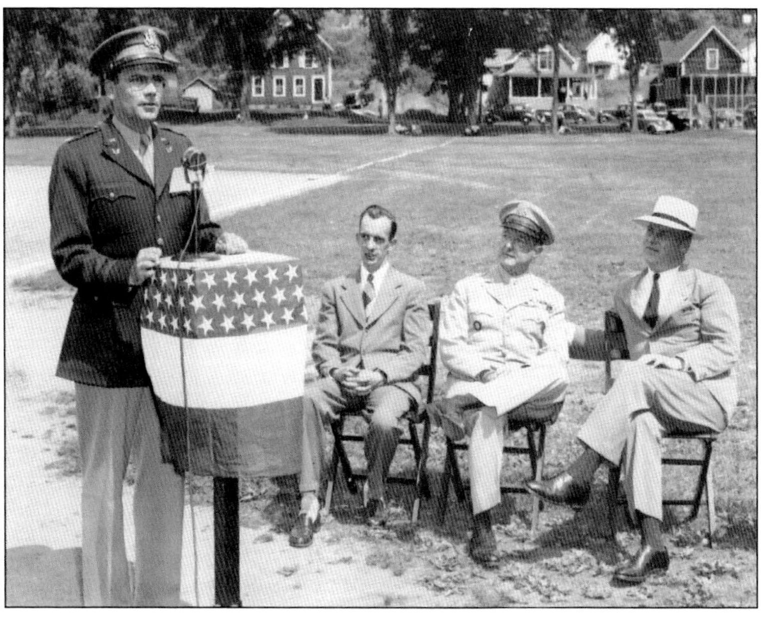

Sitting, from left to right, Mason Connary, Lt. Gen. Robert Richardson, and Hon. Sinclair Weeks listen attentively as Walter Hinkley, the spokesman for the veterans, introduces General Richardson during the veterans' celebration at the Colonel Town field on July 4, 1946.

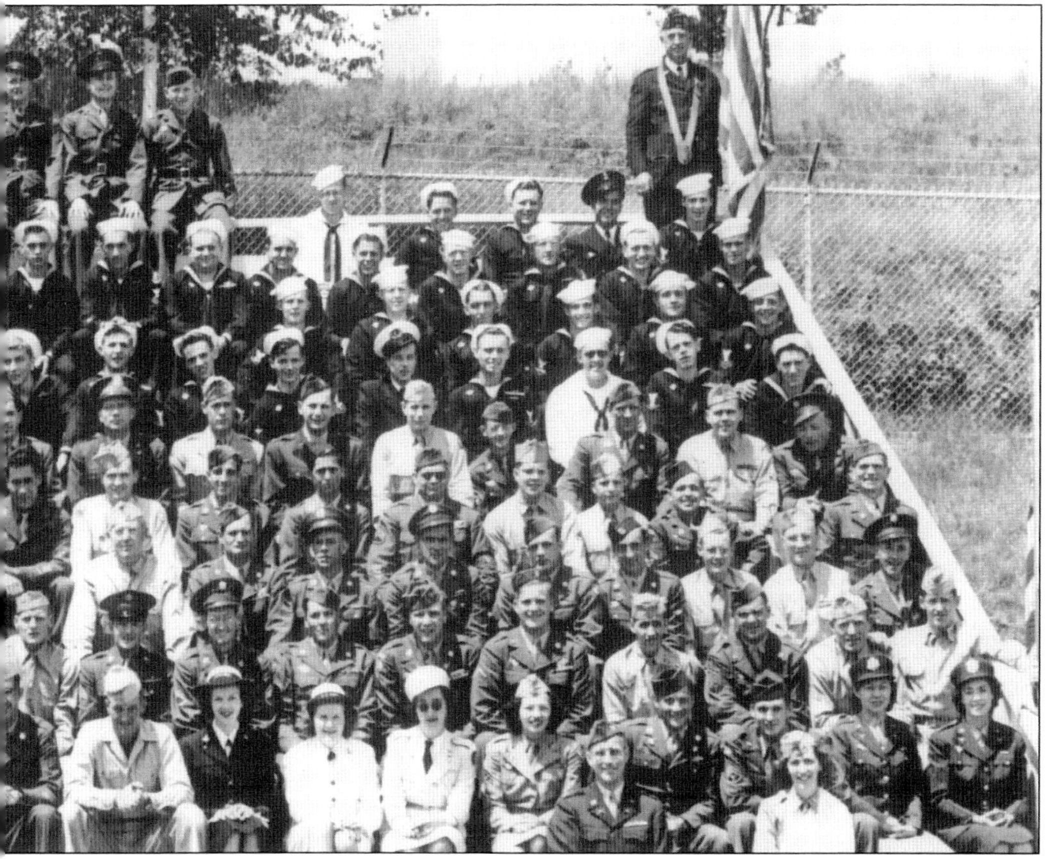

able to attend the celebration, but for the servicemen and servicewomen who could, gratitude for their service was extended to them.

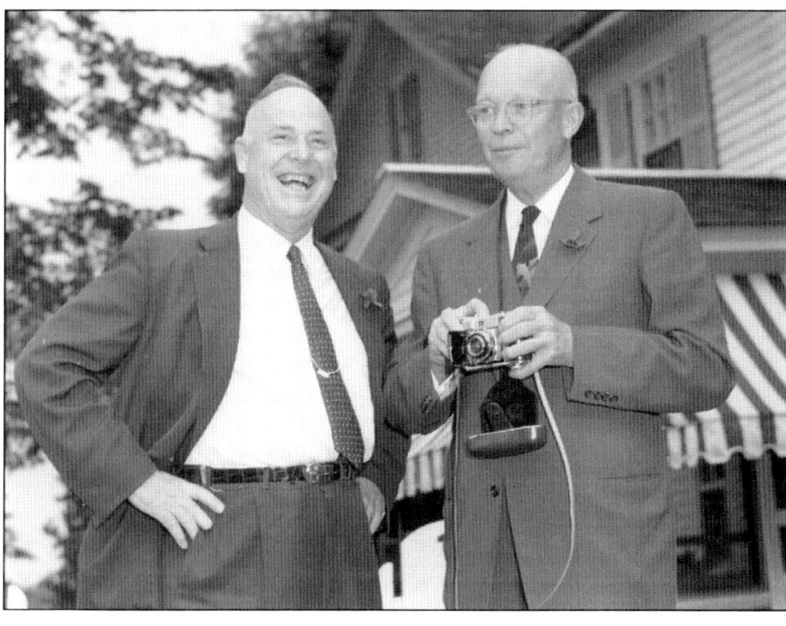

Pres. Dwight D. Eisenhower (right) visited Lancaster for two days in June 1955 as a guest of Secretary of Commerce. Sinclair Weeks.

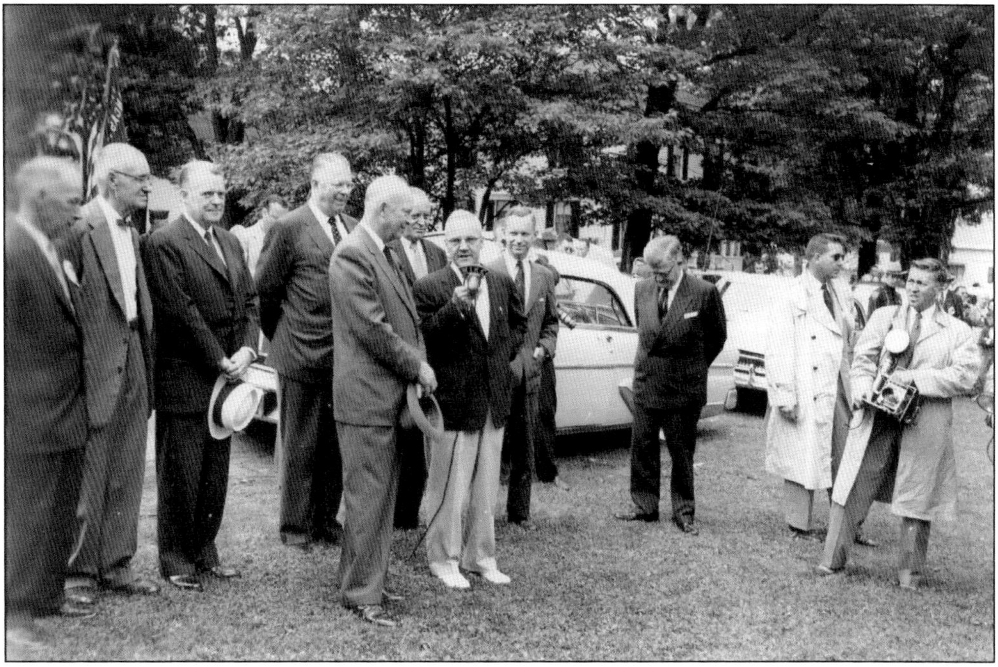

Welcoming ceremonies were held in Soldiers' Park for President Eisenhower, who is seen here being interviewed by Wilbur M. Schurman, the chairman of the Lancaster Welcoming Committee. Other dignitaries attending were, from left to right, Sinclair Weeks, Gov. Lane Swinell, US senators Norris Cotton and Styles Bridges, Rep. Perkins Bass, and Arthur Sherman, the chairman of the Lancaster Board of Selectmen.

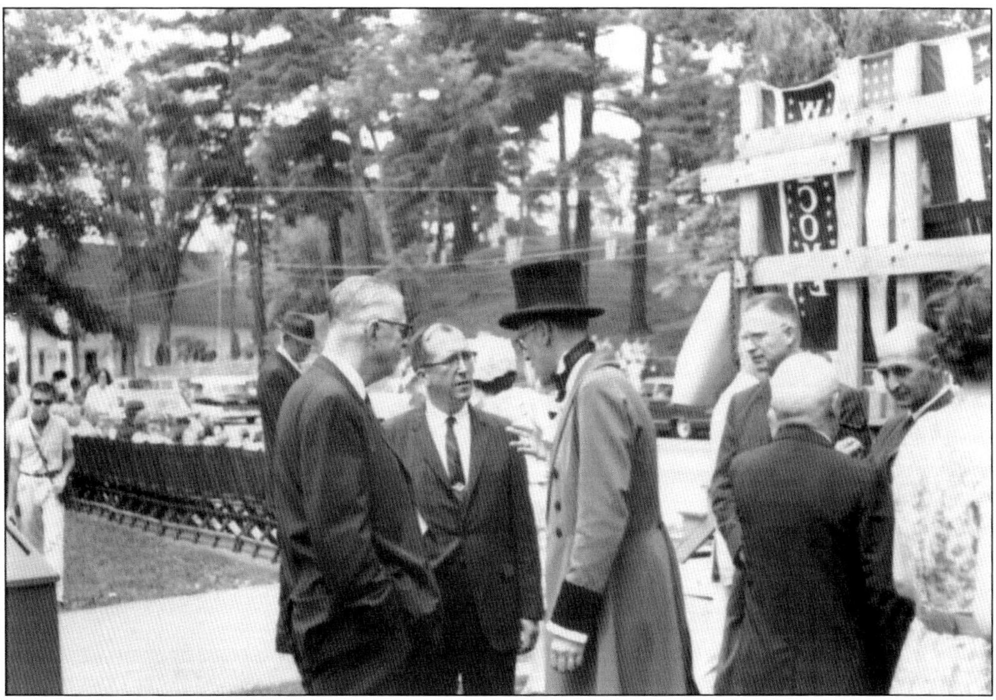

Dignitaries confer near the viewing stand during the bicentennial parade in August 1964.

Five

Homes and Businesses

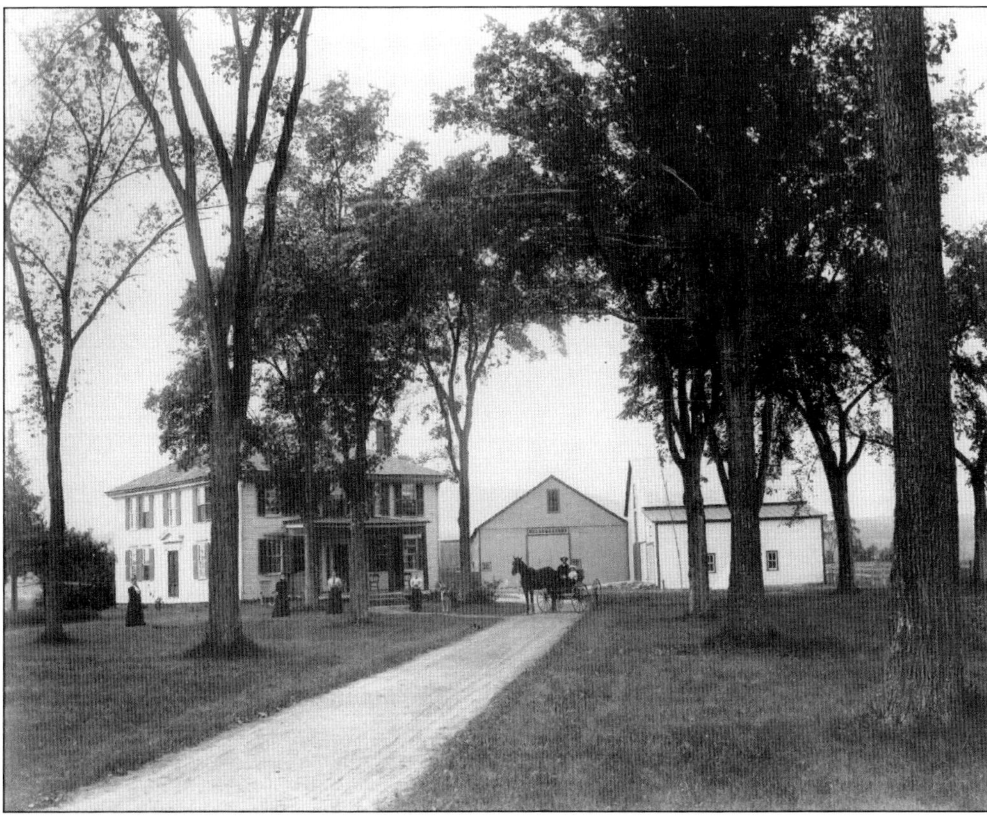

The historic Wilder-Holton House is seen here in the summer of 1899. Note the door on the left, on the Bridge Street side of the house, which was later removed.

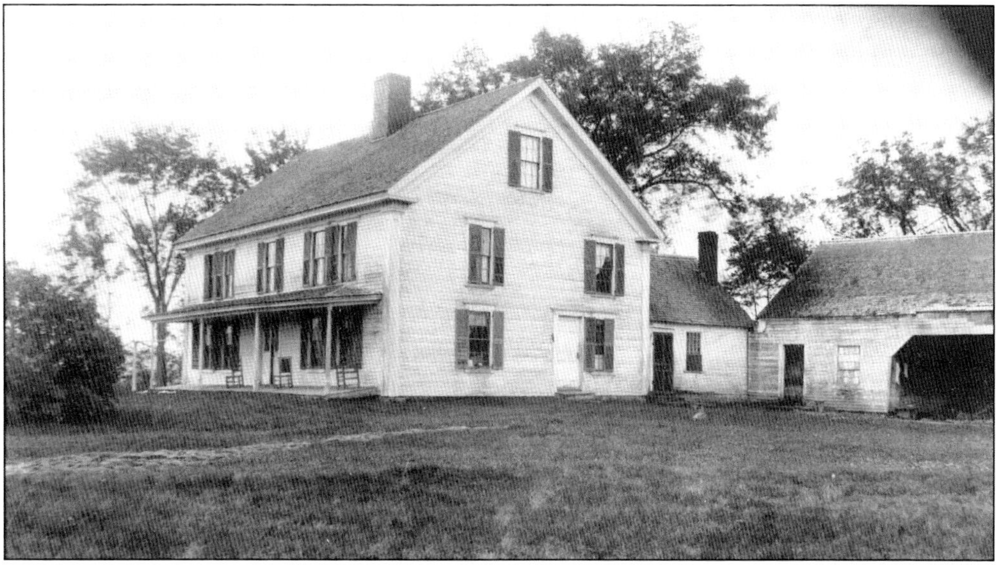

The home of early settlers Emmons Stockwell and Ruth Page Stockwell was on what is now Stockwell Road, near where Emmons had first stopped on his way back from Canada in 1759. His original cabin is possibly seen here behind the house. The home burned many years ago.

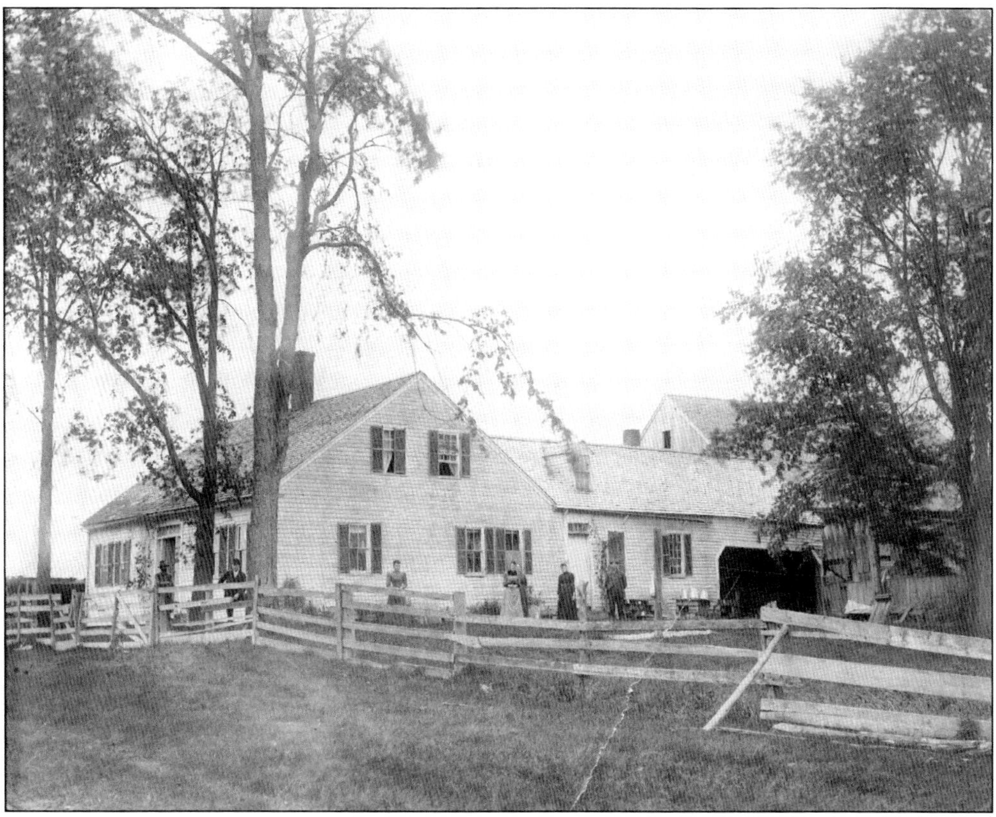

Rosebrook Farm, on Stockwell Road, is seen here in the 1890s.

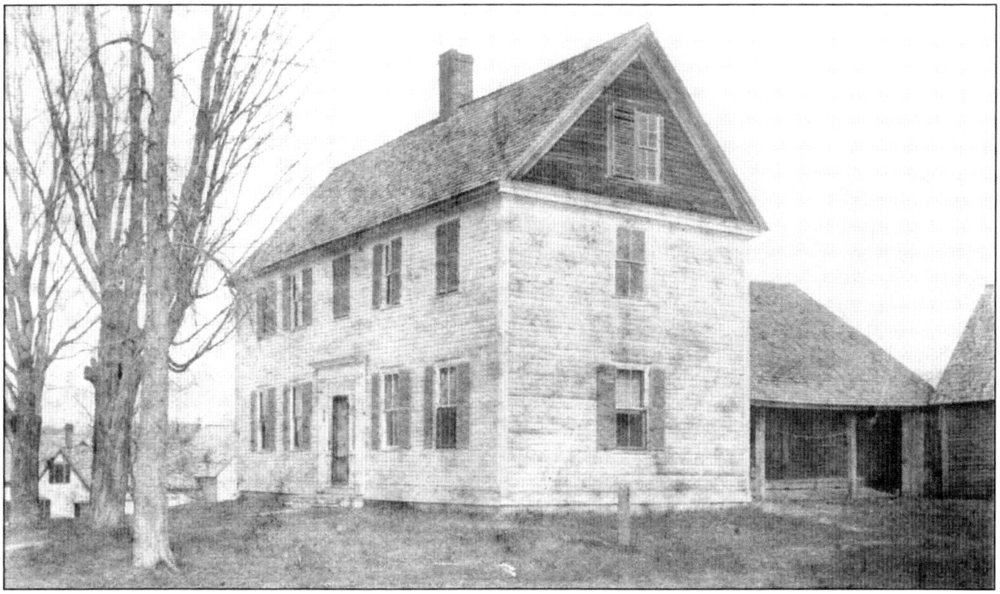

The Parson Willard house, on Elm Street, was the home of the first minister of the Congregational church, which was organized on July 17, 1794. He had served in the Revolutionary War and descended from one of the best families in New England. His brother John was the first minister of the Congregational church in neighboring Lunenburg, Vermont. The house was built by John Haven for his daughter Mrs. Willard in 1799. It is now owned by Charolette Quay.

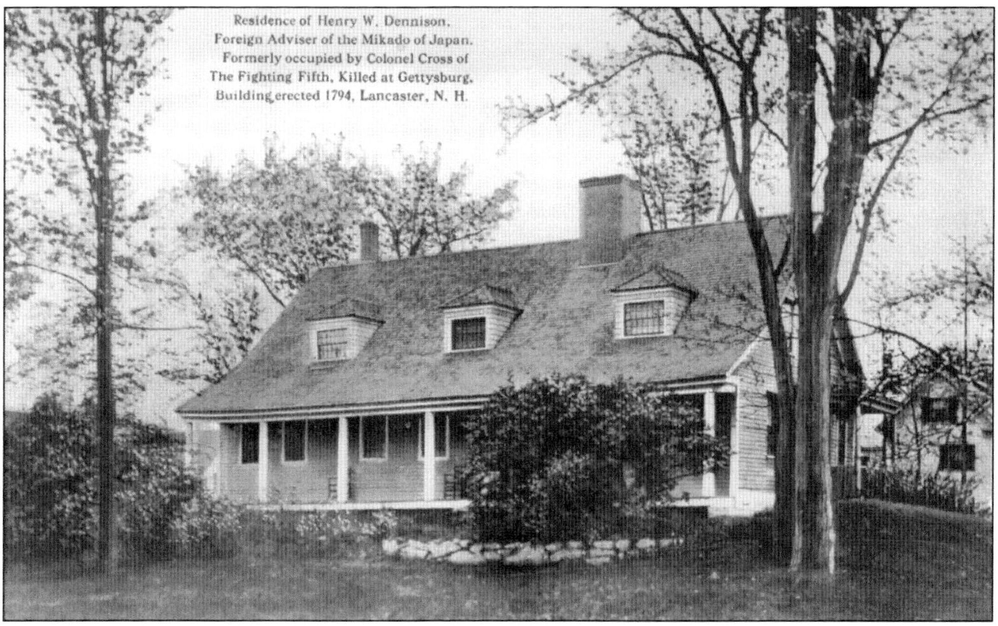

This is a rare view of the Everett-Cross house, on Main Street, where the Cross Monument now stands. It was built in 1794 by Richard Clair Everett, a prominent lawyer. Daniel Webster and other men of note were entertained at the home, and it was long occupied by Col. Ephraim Cross, Everett's son-in-law. It was also the boyhood home of Col. Edward E. Cross of the 5th New Hampshire Volunteer Infantry. Later, it was the residence of Henry W. Dennison, the foreign adviser to the mikado of Japan.

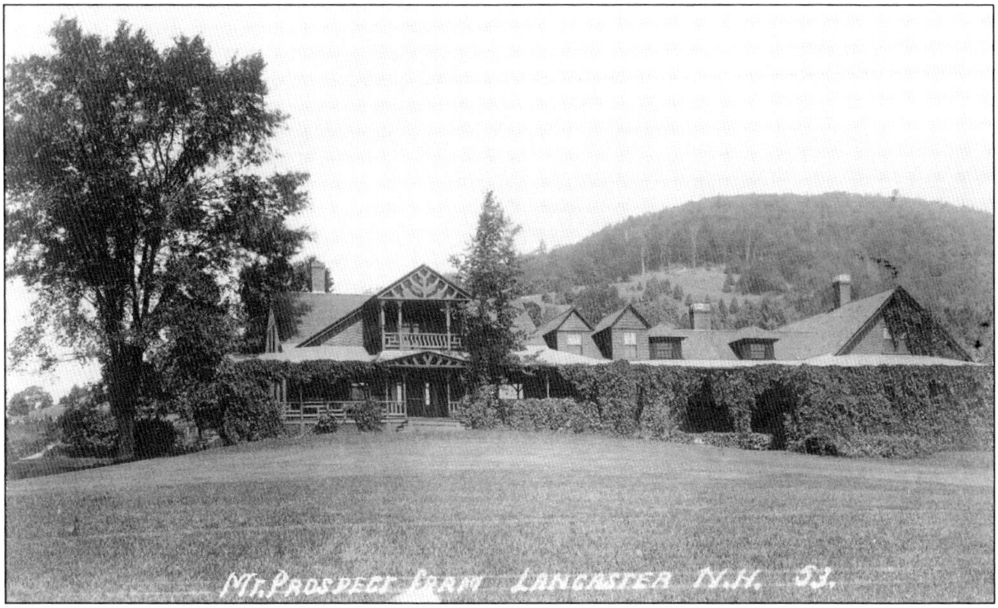

Mount Prospect Farm, seen here, was originally in the Rowell family and was later owned by John W. Weeks.

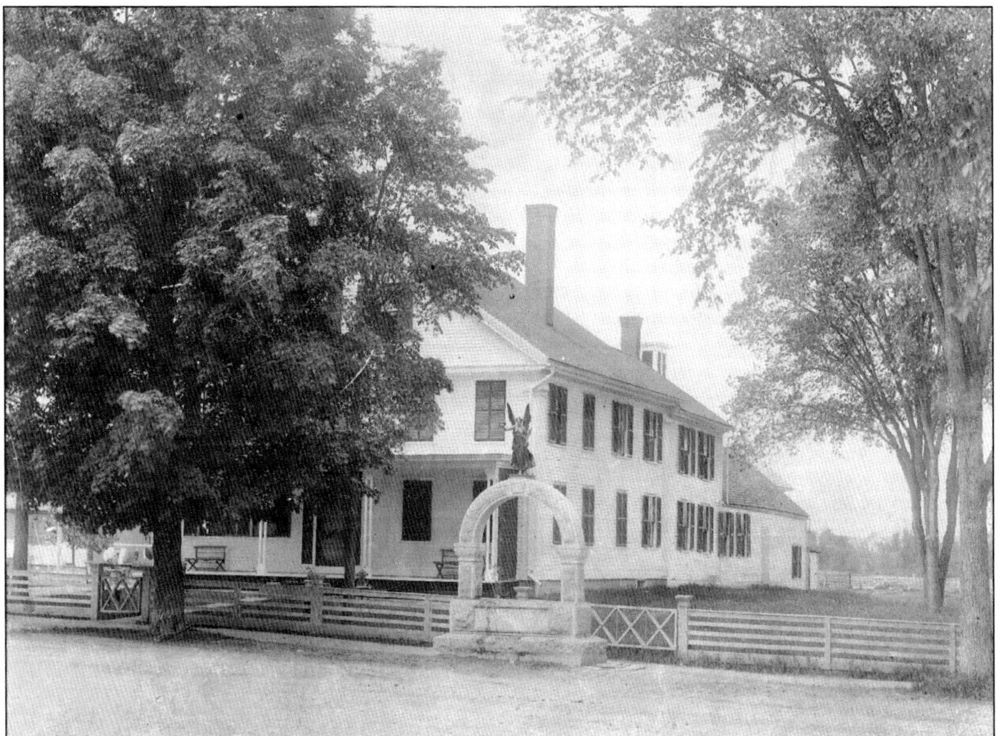

This is the Main Street home of early merchants Richard P. and Emily M. Kent, and, later, their son Edward R. Kent. It was located on the site of the present post office. The Kent Memorial Fountain was given to the town by Henry O. Kent, Edward R. Kent, and Charles N. Kent in memory of their parents. It remains to this day.

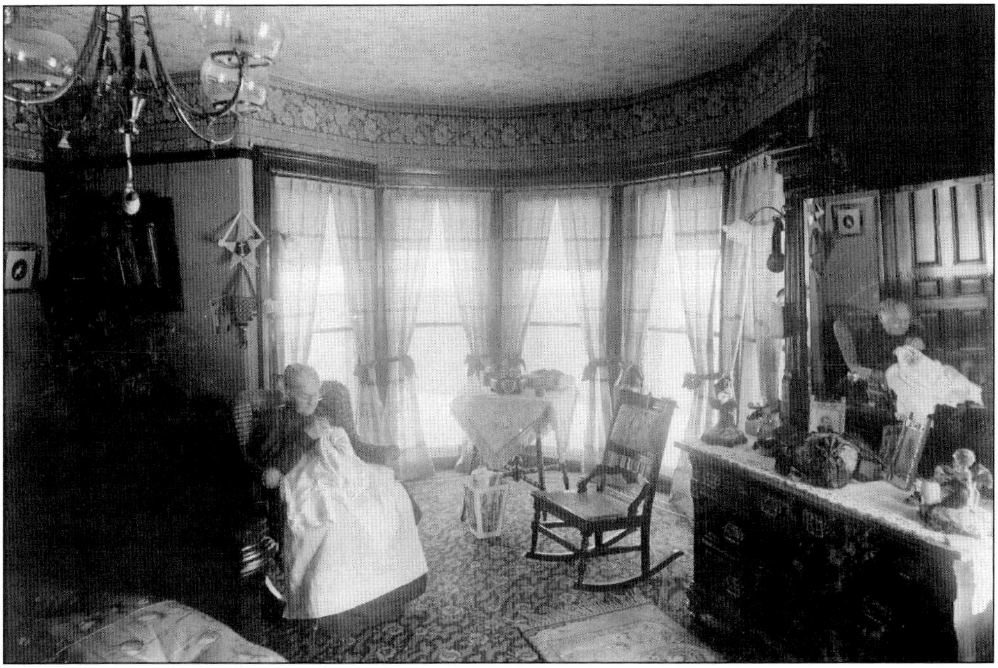

Abigail Hatch (Dixon) Van Dyke (1808–1904) is seen here in the bedroom of her home, at 119 Main Street. Originally the Benjamin F. Whidden house, it was altered and much enlarged by George Van Dyke (1836–1909), a lumber baron and one of Abigail's eight children. The Passumpsic Savings Bank now occupies the site.

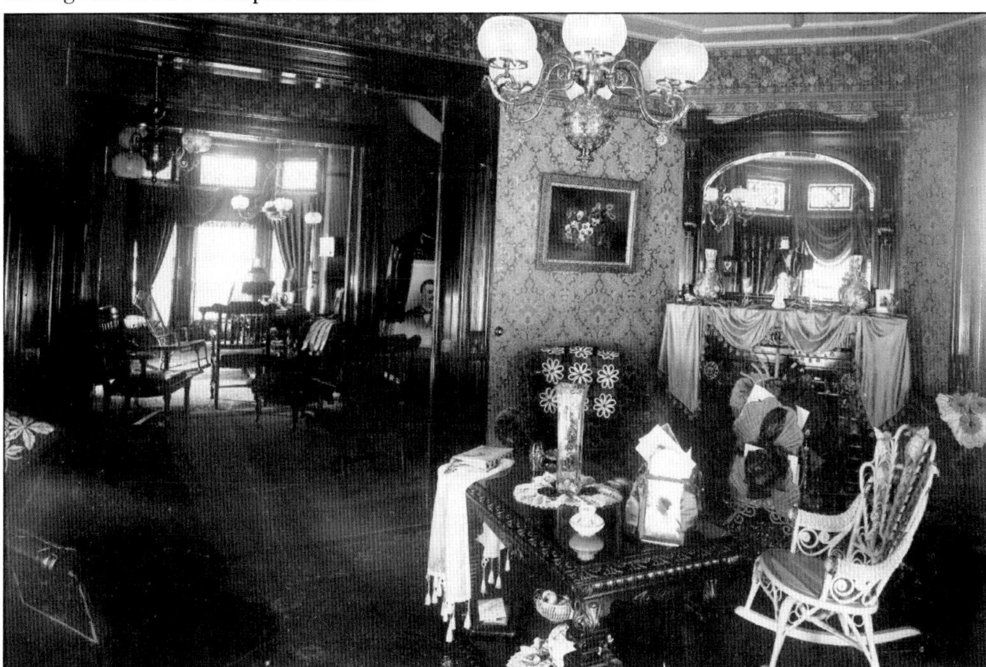

Formal parlors graced the first floor of the remodeled Van Dyke house. Notice the rare woodwork and the chandeliers lit by the mansion's own gas plant.

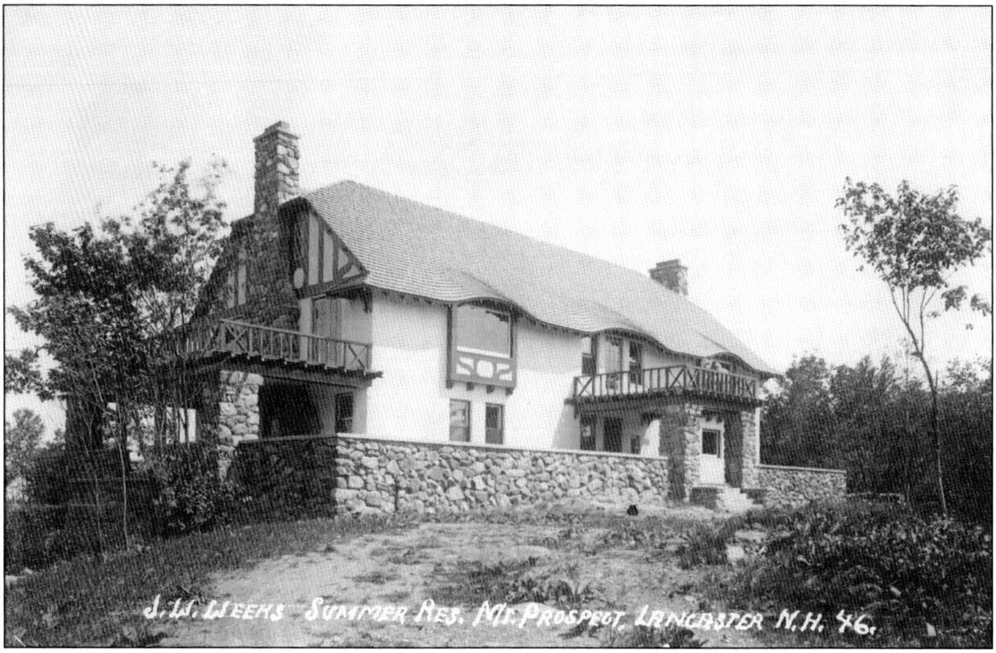

The Weeks estate on Mount Prospect was the home of John Wingate Weeks, a Lancaster native, US congressman, US senator, and secretary of war under presidents Harding and Coolidge. Weeks worked successfully to establish the White Mountain National Forest in New Hampshire. Today, Weeks State Park is made up of his land and home. It was given to the State of New Hampshire by his son Sinclair Weeks, the former secretary of commerce under President Eisenhower, and his daughter Katherine Weeks Davidge.

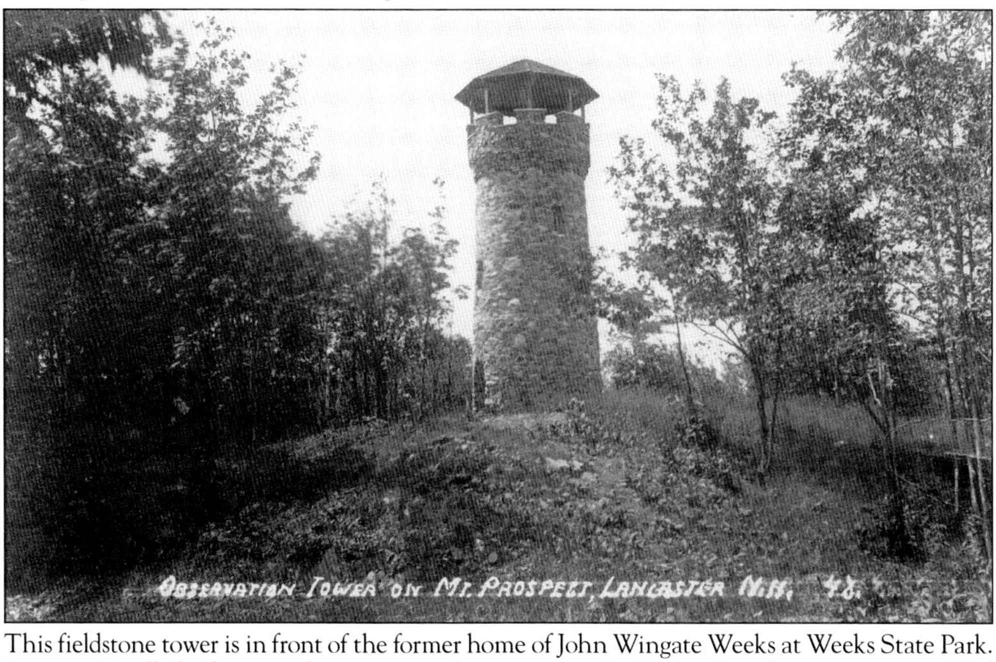

This fieldstone tower is in front of the former home of John Wingate Weeks at Weeks State Park. It was originally built as an observatory and water tower. In 1941, a fire observatory was added to the top.

Known as the Eaton house, this grand old home is located at 19 Pleasant Street, above the Mechanic Street Bridge.

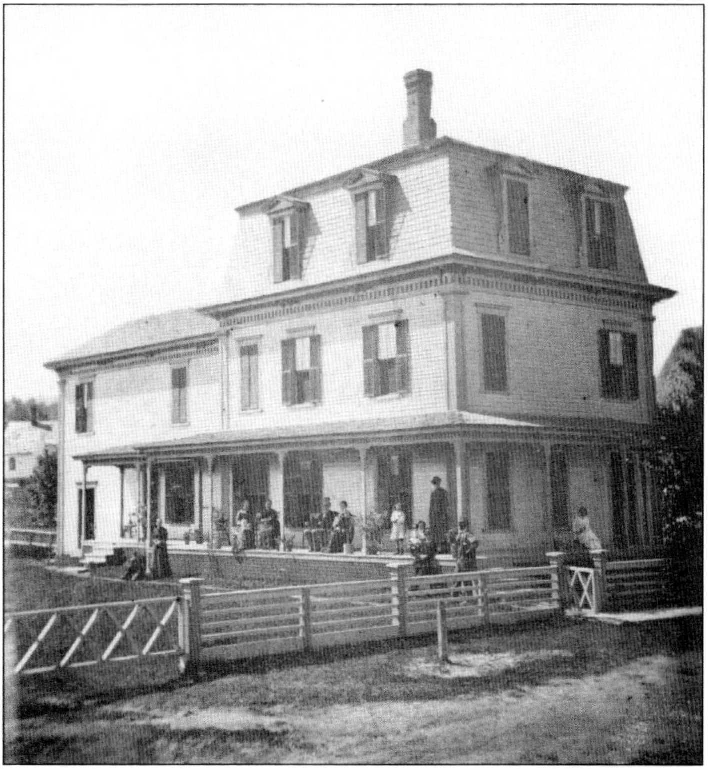

The building below, which currently houses Bailey Funeral Home, was previously Stannard's Funeral Home. Before that, it was a private residence.

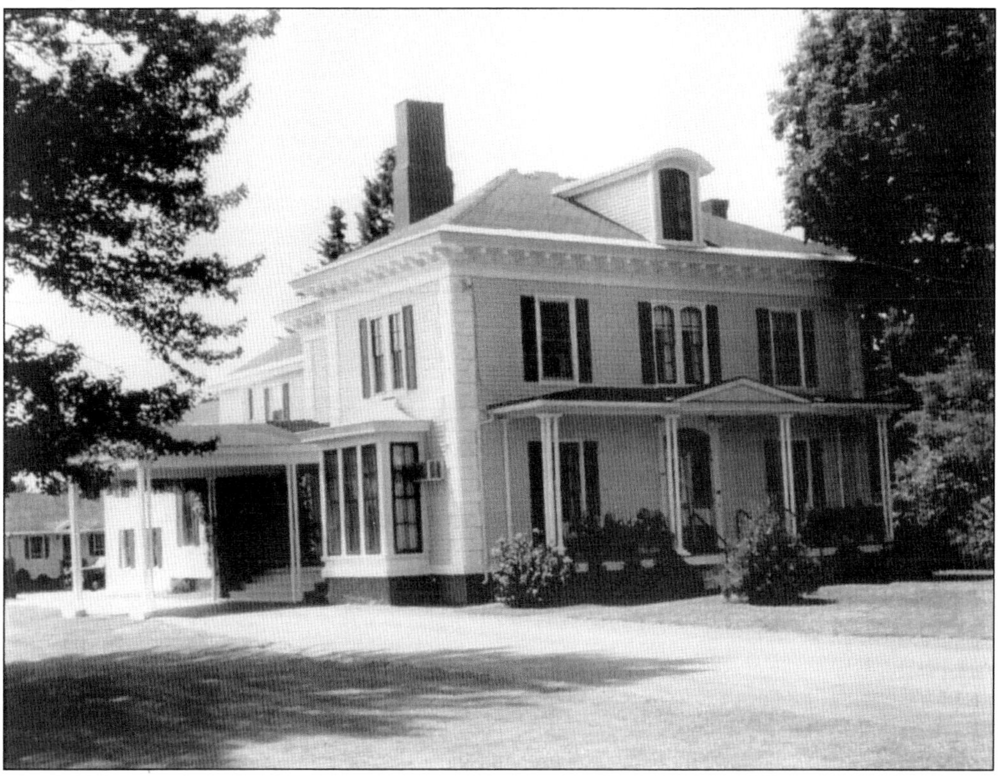

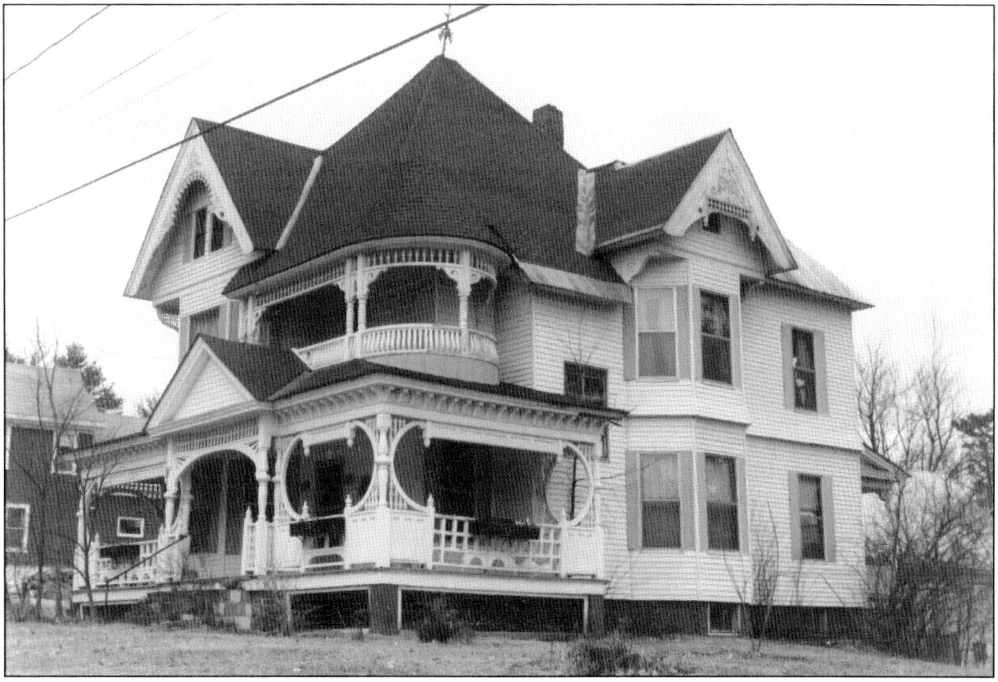

Located on Bunker Hill Street, the Curtis house is a wonderful Queen Anne Victorian with Eastlake and gingerbread-style decorations.

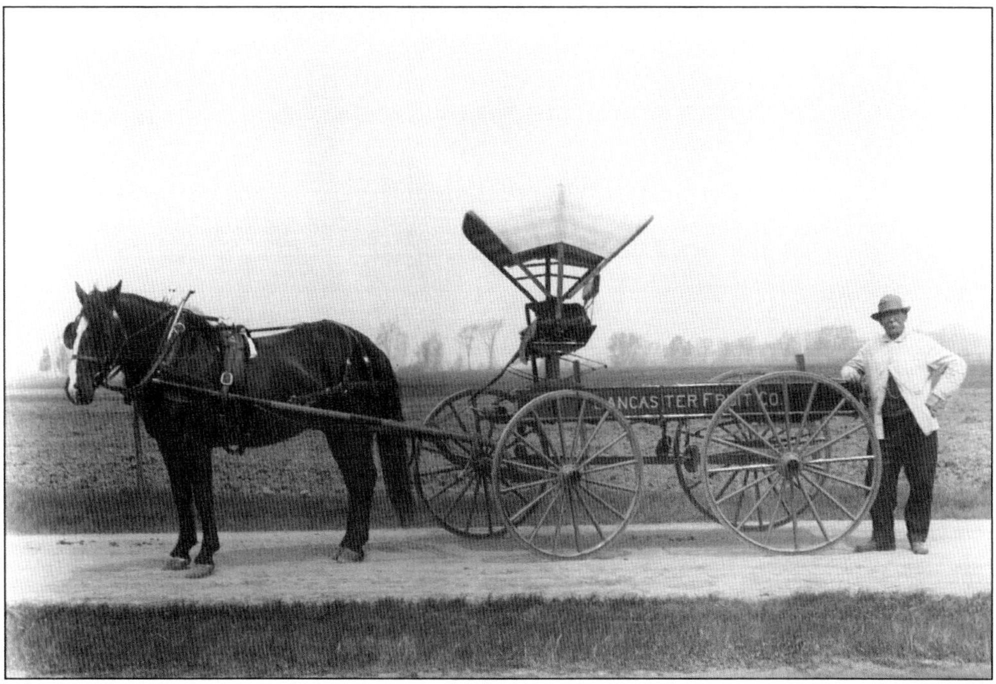

Mauro Busi, an Italian immigrant and the founder of Lancaster Fruit Company, poses in front of his peddler's wagon in the early 1900s. Busi's children, Frank, Angelo, and Angelina, worked with him. The business was eventually sold to Armand Abelli and was a must-stop for politicians on the campaign trail.

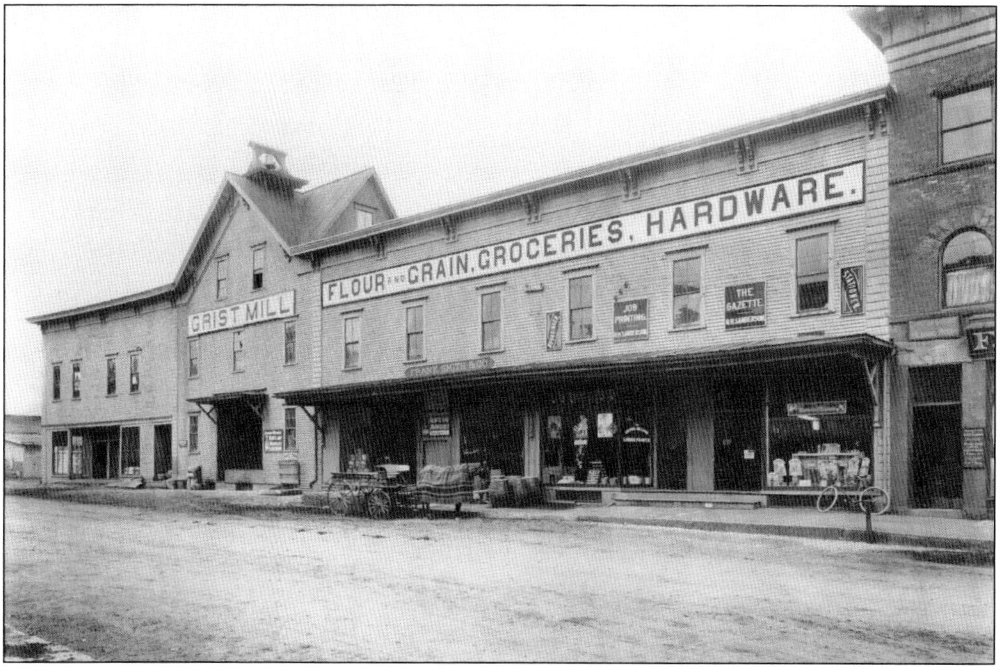

The Frank Smith & Company building is seen here. Long a fixture on Middle Street, the business included a sawmill and a gristmill and sold hardware and groceries. The buildings were torn down in the 1980s when the Lancaster National Bank added a drive-up window and a parking lot.

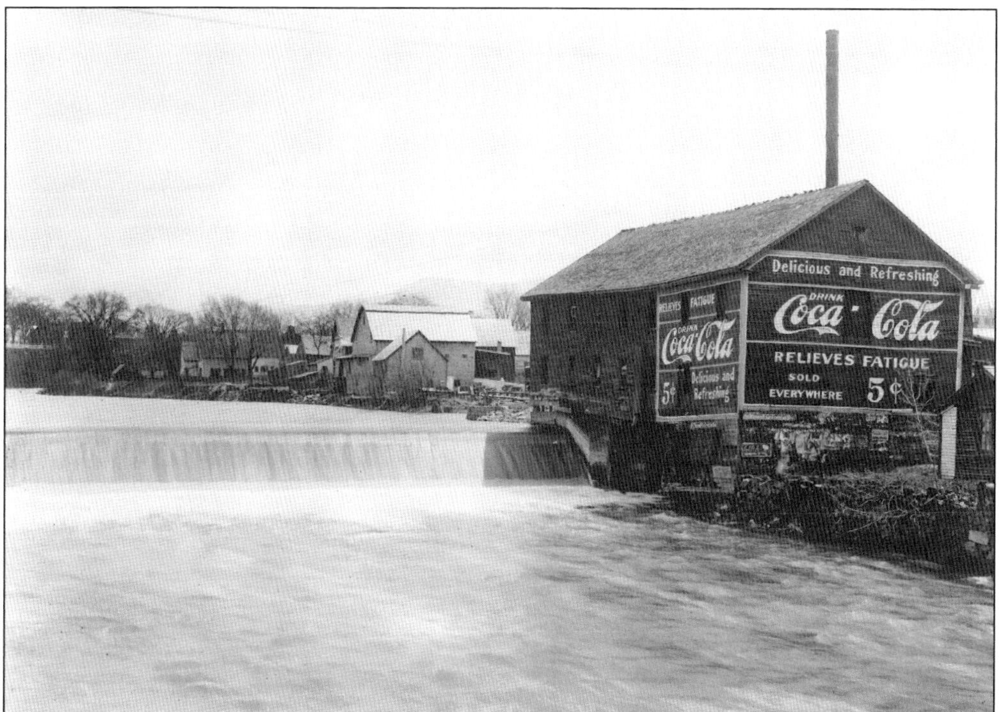

The Frank Smith & Company sawmill and upper dam on Israel's River is seen here from the Main Street Bridge in the early 1900s.

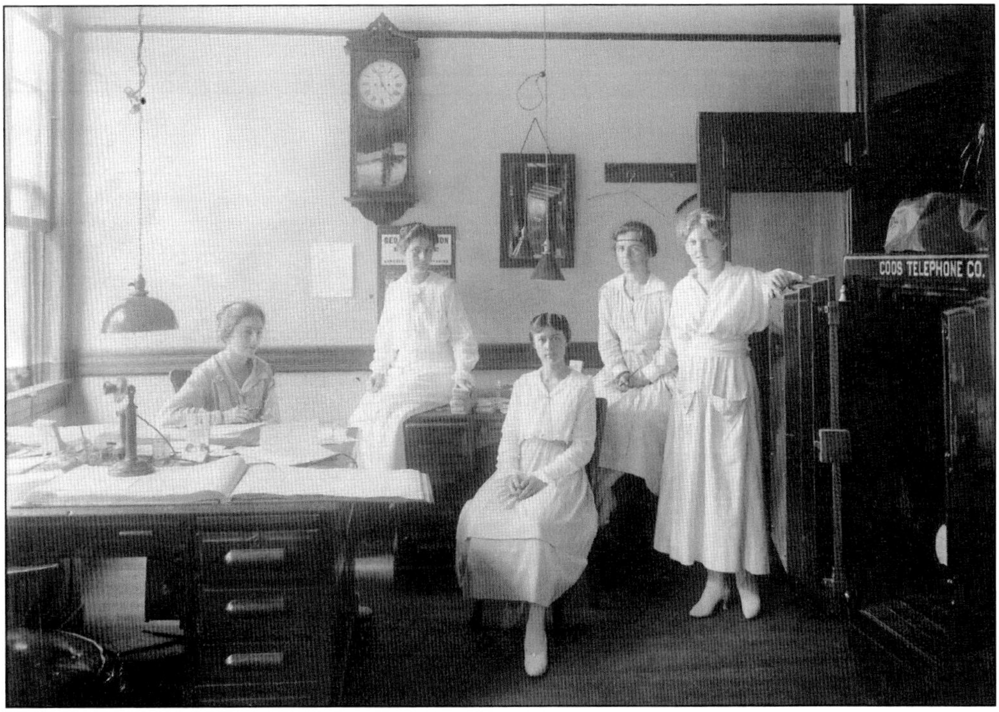

The office staff of the Coös Telephone Company is seen here in 1917.

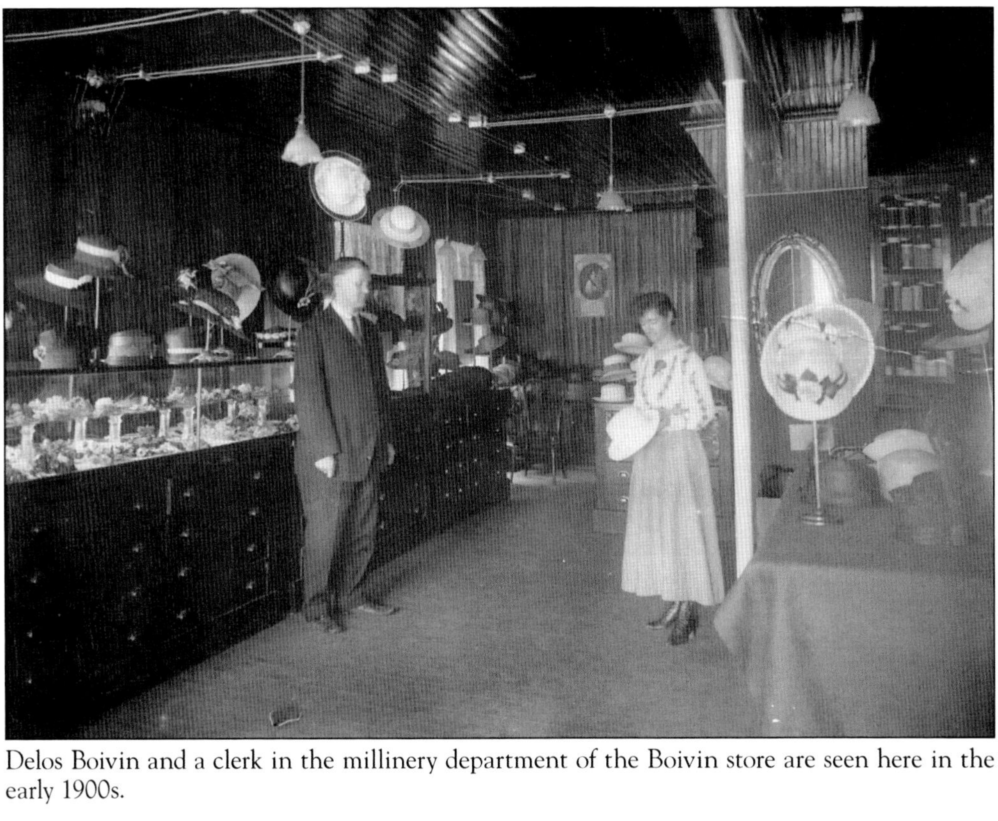

Delos Boivin and a clerk in the millinery department of the Boivin store are seen here in the early 1900s.

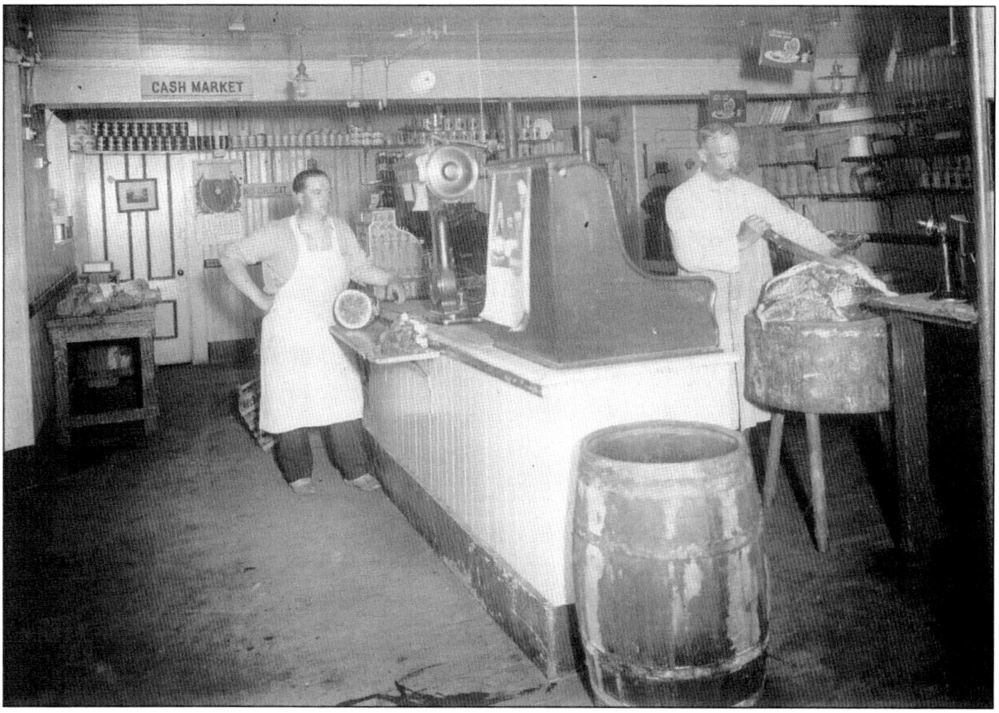

Rich's meat and fish market, underneath the S.N. Evans store on the corner of Main and Canal Streets, is seen here in the 1920s.

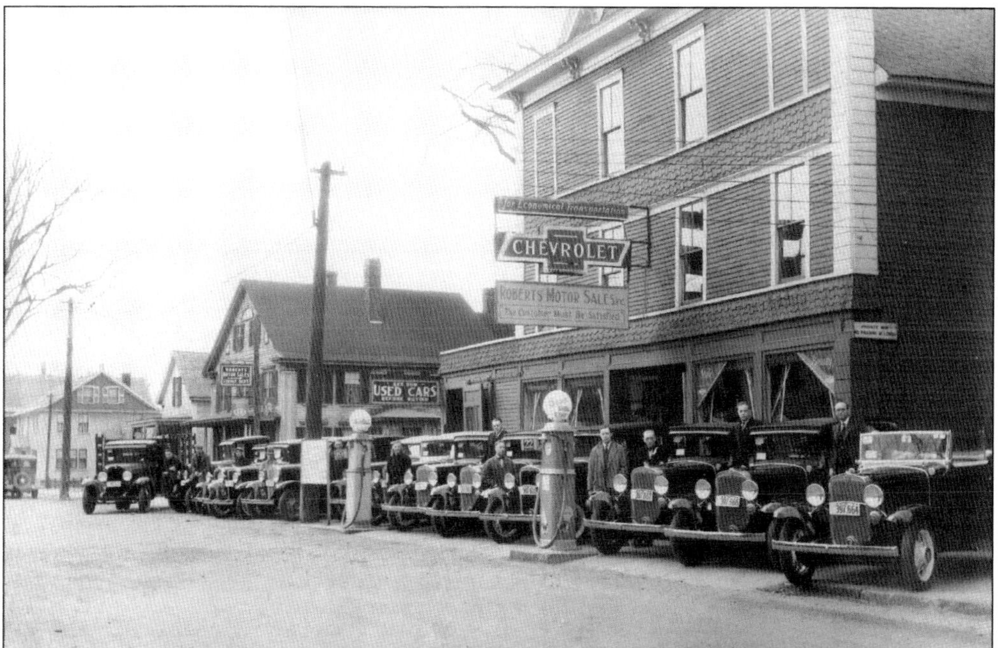

Roberts Motor Sales was in business in Lancaster for more than 50 years. The company is seen here in its Elm Street location in the 1920s. This building was behind what is now J.L. Sullivan's Pub and Restaurant on Main Street.

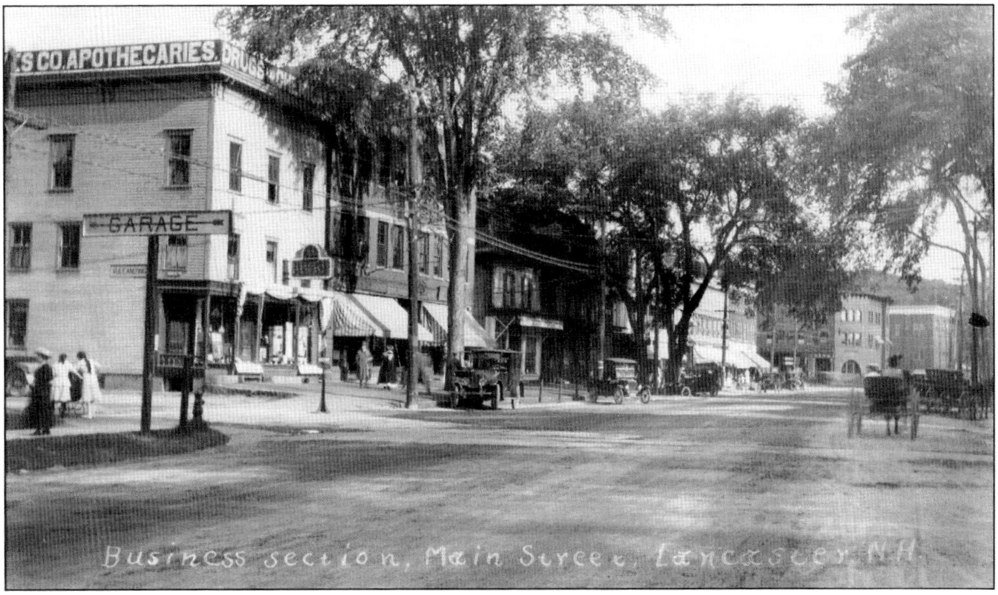

Graceful elms shade Main Street as buggies and motorcars share the broad thoroughfare along Lancaster's business section around 1915.

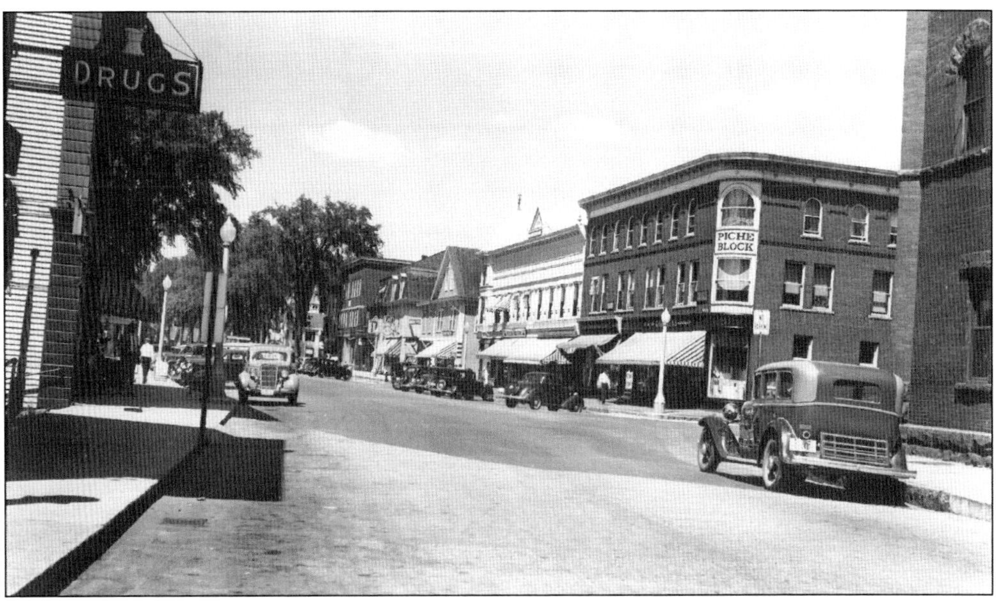

This idyllic 1930s view shows the brisk business section on Main Street.

Six

TRANSPORTATION

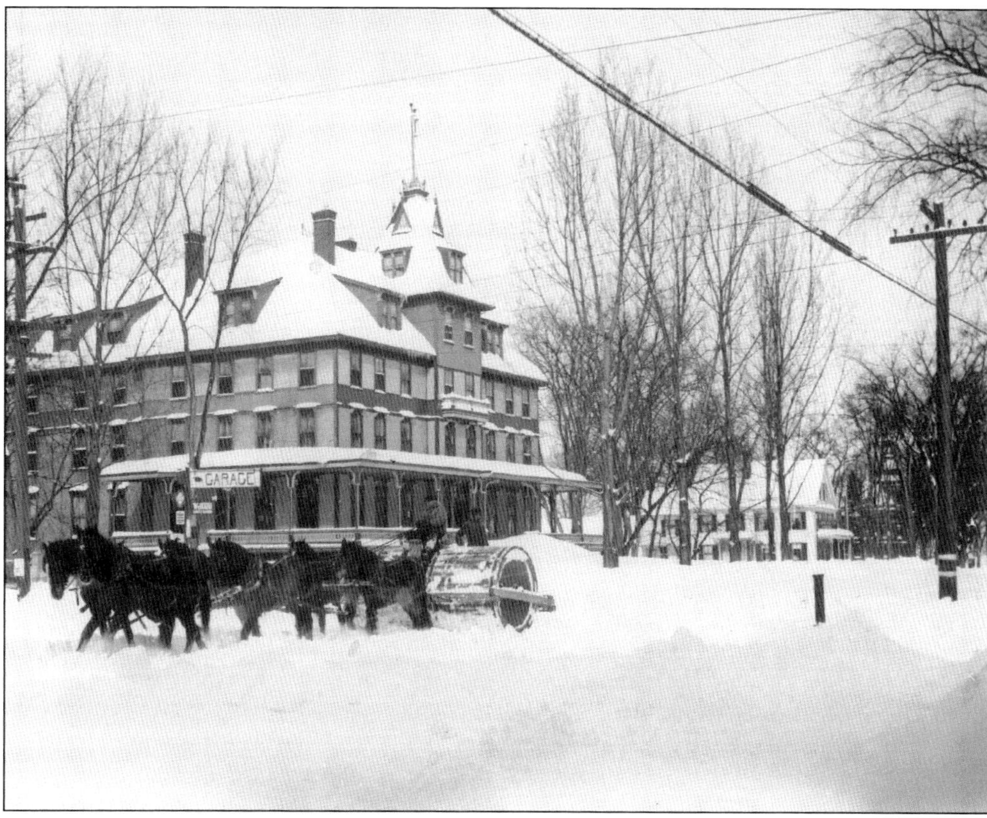

Large, heavy snow rollers were used to pack the snow down on the streets to make them passable by horse and sleigh. The Lancaster House is seen here behind the town roller, which is being drawn by six horses after a winter storm. (Courtesy of the P.J. Noyes Company.)

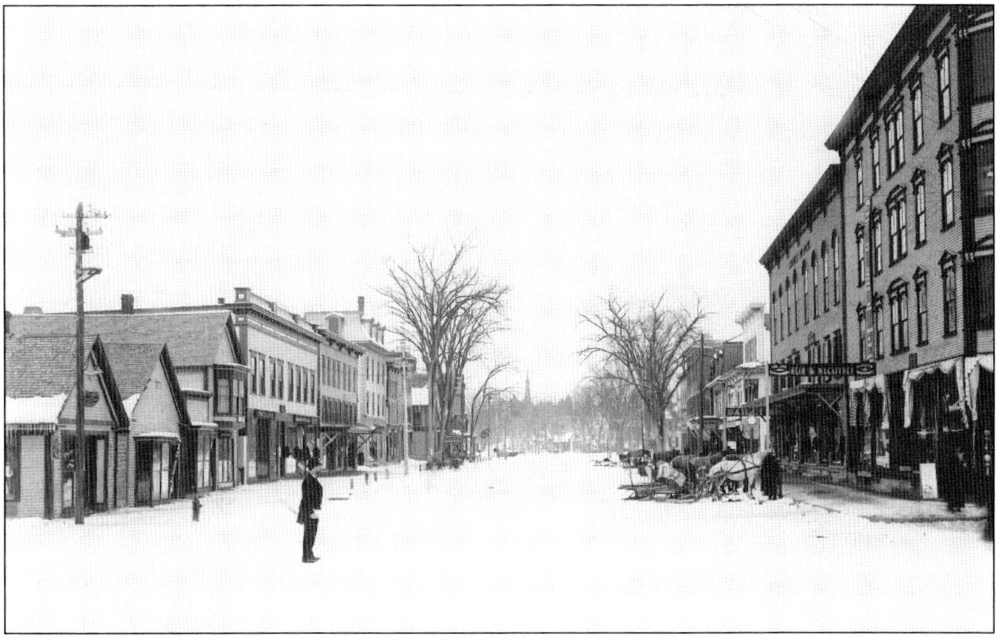

Folks came to town using horse-drawn sleds and sleighs in the winter, as seen here in this late-1800s scene looking north from the intersection of Main and Middle Streets.

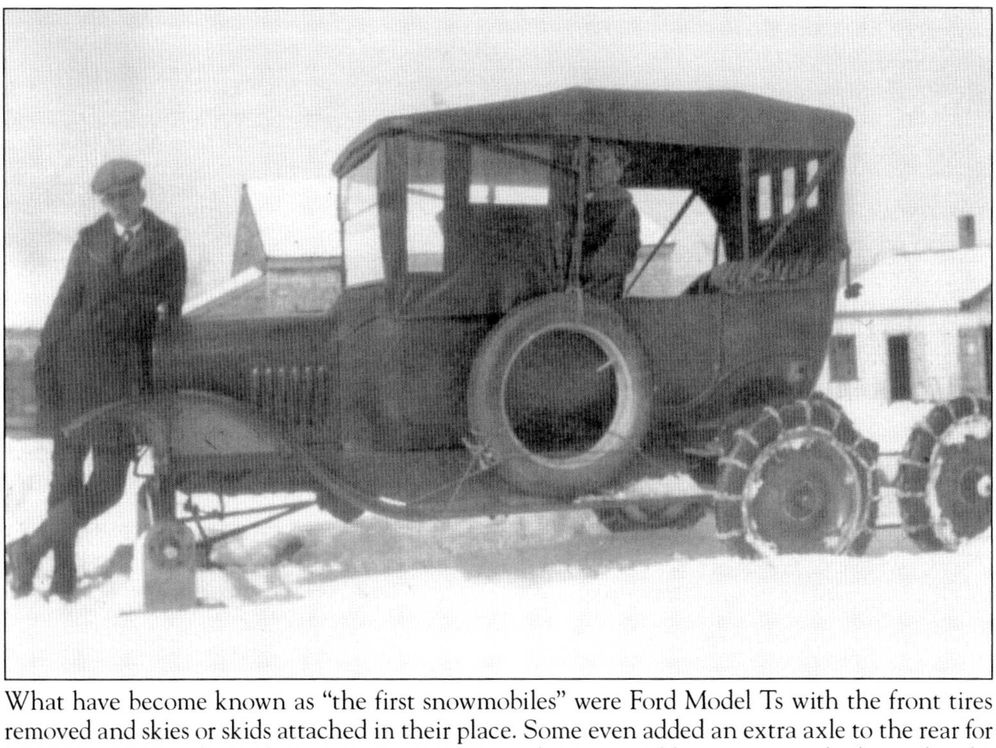

What have become known as "the first snowmobiles" were Ford Model Ts with the front tires removed and skies or skids attached in their place. Some even added an extra axle to the rear for better traction, and tire chains were a must. Soon, kits were sold to convert vehicles and make getting around on snowy roads easier.

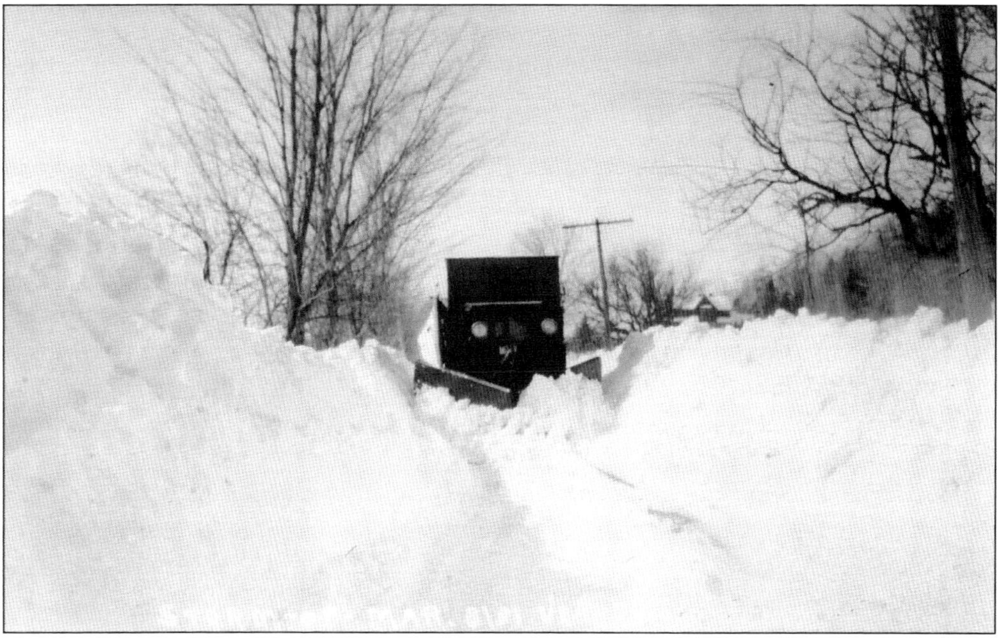

Snowplows worked hard day and night to keep the roads open, though it may have been several days before all the outlying roads were passable, especially after a blizzard.

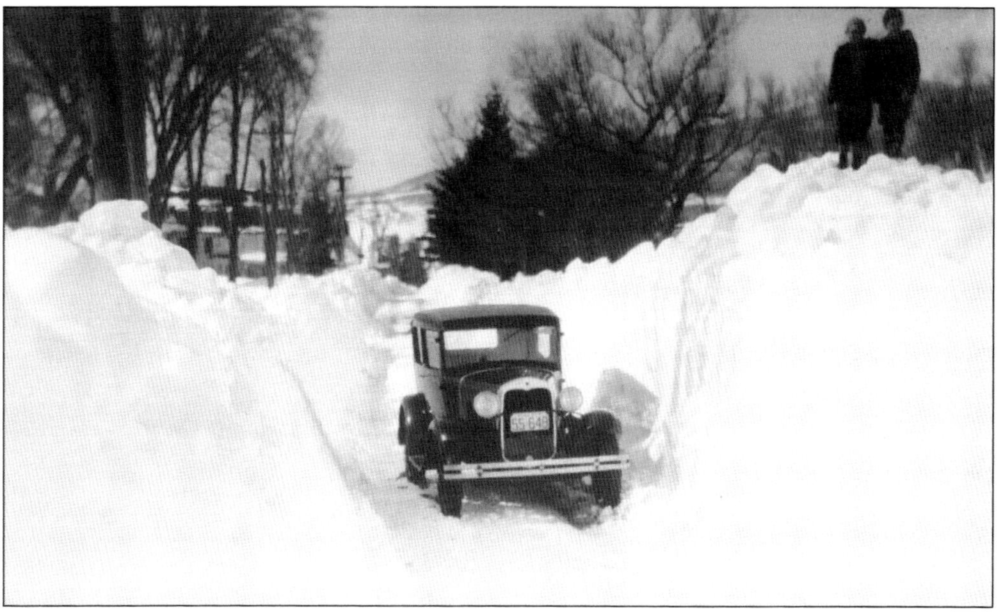

Winter in northern New England can be a challenge, with blizzards, freezing rain, and the January thaw. Lancaster experienced its share of deep snow and trying to keep the roads passable. Many diary entries tell of deep snows of two feet or more accompanied by temperatures well below zero degrees. The coldest recorded temperature was minus 55 degrees Fahrenheit. At times, snowbanks would be far above any conveyance of transportation.

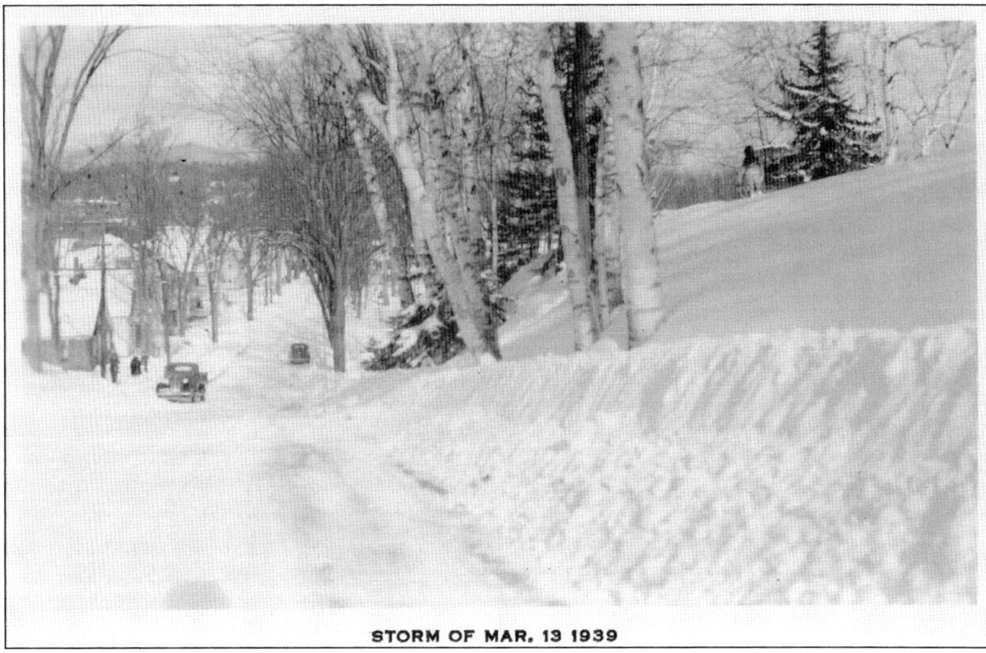

Bunker Hill Street, as the longest-steep street, became an interesting ride in the winter, both going up and coming down on the snow-covered surface. The street was also used by both children and adults for sledding, which was sometimes done on just sheets of cardboard.

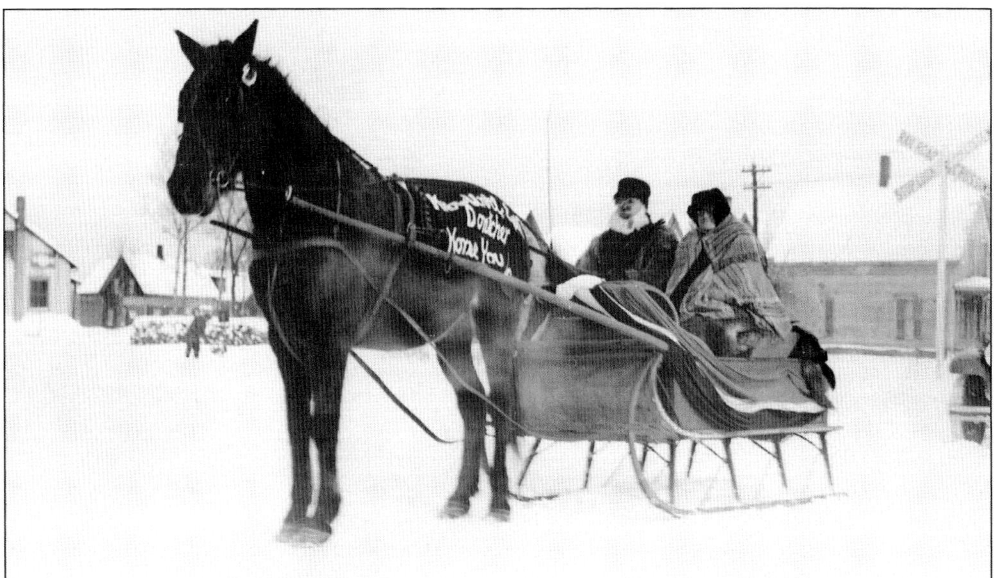

Wintertime travel by horse and sleigh meant bundling up well. Most likely, a heated soapstone was tucked in to keep feet warm. Snow-covered streets were rolled rather than plowed in the early days, making sleigh rides possible.

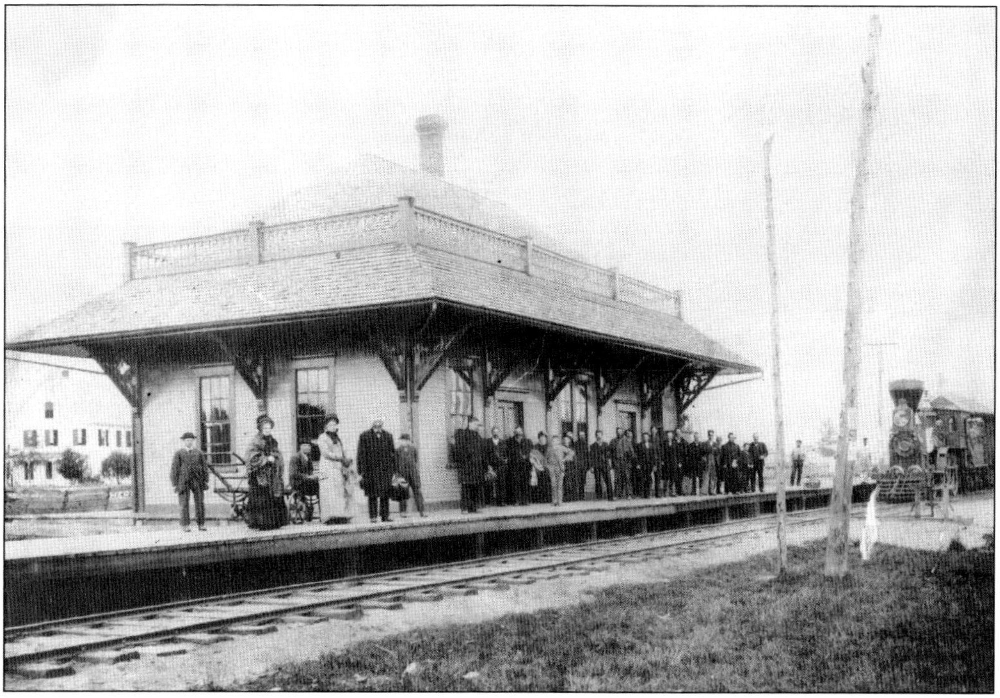

Seen here is Lancaster's first railroad station, built in 1871. Townspeople await the arrival of the *Granite State*, the first engine to arrive.

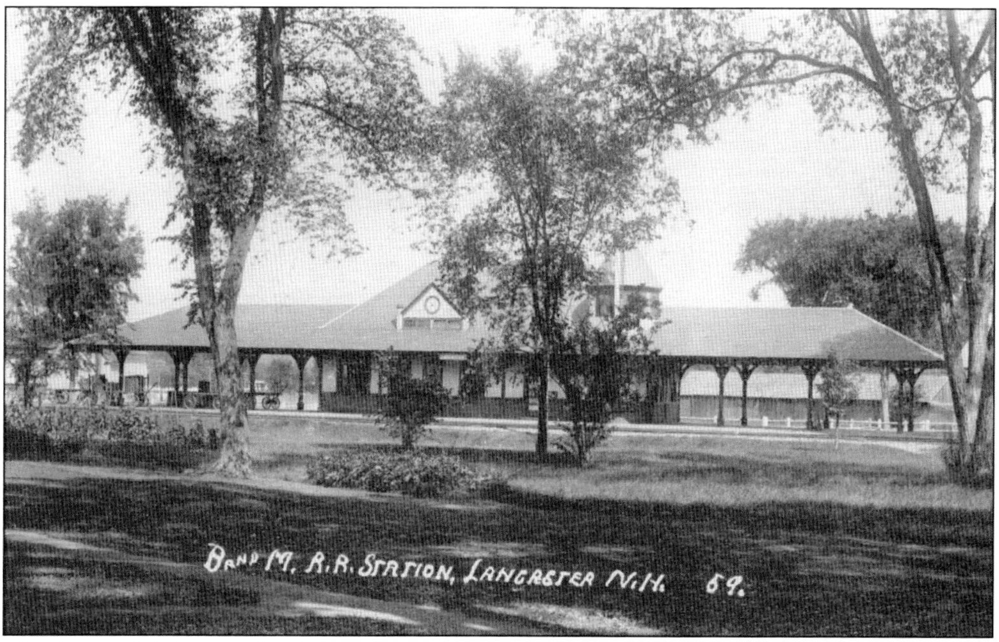

The Boston & Maine railroad station was on the corner of Main and Railroad Streets, where Rite Aid is today. The station was built in 1893 to replace the original depot, built in 1871. With the decline of train service, it fell into disrepair and was torn down around 1940.

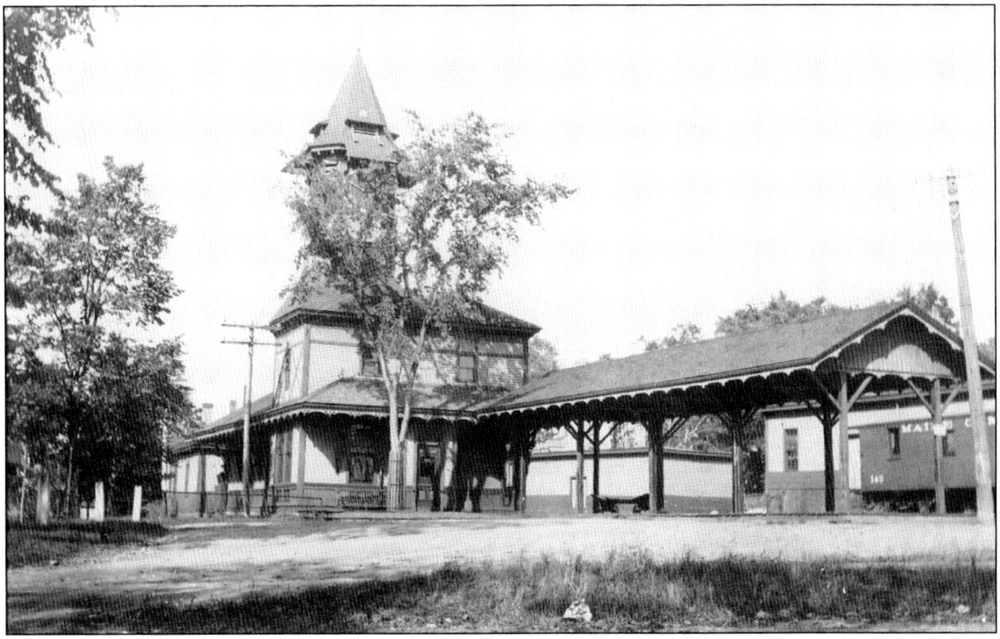

The Maine Central railroad station, on Bunker Hill Street, was built around 1890 and served for many years. The tower clock was a town landmark. In addition to the passenger terminal, it housed the offices of the superintendent of the White Mountain Division and the maintenance and freight offices.

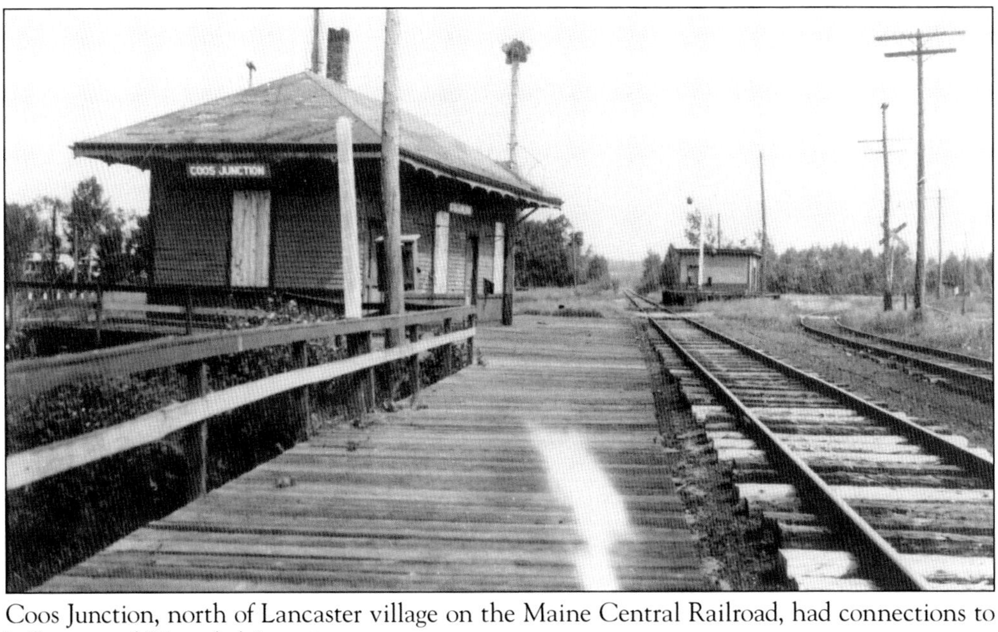

Coos Junction, north of Lancaster village on the Maine Central Railroad, had connections to Jefferson and Waumbek Junction.

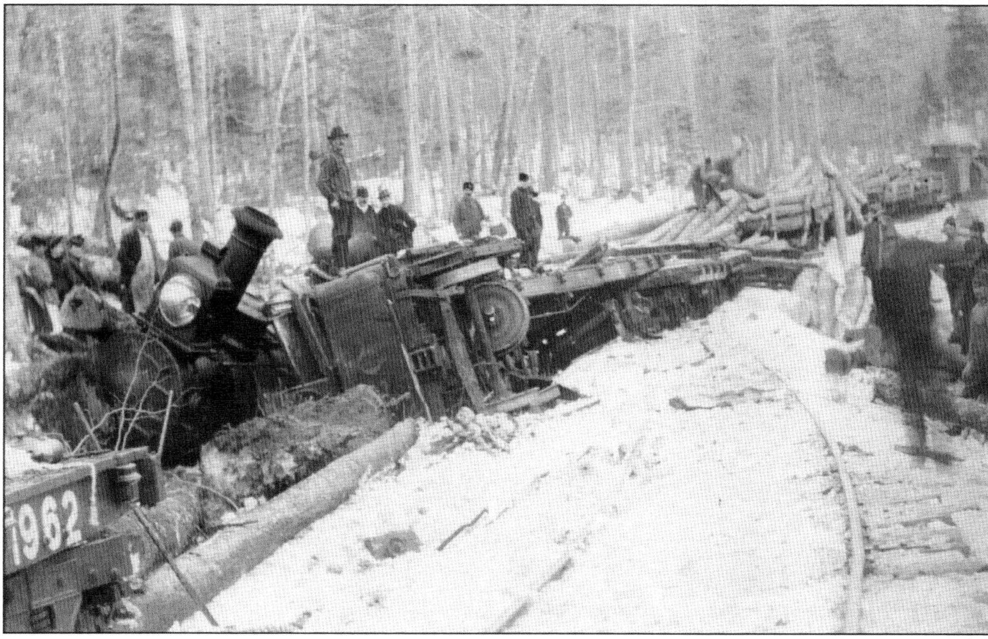

On January 31, 1890, the engine *Triton*, of the Concord Line, made its first and last run, as a replacement for the regular engine on the Lancaster & Kilkenny Railroad. Engineer Leonard Crouch was pulling a string of 10 cars loaded with 50,000 board feet of logs when a pin between the fourth and fifth set of logs snapped. The engine left the track on the curve near the old Rowell farm. Crouch was killed instantly. It was the only fatal accident that ever occurred on the Lancaster & Kilkenny Railroad.

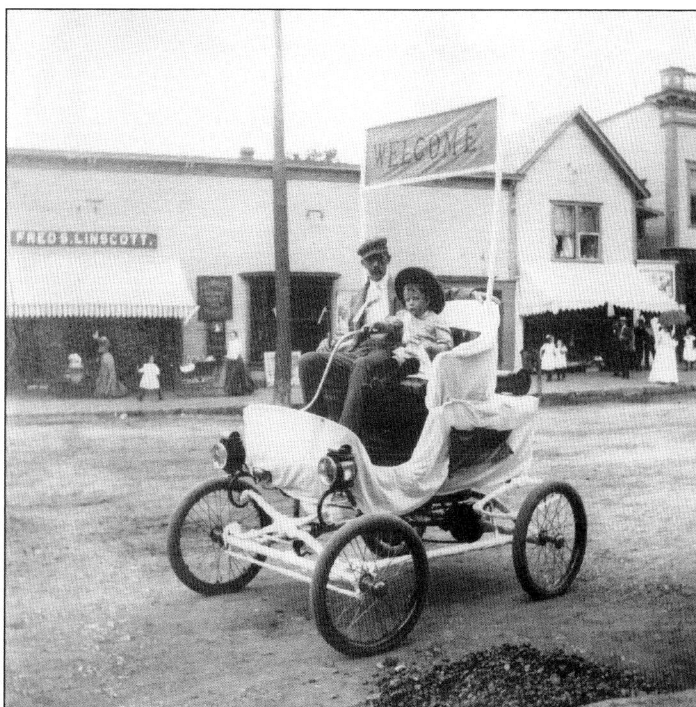

Abner Bailey and Allin Moore parade through Main Street in the first automobile in Lancaster.

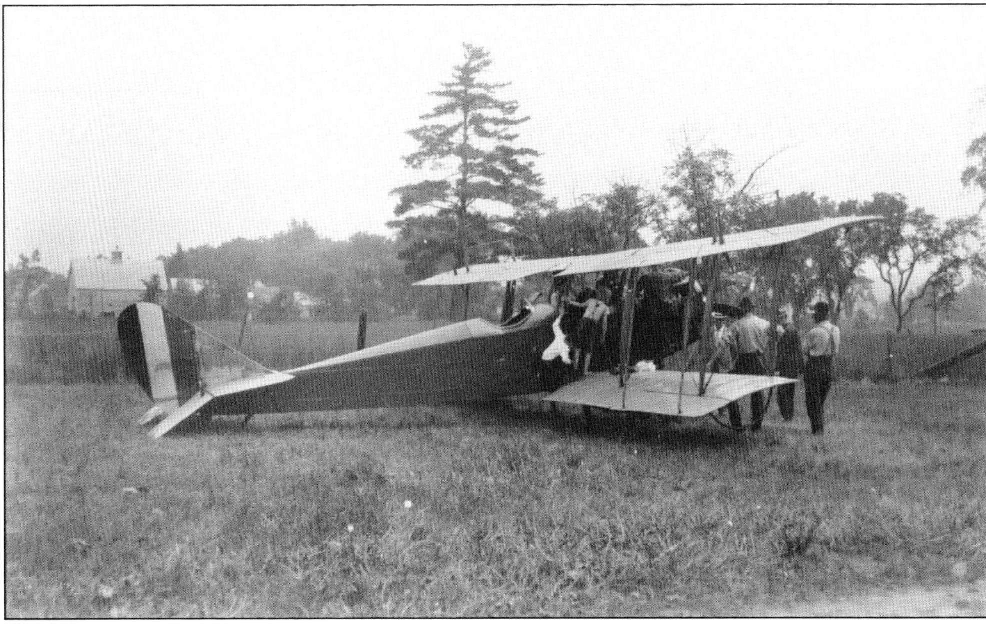

The arrival of an airplane on one of the Holton fields was quite the curiosity. Eventually, a landing strip was built behind the Timberland Machine buildings that extended down to the Connecticut River.

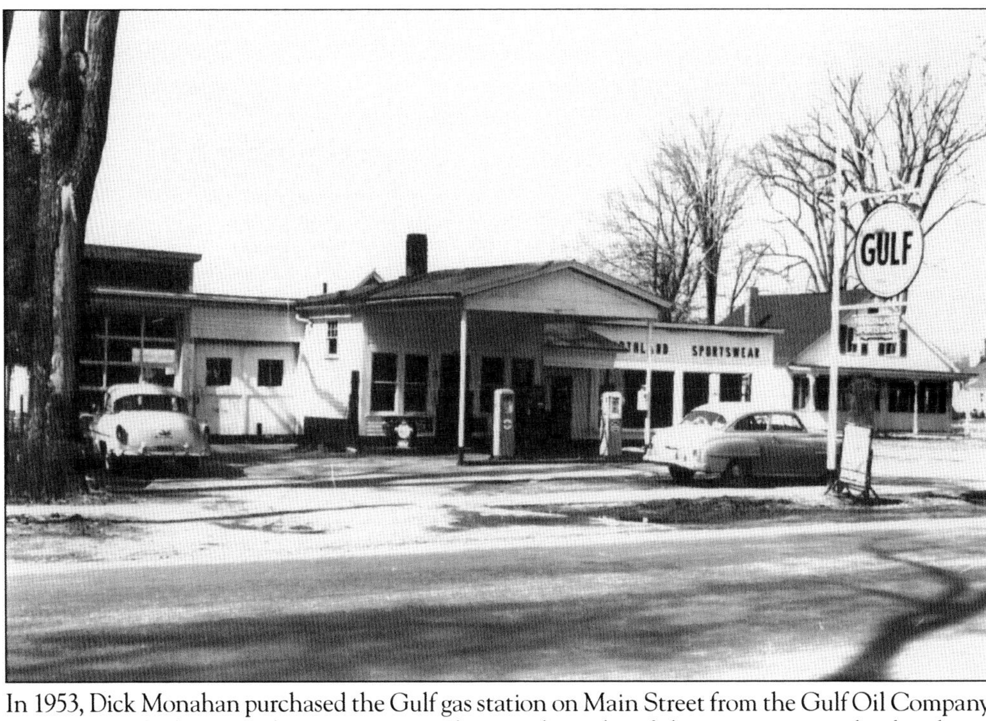

In 1953, Dick Monahan purchased the Gulf gas station on Main Street from the Gulf Oil Company. It was located where Dunkin' Donuts is today. To the right of the gas station is the first home of Gladys and Earl Rosebrook, which was later removed to make room for a parking lot at Earl Whitney's Rambler dealership. The station was sold in 1989 and then removed. (Courtesy of Midge Rosebrook.)

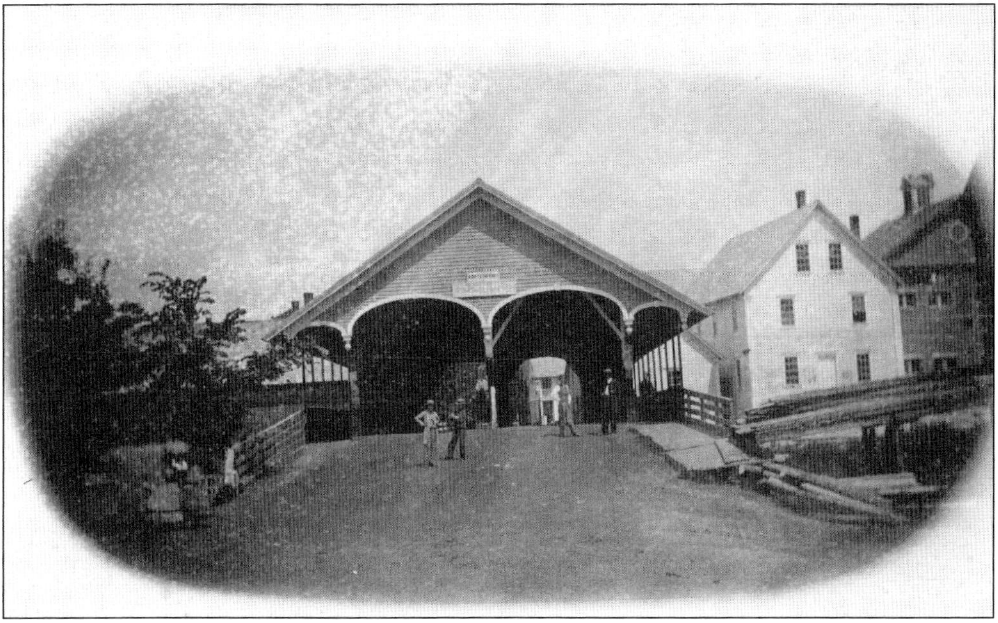

Crossing Israel's River on Main Street, this double-barreled bridge with covered walkways on each side was constructed in 1862 to replace the uncovered wooden bridge. It was a Paddleford truss style, featuring curved openings with ornamental carvings. This bridge was damaged by the flood of 1870 and ultimately destroyed by the big flood of 1886.

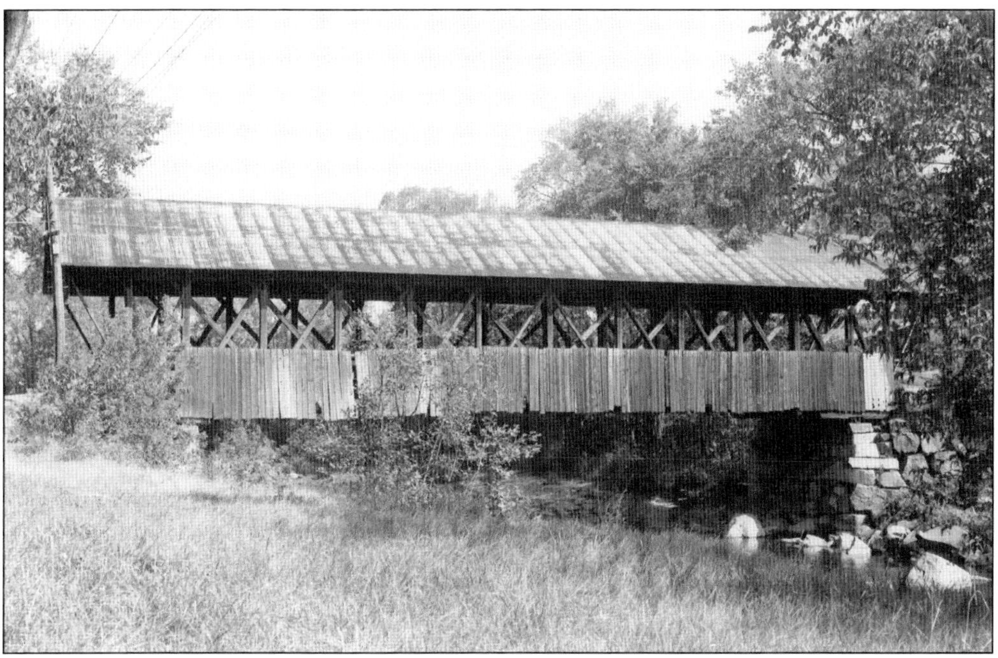

The Mechanic Street Bridge goes over the scenic Israel's River east of Routes 2 and 3. Built in 1862 in the Paddleford truss style of construction, it has been kept in good repair, with a rehabilitation in 1962.

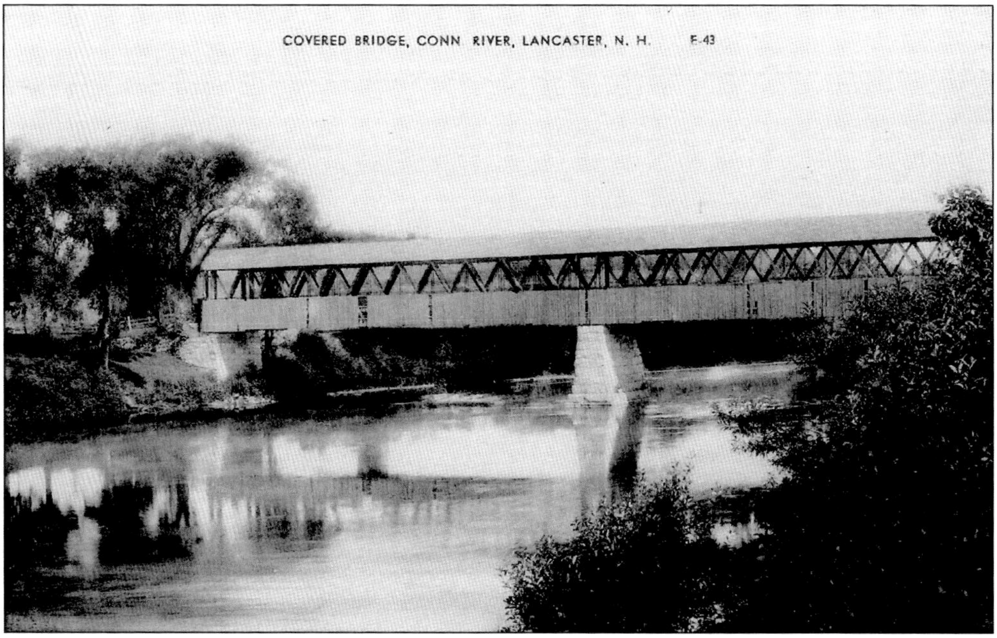

A covered toll bridge was built in 1804 crossing the Connecticut River from Lancaster to Guildhall, Vermont, on Bridge Street. It was destroyed in the 1890s by a logjam. It was replaced by this 280-foot-long, two-span, Howe truss–style covered bridge, built in 1902.

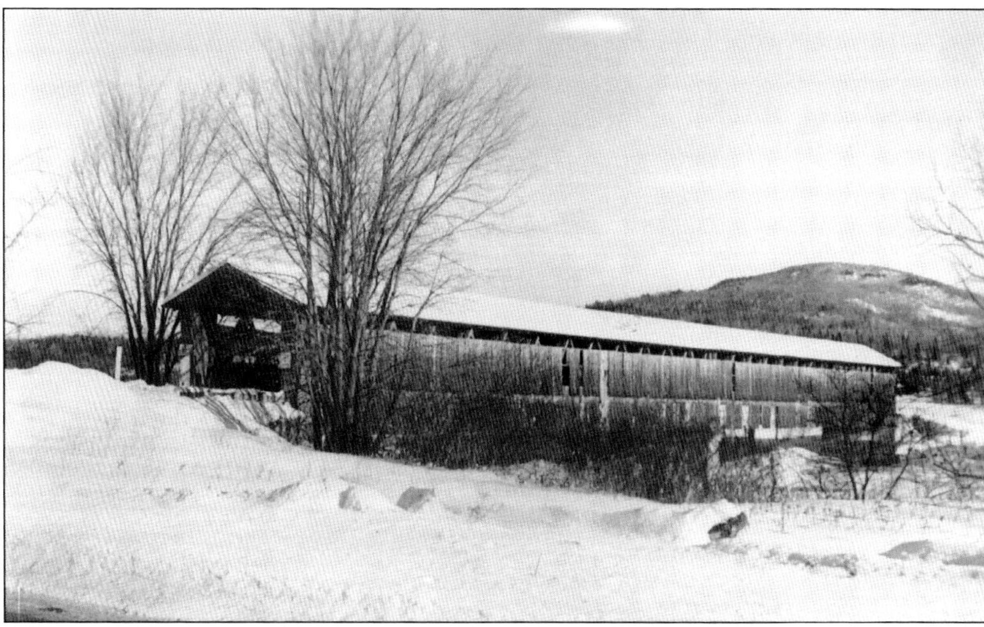

The Mount Orne Bridge, a two-span Howe truss bridge crossing the Connecticut River, is located west of Lancaster on Route 135. The original bridge was built in 1864 as a toll bridge and was washed out in 1908 by a log jam. The present 266-foot-long bridge was erected in 1911 of timber precut and assembled on-site. It has been repaired several times due to damage caused by trucks trying to go through.

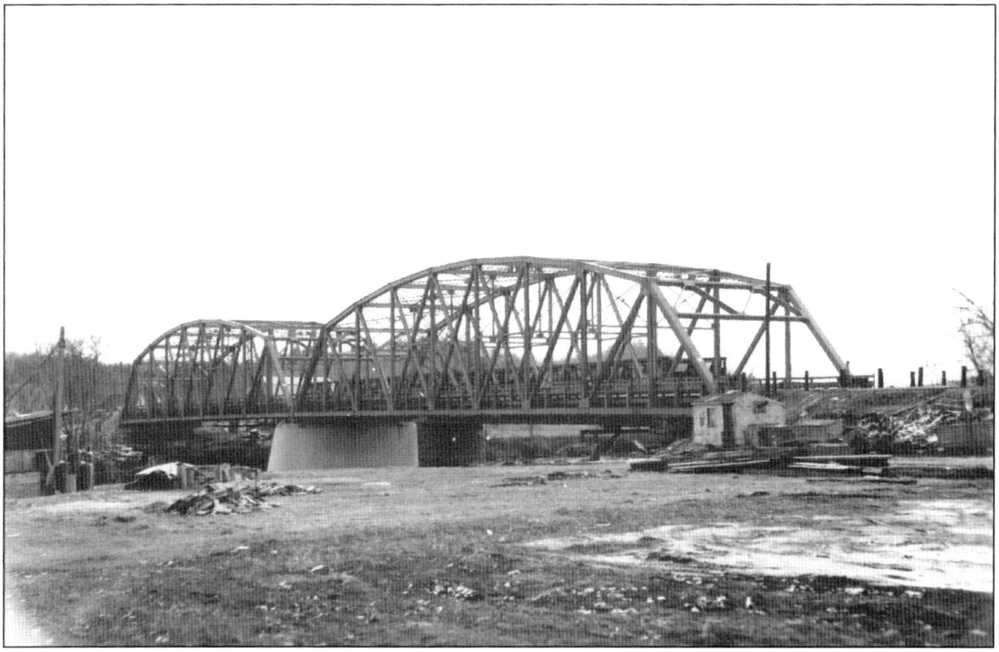

The Bridge Street covered bridge was replaced in 1950 by this 398-foot-long, two-span iron bridge. It was named the Rogers Rangers Bridge in honor of the Rogers Rangers, who went through the Lancaster area on their way to Canada. (Courtesy of Lawrence "Gomer" Powell.)

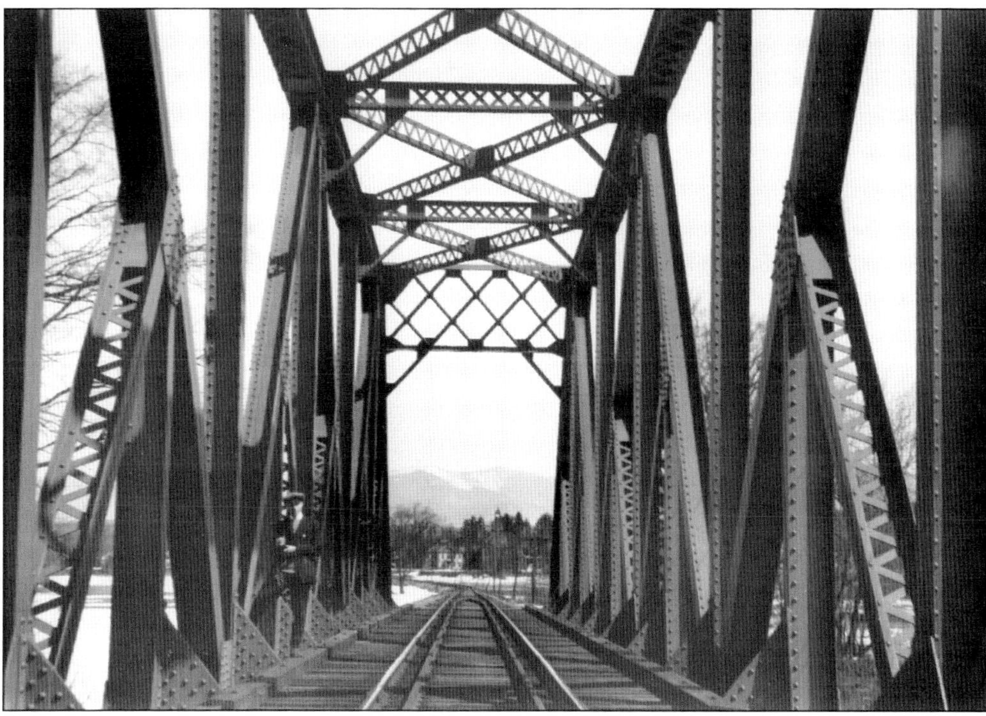

The Boston & Maine Railroad trestle crossed Israel's River below the current Coös County Courthouse. This photograph, taken around 1910, frames the old courthouse tower and the Kilkenny Mountains in the middle of the trestle.

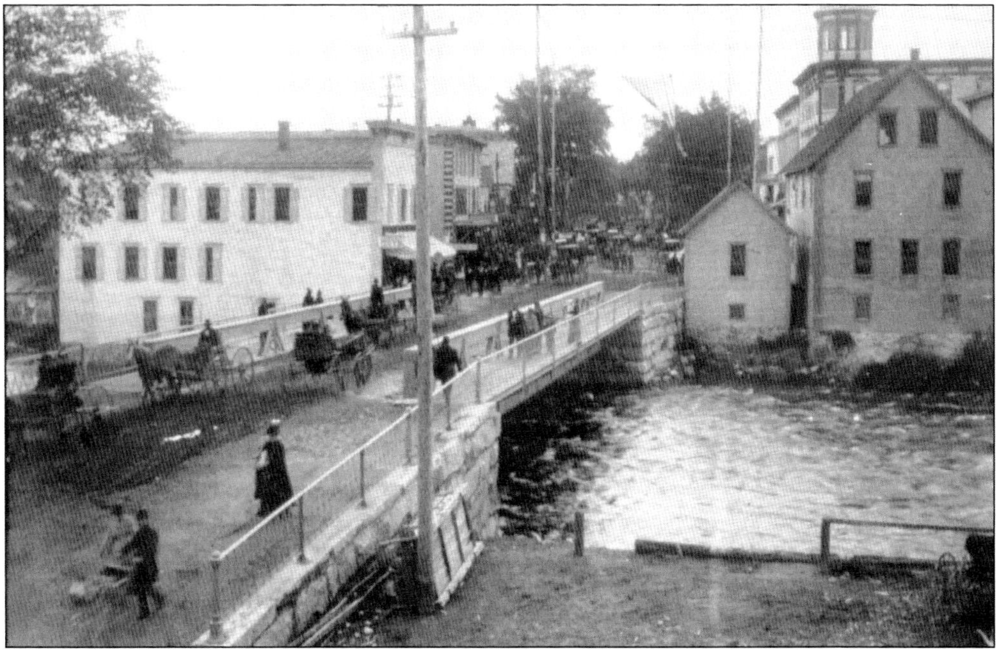

The first iron bridge over Israel's River on Main Street was built in 1888 after the previous covered bridge was destroyed by the 1886 flood. This bridge was also washed out two years later by a flood. The next iron bridge was raised two feet higher and survived until it was replaced by the concrete bridge seen in the photograph below. The tower of the Richardson building on the corner of Main and Middle Streets can be seen in the background.

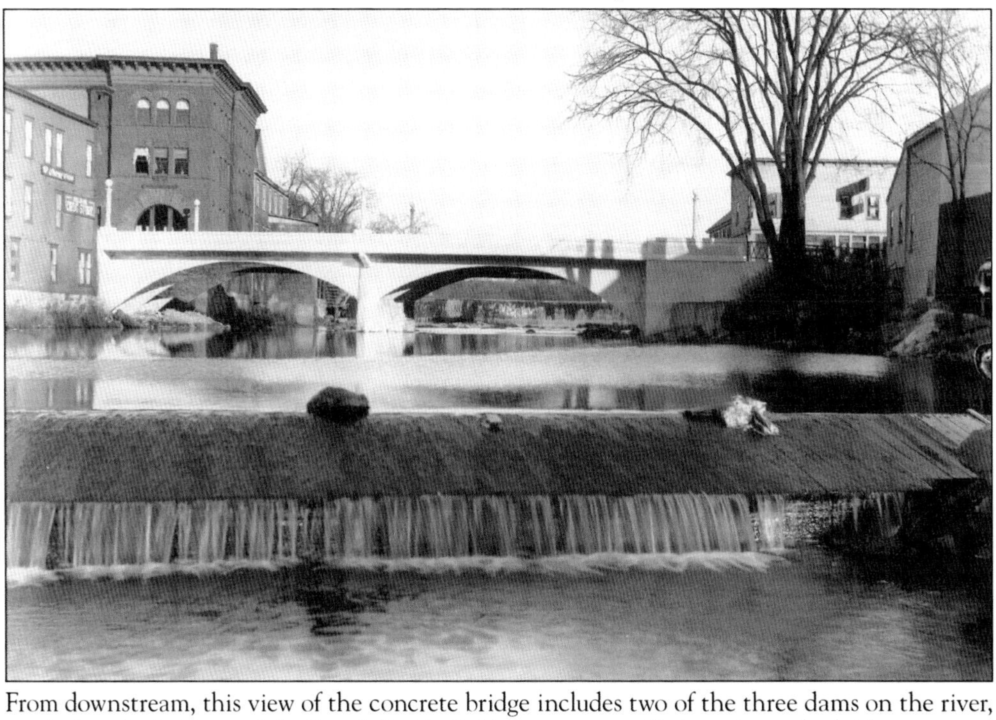

From downstream, this view of the concrete bridge includes two of the three dams on the river, one below the bridge and the Frank Smith & Company sawmill dam above the bridge.

Seven

WINTER ACTIVITIES

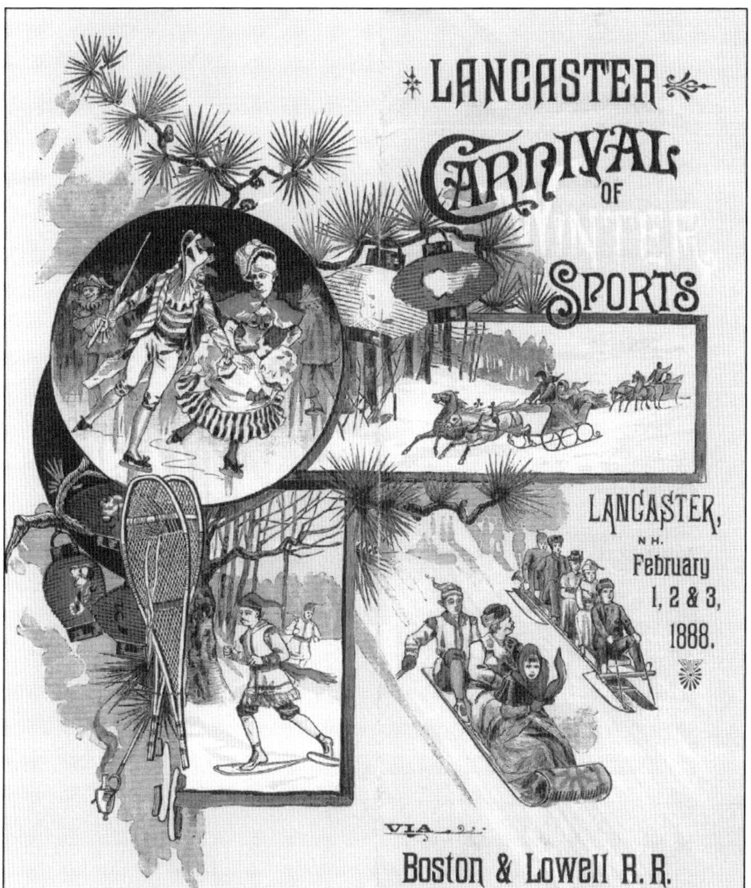

Sponsored by the Lancaster Toboggan Club and promoted by the Boston & Lowell Railroad and the Lancaster House, the Lancaster Carnival of Winter Sports was held over three days in February 1888. It included tobogganing, baseball on snowshoes, horse races, a citizen's parade, and a masque ball.

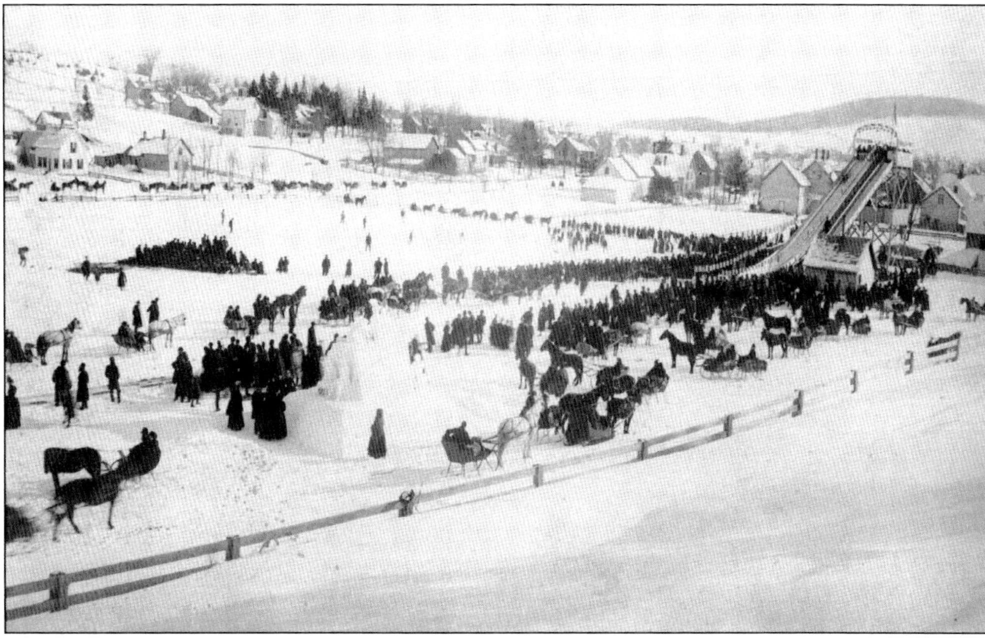

At the height of the winter carnival of 1888, the number of visitors increased with every train until it was estimated that between 4,000 and 5,000 people were in attendance. At the chute in Ray's field (now the Colonel Town Community Field), coasting was indulged in until a late hour, with the help of bonfires and Chinese lanterns.

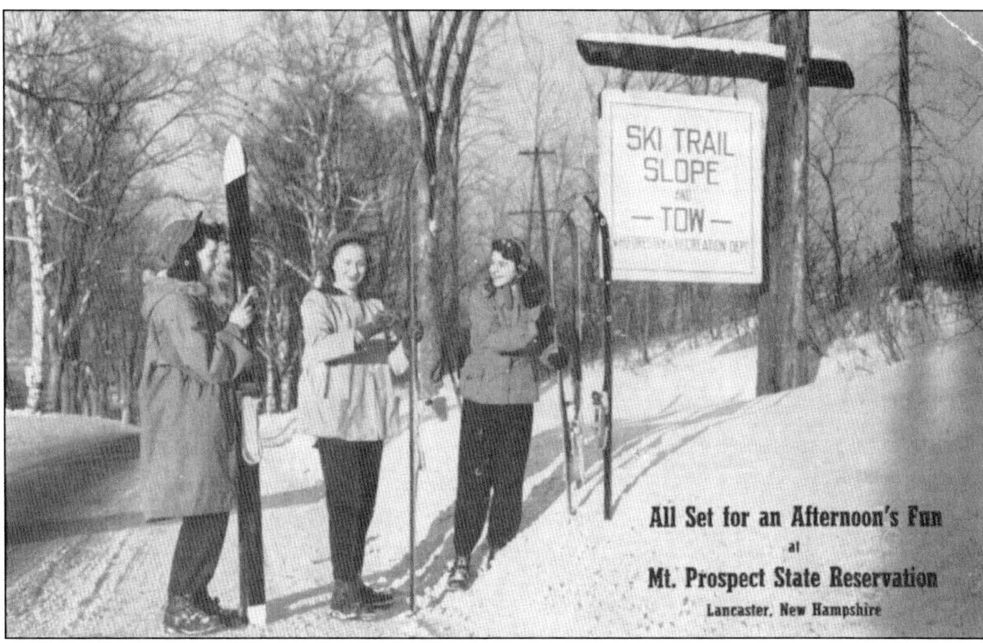

Started in the 1940s, this ski slope and rope tow still operates at Weeks State Park under the direction of the Mount Prospect Ski Club. In this postcard from the 1940s, from left to right, Janice Lynch, Joanne Roberts, and Nancy Hodgdon are eager to hit the slopes.

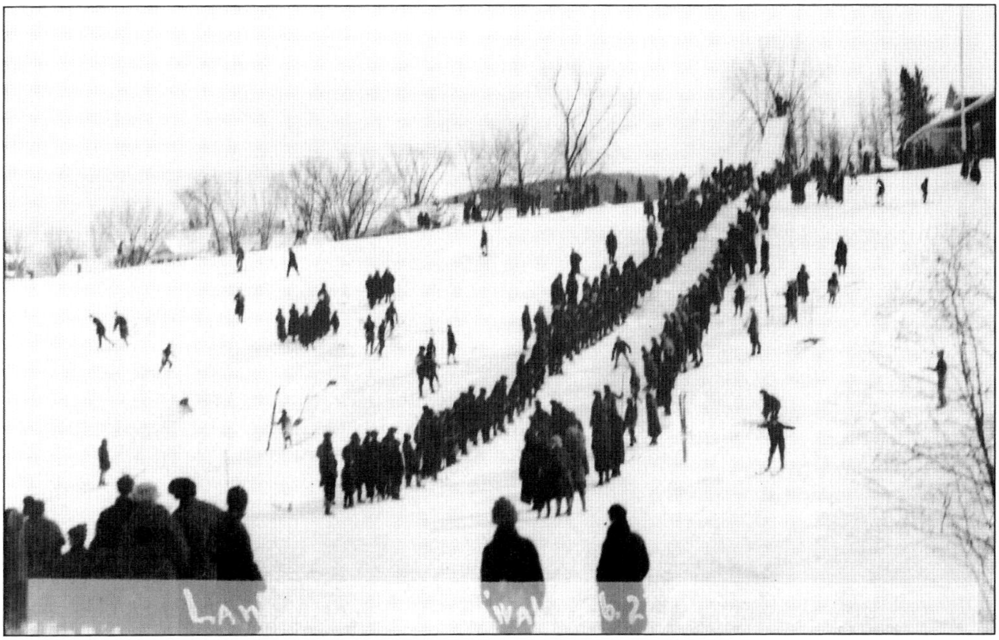

For the winter carnival of 1924, a ski jump was built on Cook's Hill on Williams Street. Throughout the years, Cook's Hill has been a favorite sledding hill for all ages, right up to the present day.

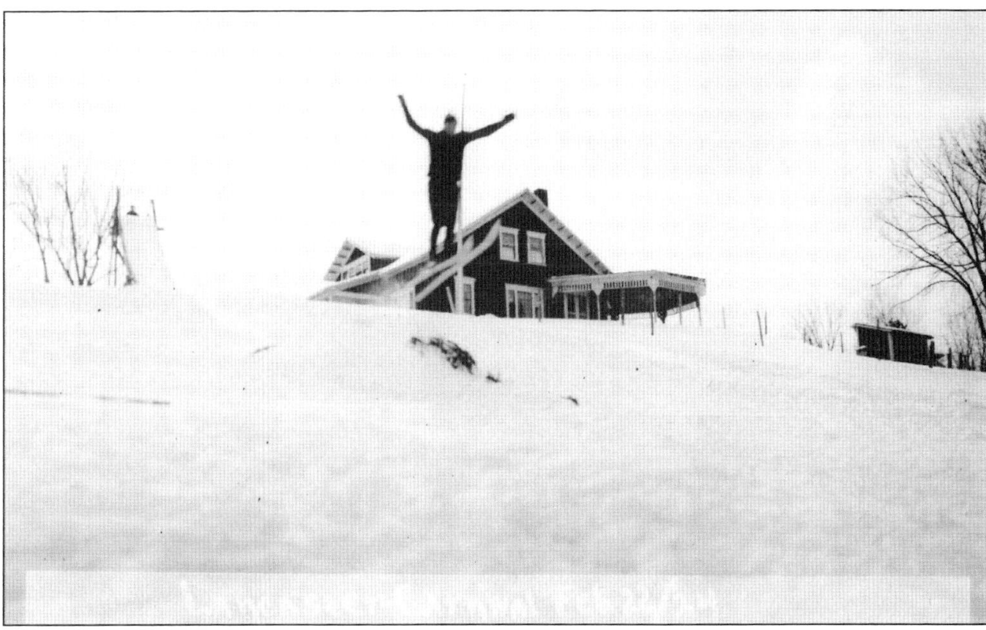

A skier leaves the jump on Cook's Hill during the winter carnival on February 22, 1924. The current owner of this home, centenarian Margaret Carr, a niece of the Cooks, is in the background.

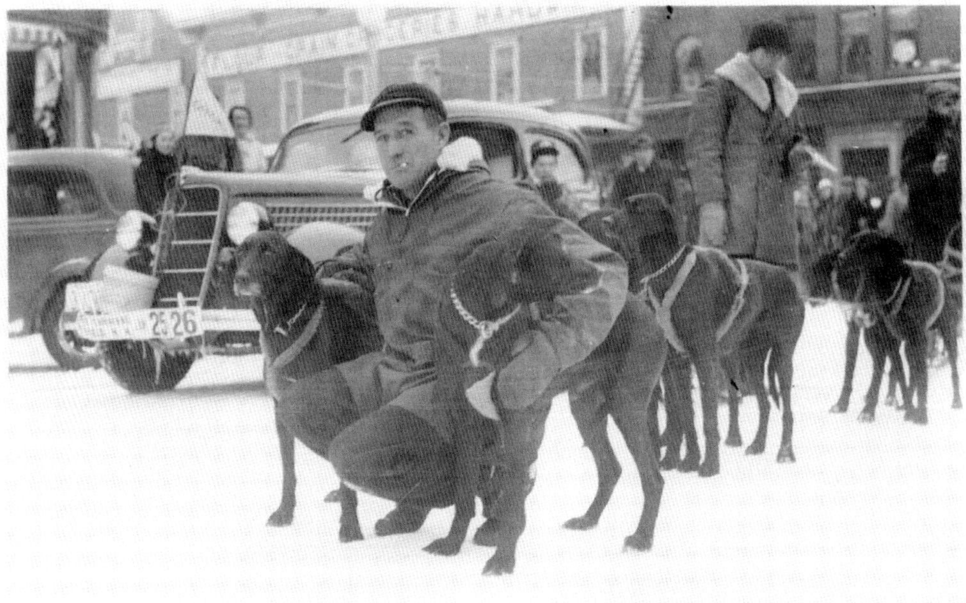

LANCASTER CARNIVAL.

Sled-dog racing was a big part of Lancaster's 1936 winter carnival. Local driver Ross Stanard (above and below), with his team of crossbred Irish Setter–Dobermans, won the 17.1-mile race, which began at the corner of Main and Middle Streets, went down Bridge Street to Lunenburg, Vermont, and returned by way of South Lancaster.

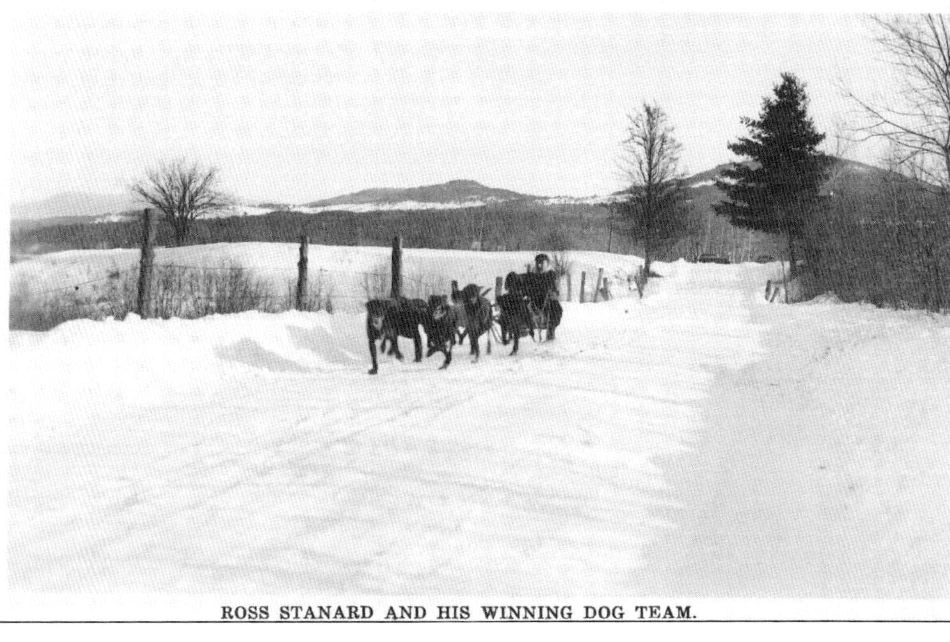

ROSS STANARD AND HIS WINNING DOG TEAM.

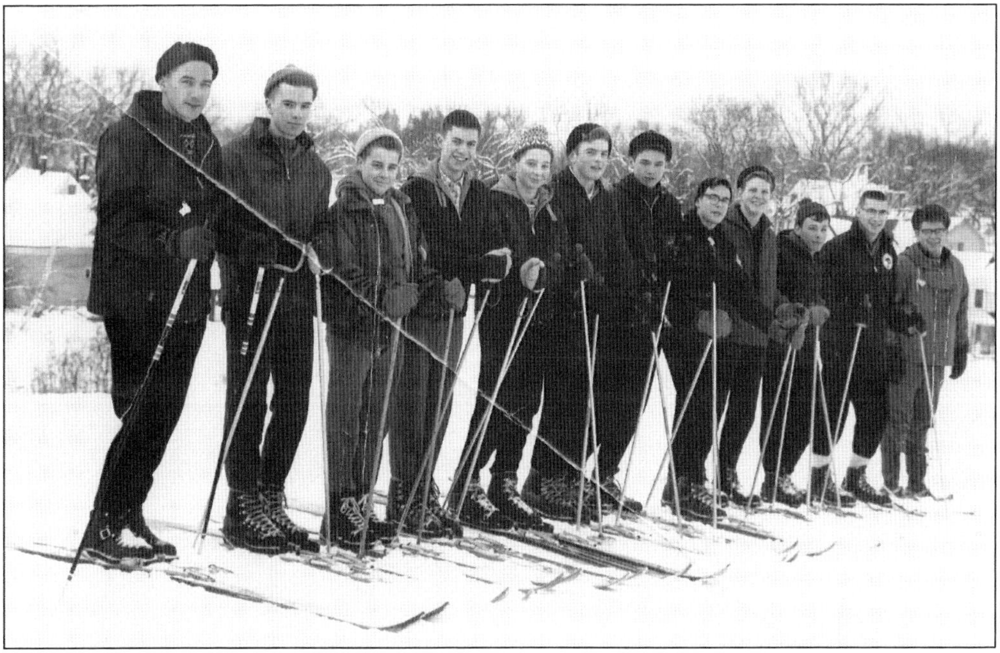

The Lancaster High School boys' ski team is seen here in the winter of 1962. From left to right are coach and mathematics instructor Paul Wilkinson, Ronald Kay, Stephen Abbott, Richard Kay, Alan Livingstone, Stephen Berry, Mitchell Moody, Stephen Stinehour, Eric Livingstone, Ernest Blodgett, Stephen Martin, and Jeff Tenney.

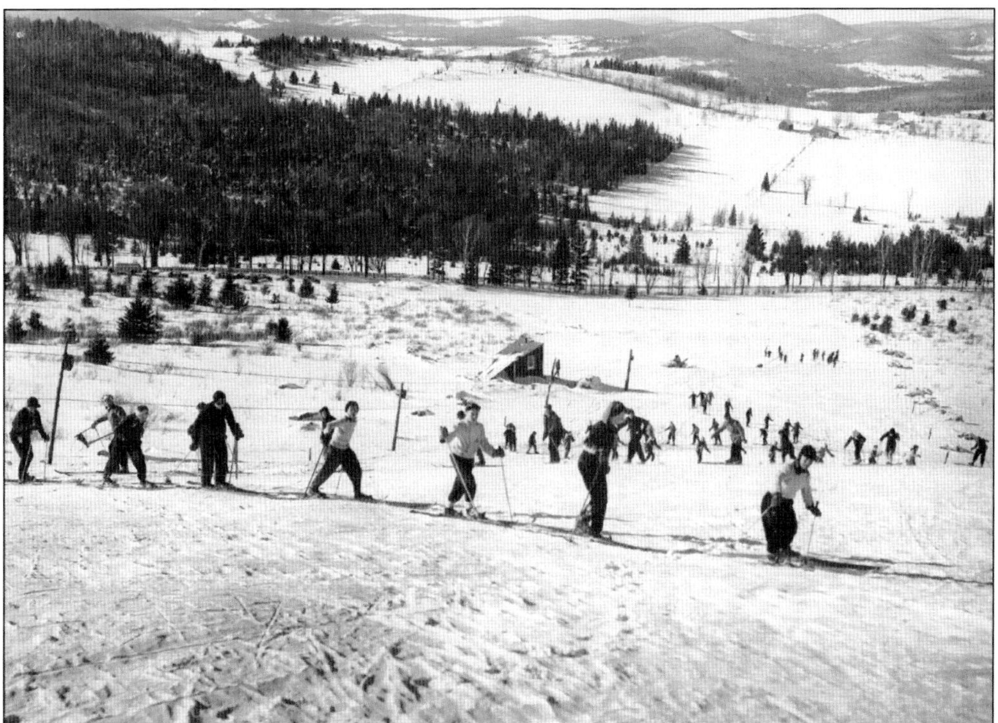

Community skiing on Mount Prospect was part of the bicentennial winter carnival in 1964.

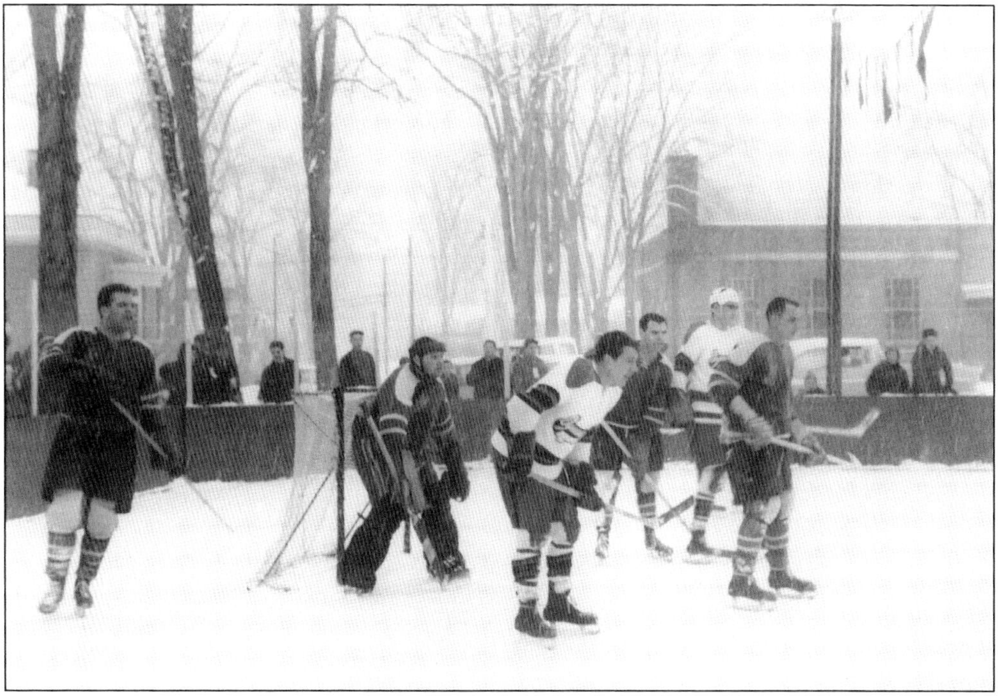

Always a favorite in Lancaster, ice hockey was played all winter at the rink in Centennial Park. Seen here is one of the exciting games from the bicentennial winter carnival in 1964.

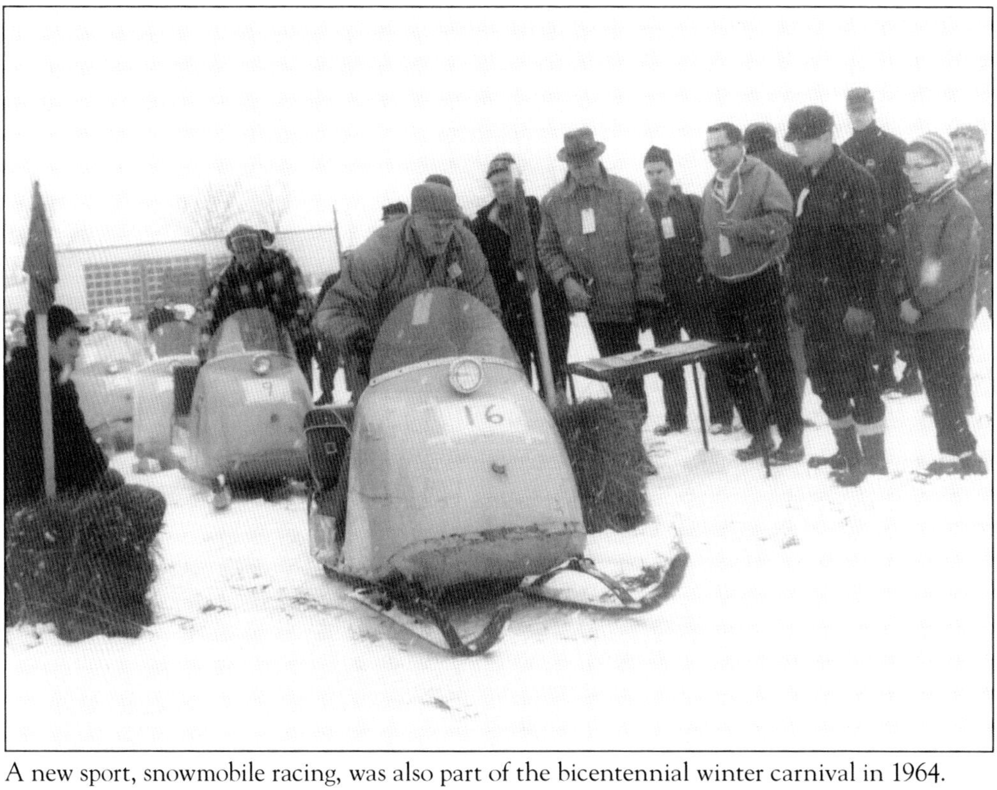

A new sport, snowmobile racing, was also part of the bicentennial winter carnival in 1964.

Eight

EDUCATION

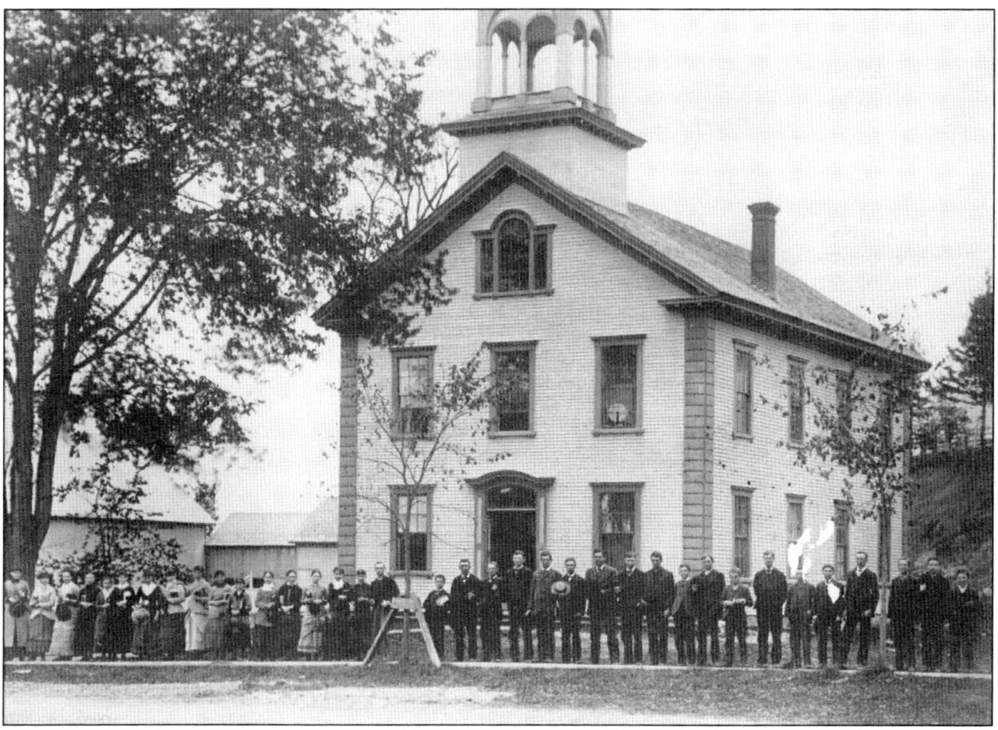

In 1862, a new school building was constructed on the site now occupied by George M. Stevens Insurance. This graded school continued until 1952, when an elementary wing was added to the high school across the street.

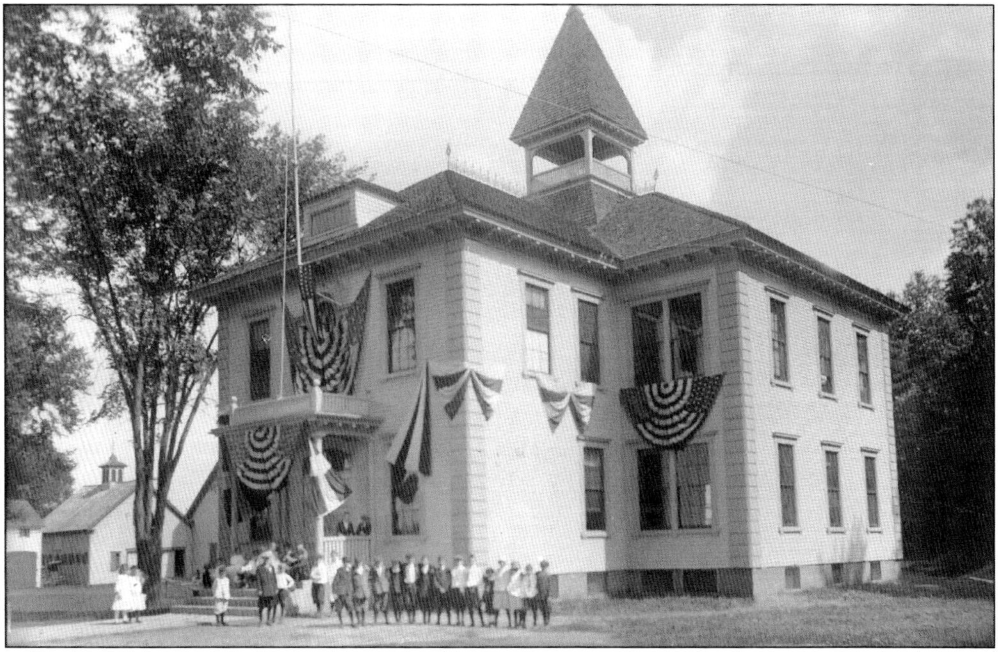

The graded school underwent changes sometime after it was constructed, presumably to accommodate increased student enrollment. The building is seen here decorated for the 150th anniversary of Lancaster in 1914.

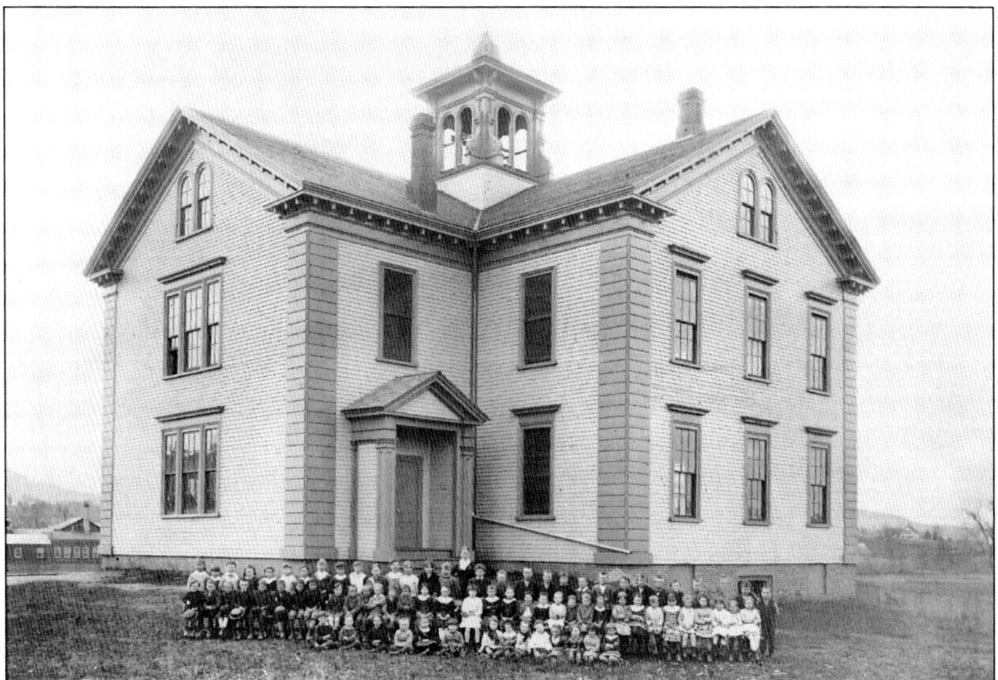

The graded school built behind Centennial Park was finished in 1870. Mary Aldrich's primary room class of 1885 posed for this photograph. This building was replaced in 1912 by a brick building. Thompson Manufacturing buildings are in the background.

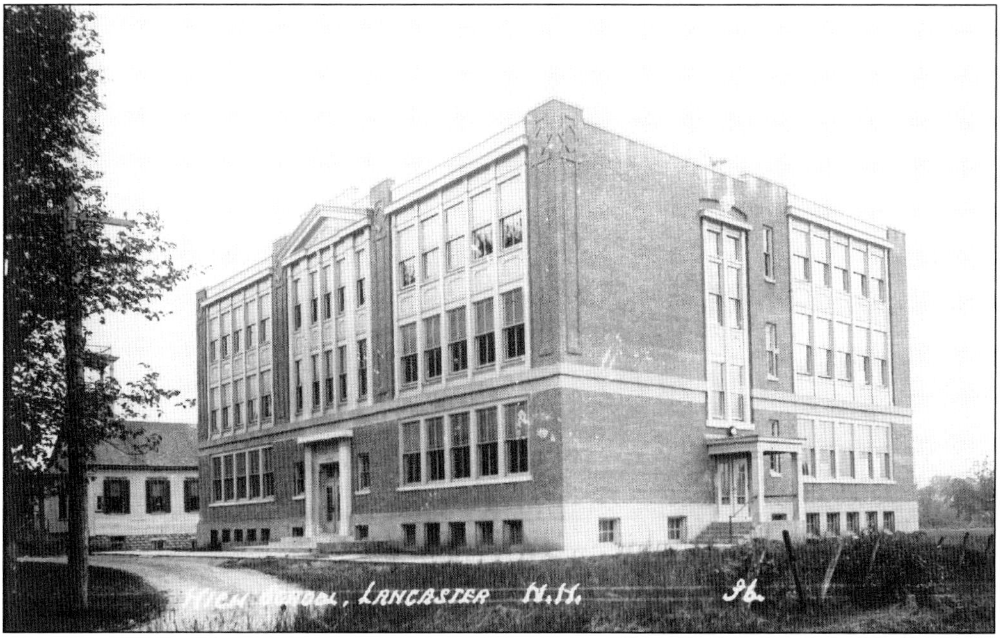

Lancaster Academy, built in 1912, later became Lancaster High School. To the left of the building is the old Unitarian church, which was once used as the town's library.

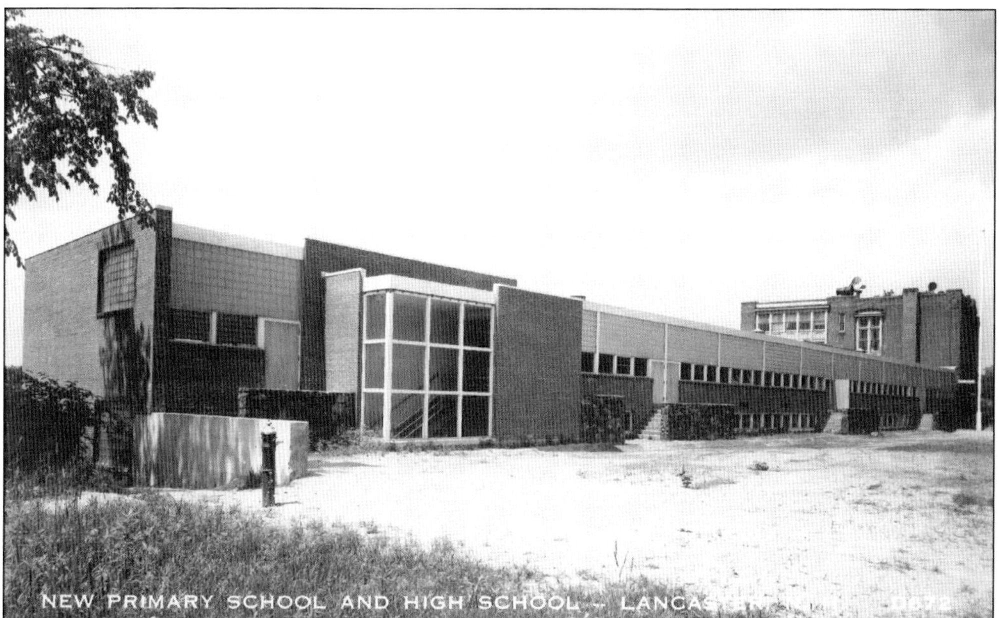

After the new primary school was built in 1952, grades one through six moved across from the old school.

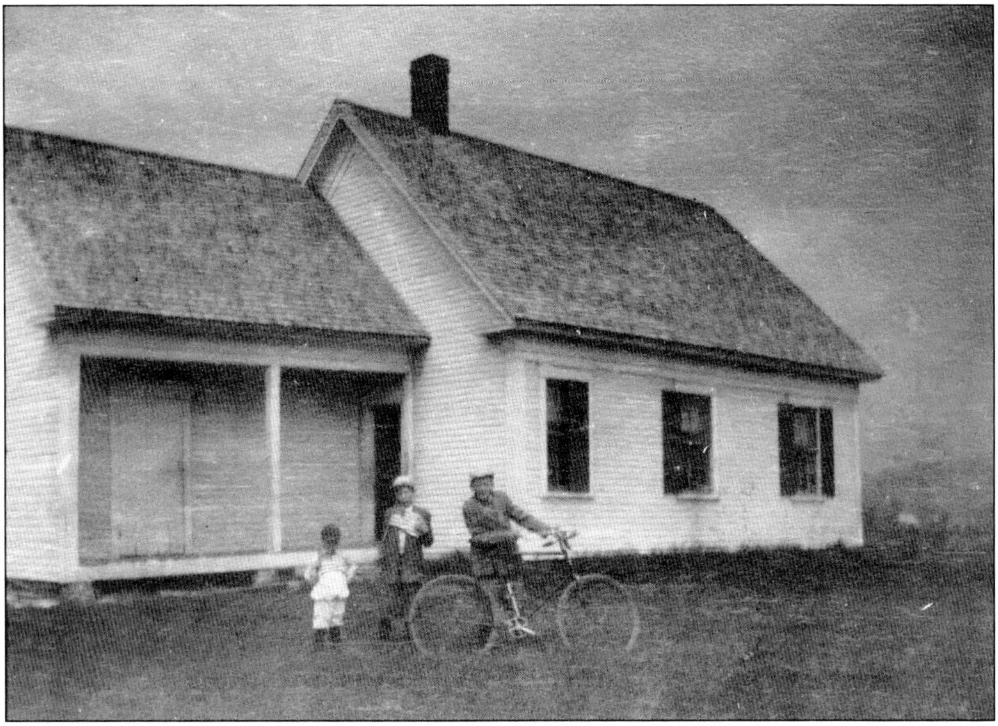

In 1794, Lancaster was divided into educational districts, with a schoolhouse to be constructed in each district. District No. 2, the South Lancaster School, was one of the first three schools funded. The first of the three schools was a log cabin. The fourth building, built in 1889, is seen here in 1912.

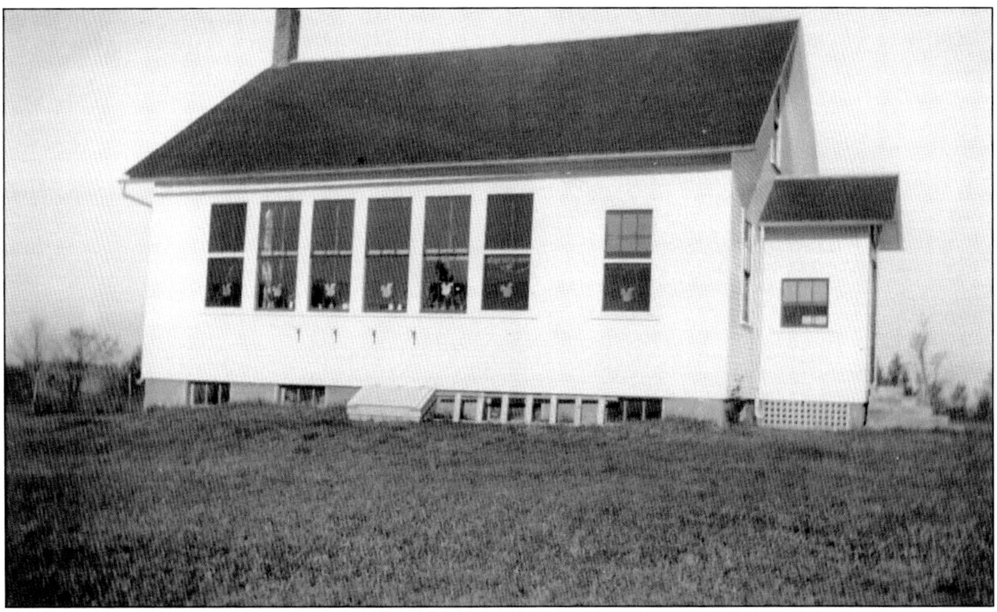

The last of the rural schools to be built in the state was the Mount Cabot School, which closed its doors in 1957. When it was built, it was considered modern, as it had running water, flush toilets, and electricity.

Nine

DISASTERS

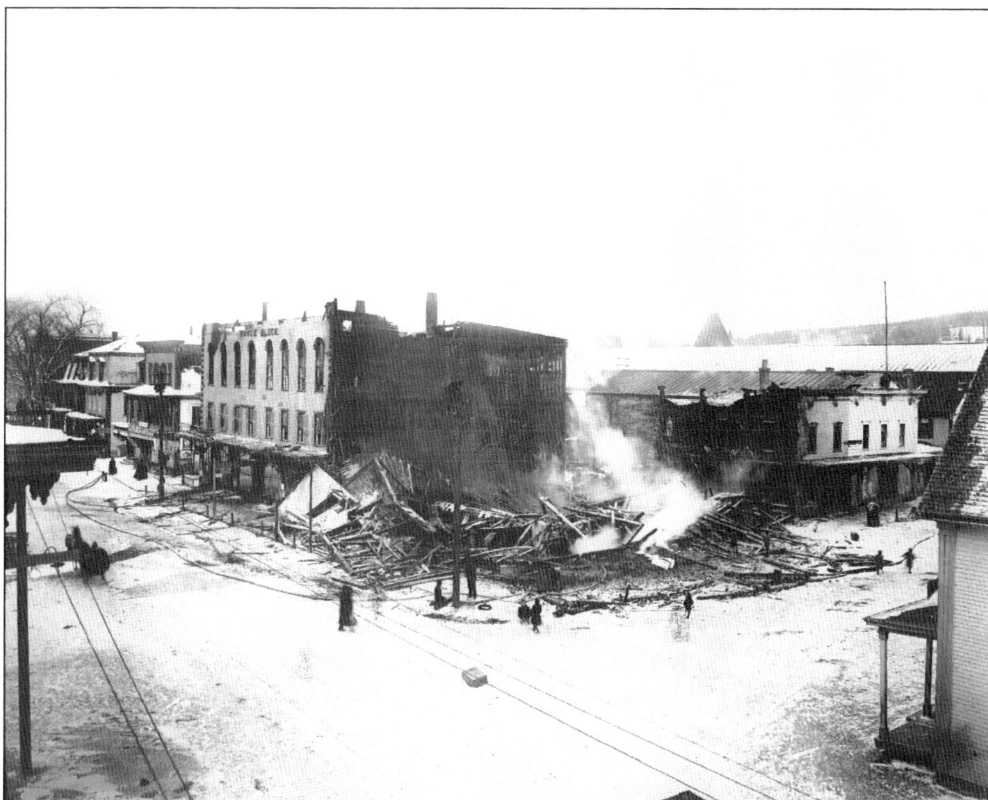

The Richardson Building, on the corner of Main and Middle Streets, and the adjacent Eagle Block, were destroyed by fire in January 1899. The Bailey brothers replaced the building with a brick structure that was finished and occupied by the end of the year.

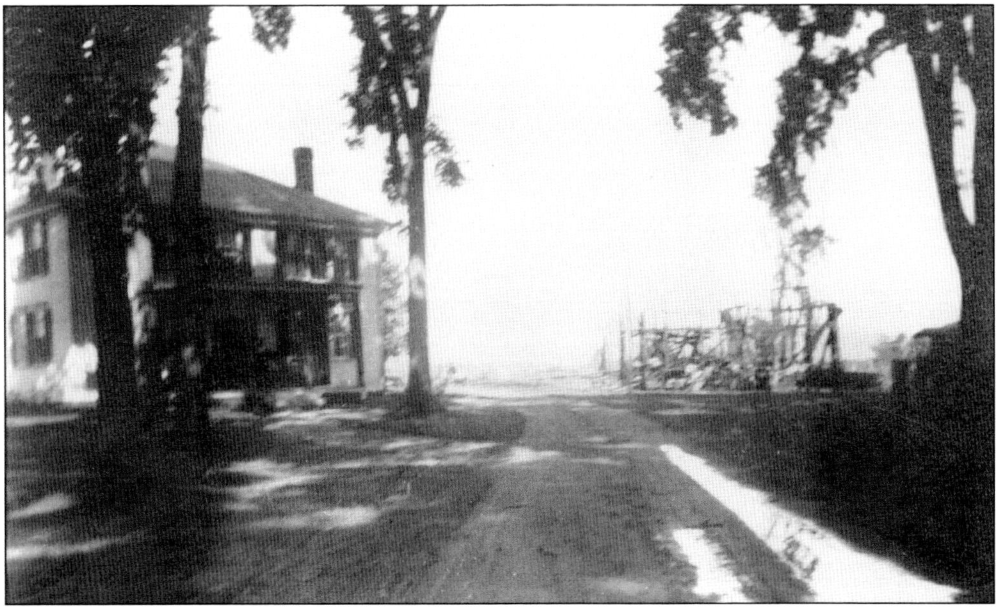

The Wilder-Holton House, now the home of the Lancaster Historical Society, was the first two-story frame house constructed in Lancaster. It was built in 1780 by Maj. Jonas Wilder, who had purchase a square mile of land after learning of rich land discovered in the Upper Coos. From 1807 until 1964, it was owned and occupied by five generations of the Holton family. A fire on September 10, 1917, destroyed eight barns and silos in one hour, forcing Sally Holton to discontinue farming.

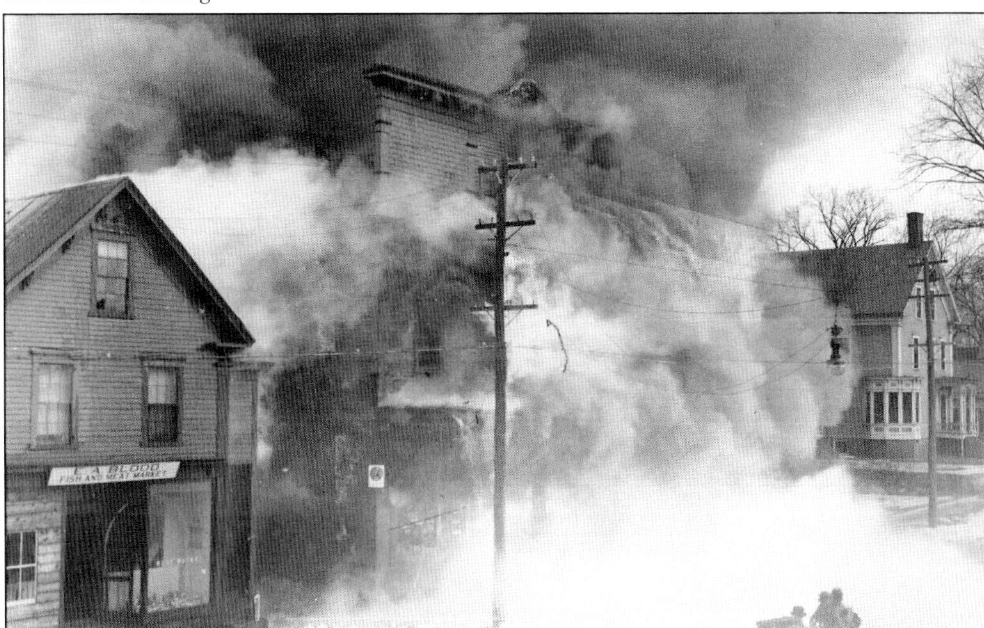

The great L.F. Moore fire on Middle Street occurred on March 14, 1922. It was caused by the overflow of a 10-gallon gas can in front of the store. L.F. Moore sold hardware, mercantile, and building materials and was never known to be "out" of anything. The fire was the greatest since the conflagration of 1899.

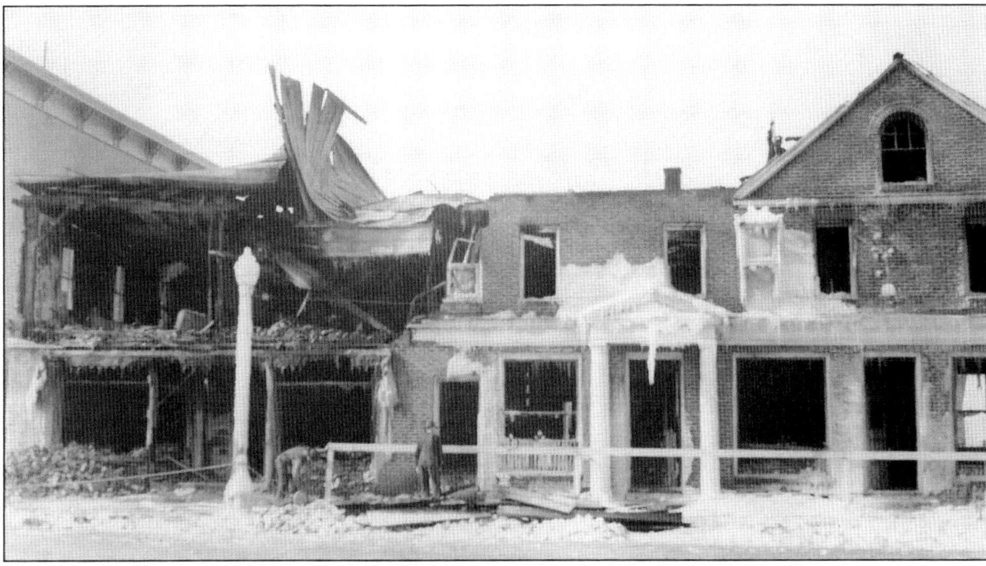

This photograph shows the aftermath of a devastating fire in the Kent Block on February 9, 1941. The temperature was minus 28 degrees.

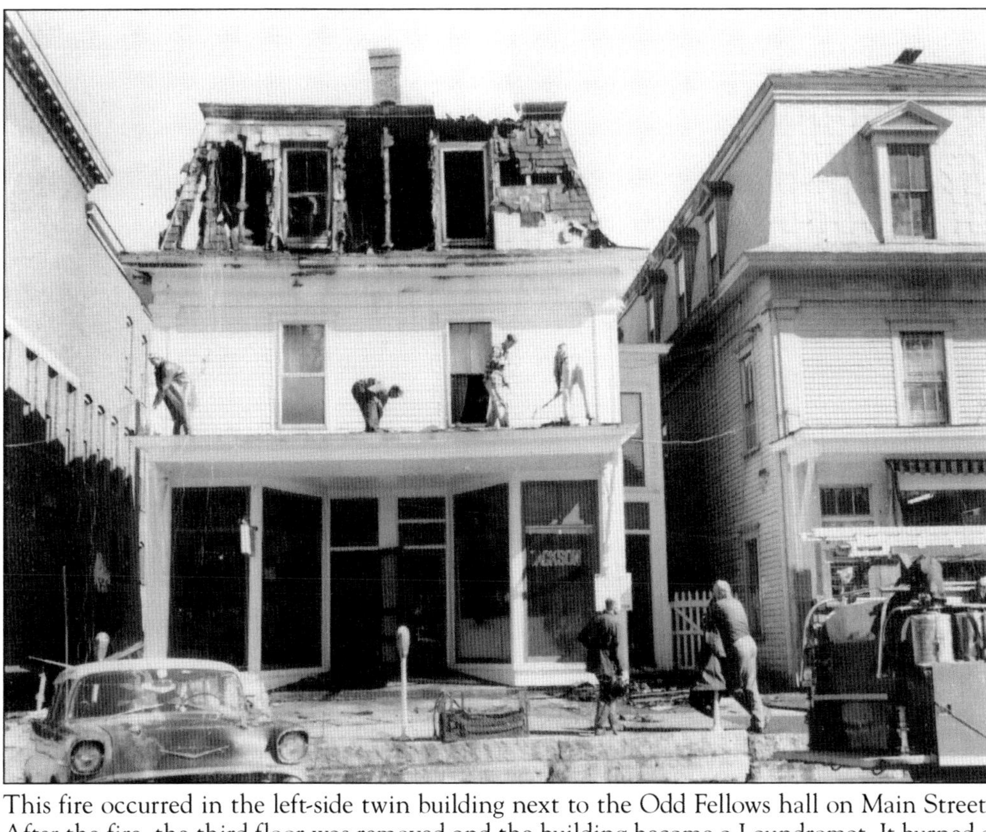

This fire occurred in the left-side twin building next to the Odd Fellows hall on Main Street. After the fire, the third floor was removed and the building became a Laundromat. It burned a second time in 1970. Today, it is used as a Re/Max Realty office.

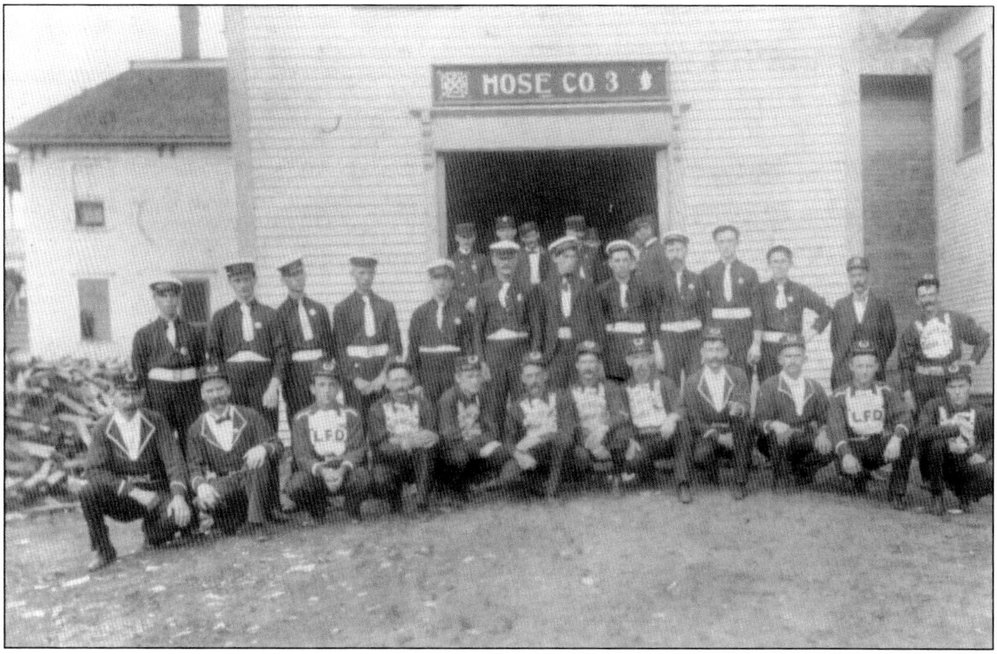

Lancaster Fire Department Hose Company No. 3 poses for a group photograph in front of its firehouse.

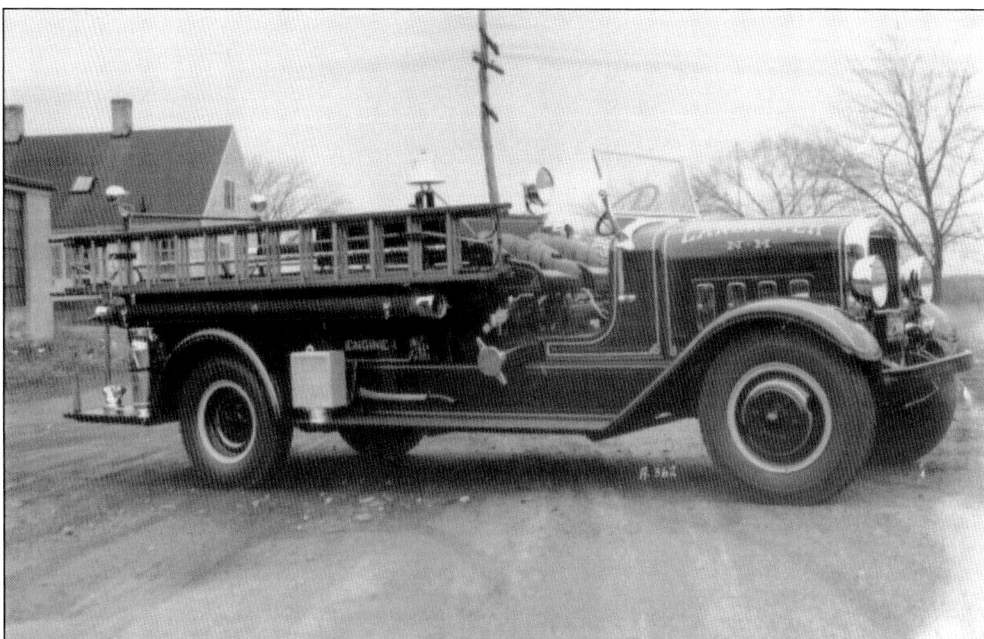

The first pumper purchased for the fire department, seen here, was bought in December 1934 from the Maxim Motor Company.

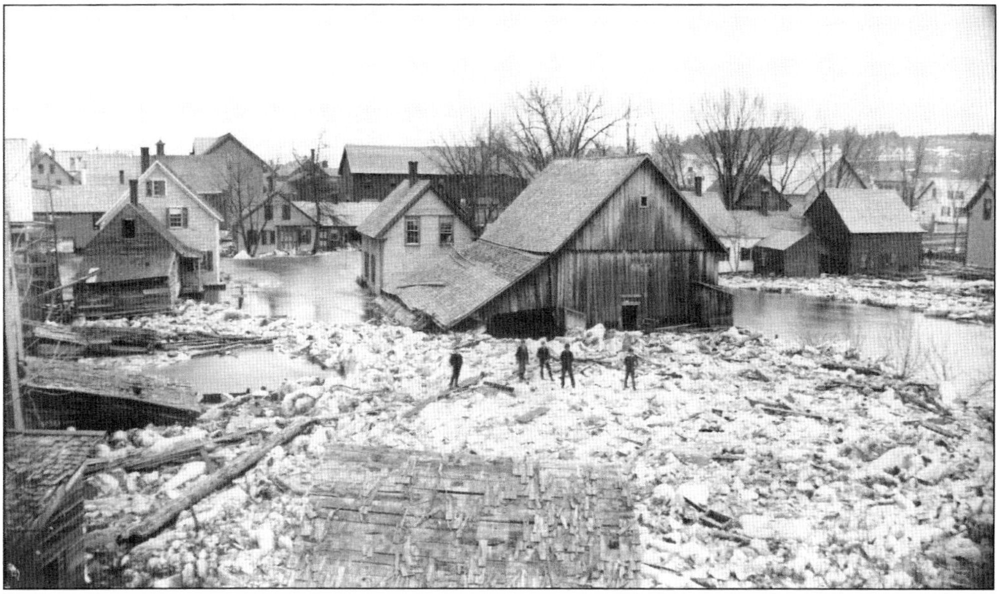

Mechanic Street homes and businesses are seen here surrounded by floodwaters and ice during the 1886 ice flood.

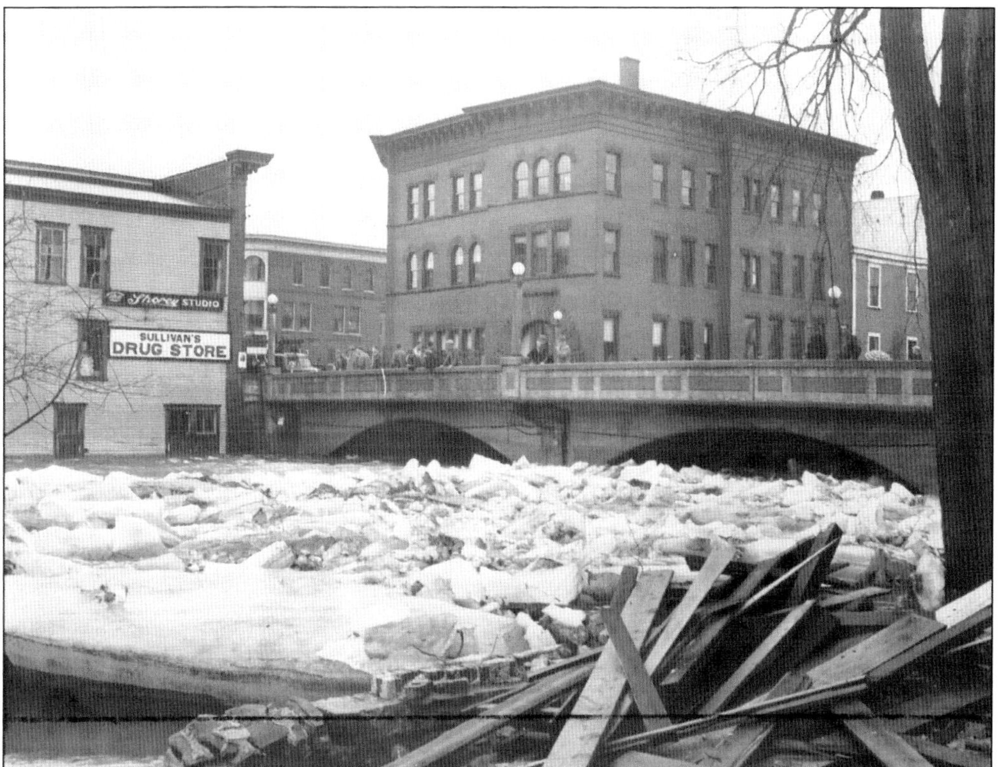

As happened every spring, a crowd of spectators gathered to watch the ice on Israel's River and anticipate further river action. In the background is the bank, the basement of which was frequently flooded.

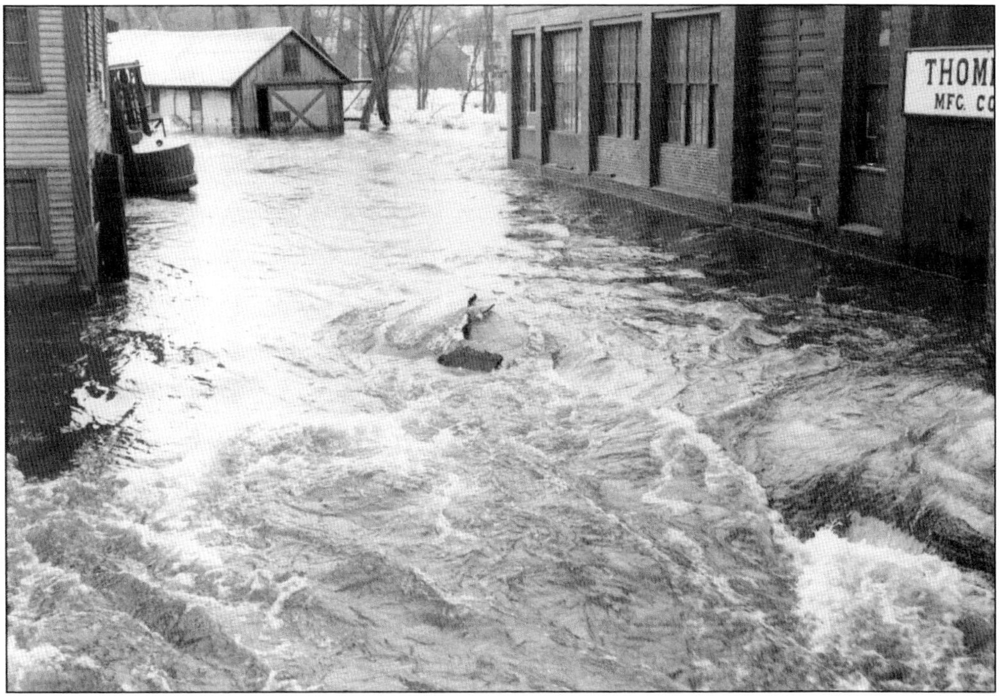

Thompson Manufacturing Company, on Canal Street, makers of furniture and wooden cogs among other items, fell victim to the flooded Israel's River as it changed course due to the ice jam seen in the background.

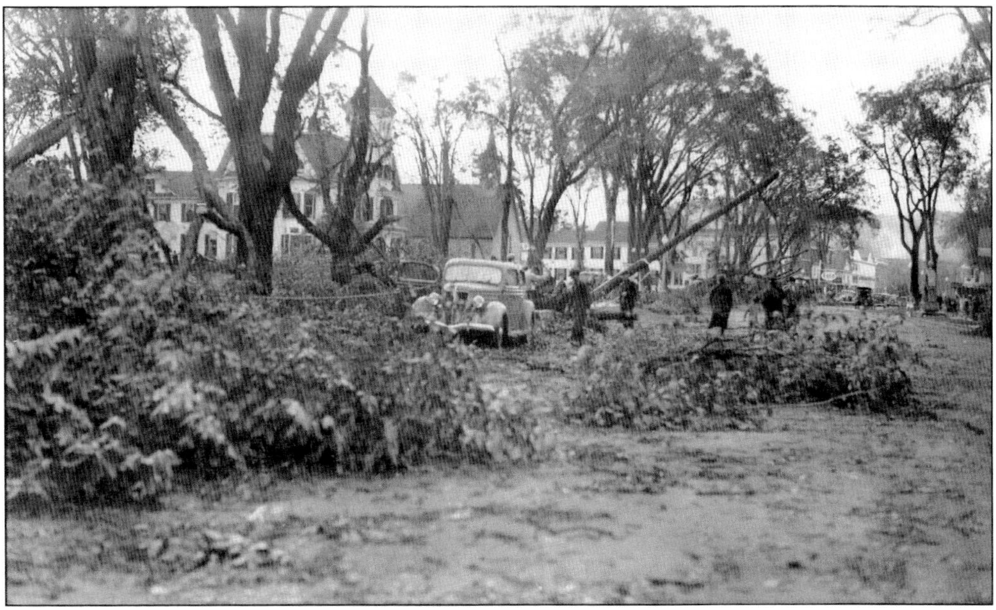

On September 21, 1938, a powerful hurricane traveled up the Connecticut River Valley and pounded Lancaster for about two hours beginning around 8:00 p.m., leaving great destruction in its path. Henry P. Kent's Ford sedan, which was parked near the Van Dyke house, had a tree come down on it. Fortunately, only minor injuries were suffered by its passengers, Bernice E. Kent and M. Faith Kent.

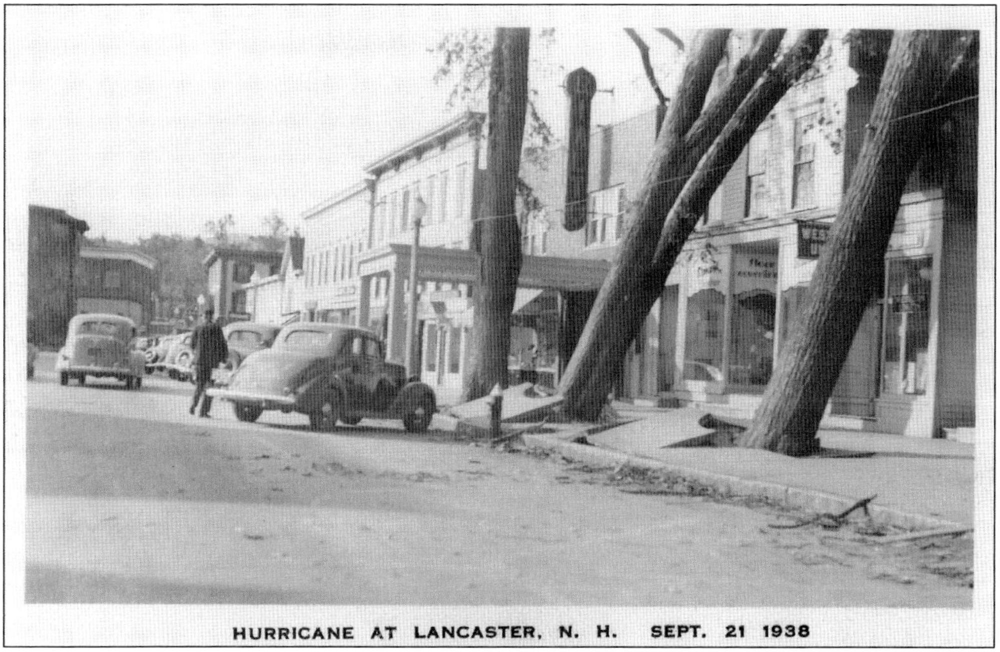

It took several days to clear the streets and make them passable, but major tree removal had to wait. These large trees near the Rialto Theater testify to the strength of the hurricane's winds.

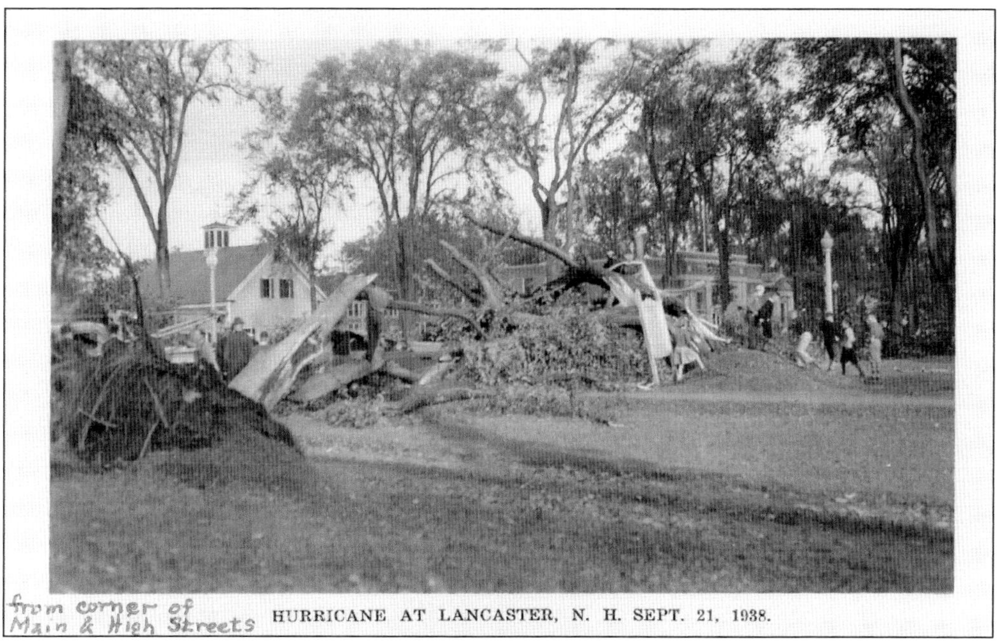

Lancaster lost many of the beautiful trees that lined its streets in the hurricane, as seen here at the corner of High and Main Streets. As soon as the hurricane passed, crews were out clearing away trees and debris. The electricity was turned off to prevent fires starting from downed electric wires.

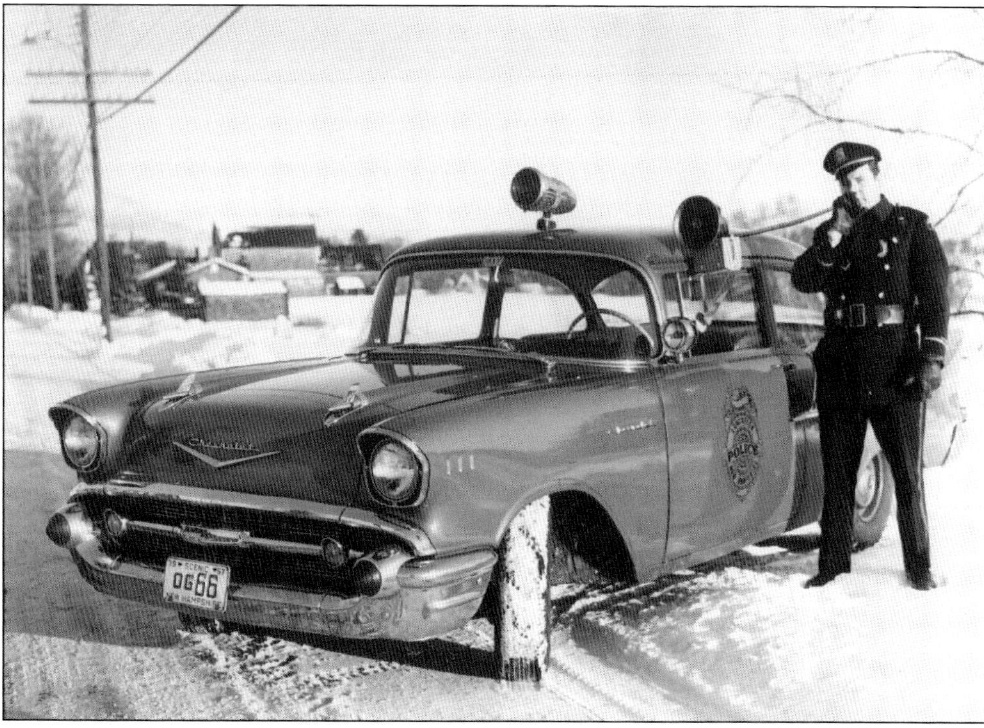

Kenneth Hinkley uses the police cruiser radio in the winter of 1958. (Courtesy of the Town of Lancaster.)

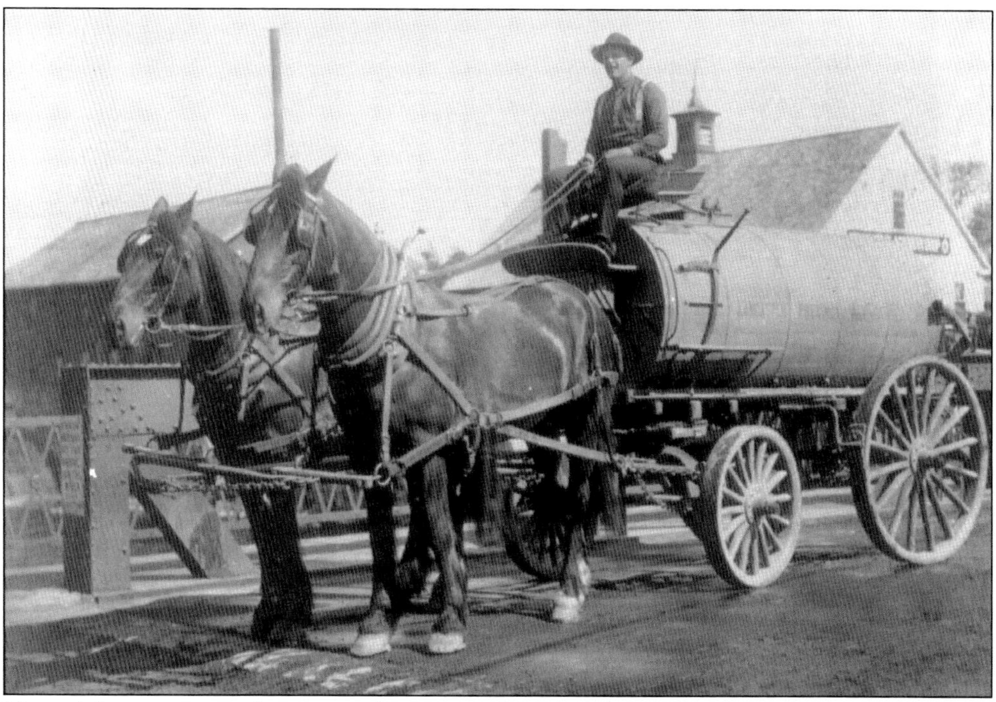

Most of the streets were dirt or gravel, meaning they were dusty when they were dry. To keep the dust down, Nelson Merrow drove the town water wagon, spraying water onto the dry roads.

Ten

RURAL LIFE

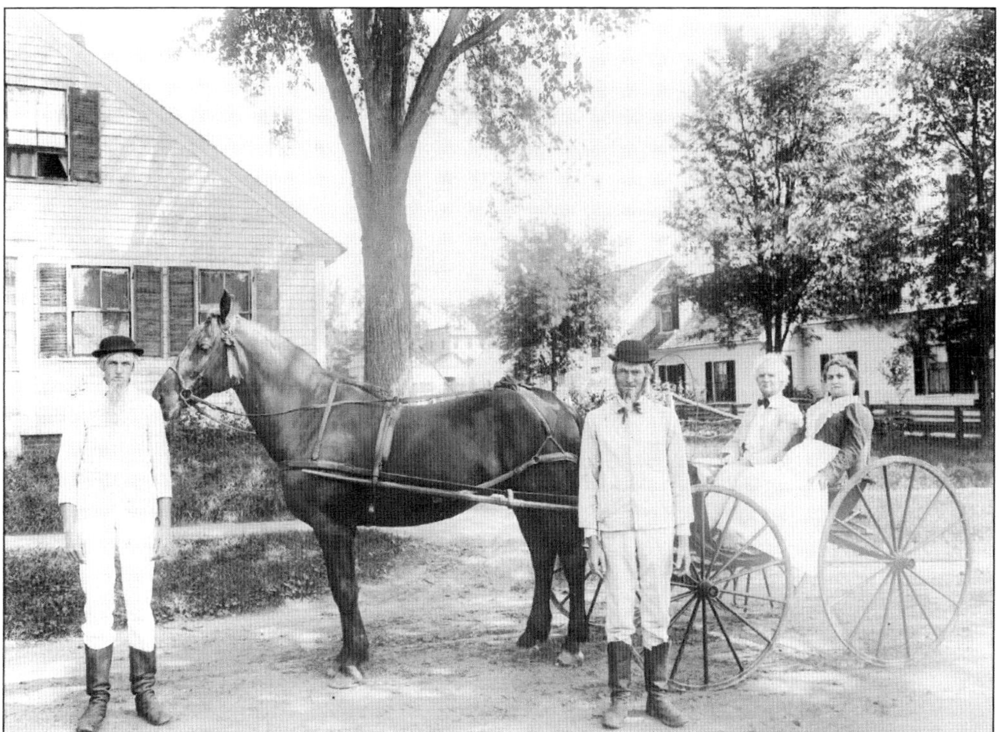

Rural residents from the local area came into town for the 150th anniversary in 1914. Seen here in costume are, from left to right, Ralph Shute, Carl Simonds, H.F. Olmstead, and Lorna Barnett.

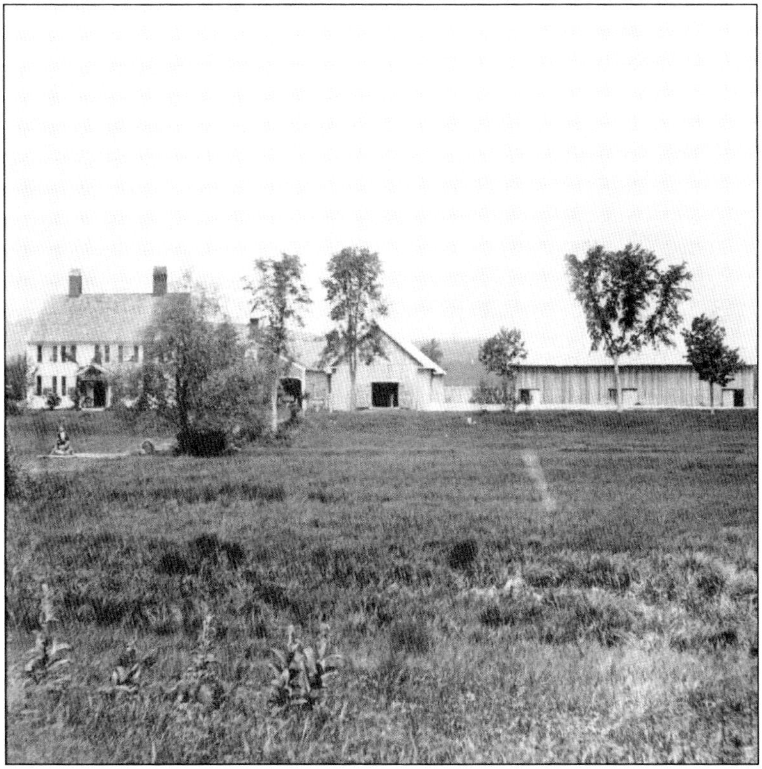

Gen. Moses Hazen, a retired colonel in the British army, purchased land along a bend in the Connecticut River known as "the cat bow" from Charles Apthorp in October 1783. General Hazen never occupied the land, but a farm was eventually established there on South Lancaster Road. This is not to be confused with Sinclair Weeks's Cat Bow Farm on Martin Meadow Pond.

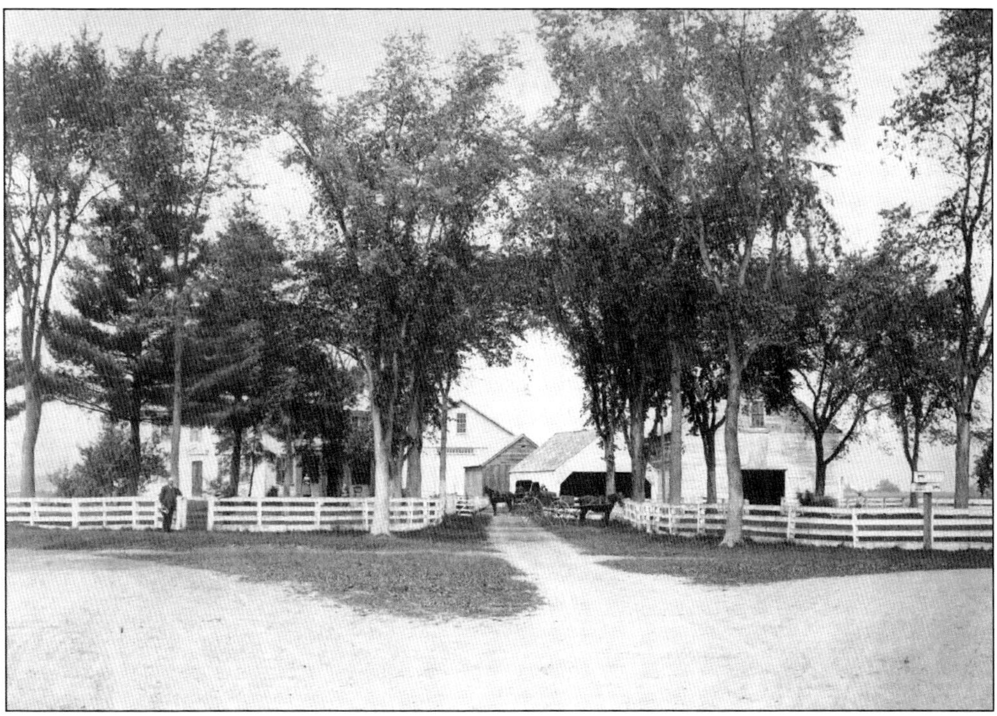

The Holton homestead is seen here before the 1913 fire that destroyed the barns. Note the original entrance on the south side.

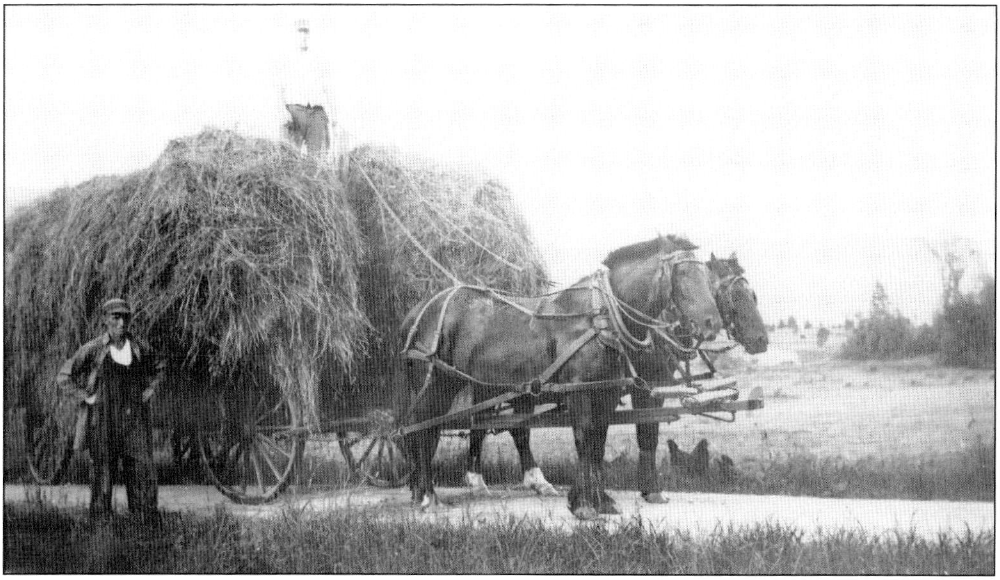

The rich meadows of the Connecticut River and Israel's River attracted the early settlers to the area, with farms established as the first means of making a living. The first crop was hay, which was cut and stacked by David Page Jr. and Emmons Stockwell in the fall of 1763 for the cattle they planned to bring north in the spring. Over the years, many farms were established throughout the town. The early farmers cut the hay by hand using scythes, and then it was raked into rows and piled onto the hay wagon, which was drawn by a team of horses.

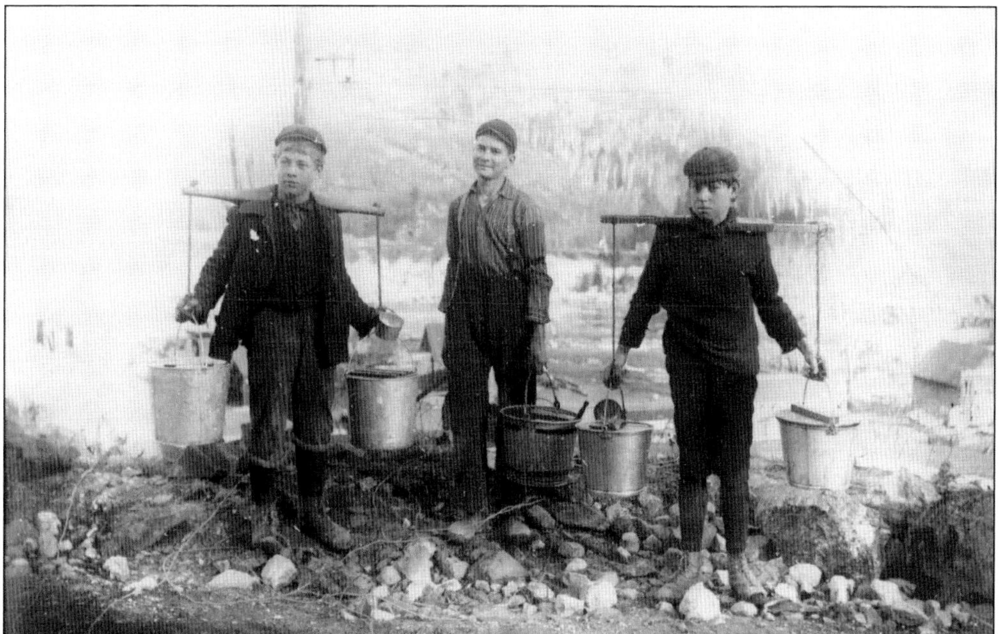

Before there were horse-drawn sleighs with tubs for sap to be gathered in, sap was carried in gathering buckets to the sugarhouse. To ease the strain on the arms from the heavy buckets, yokes were used across the shoulders, with the buckets hanging from ropes. Needless to say, they were not comfortable for the wearer.

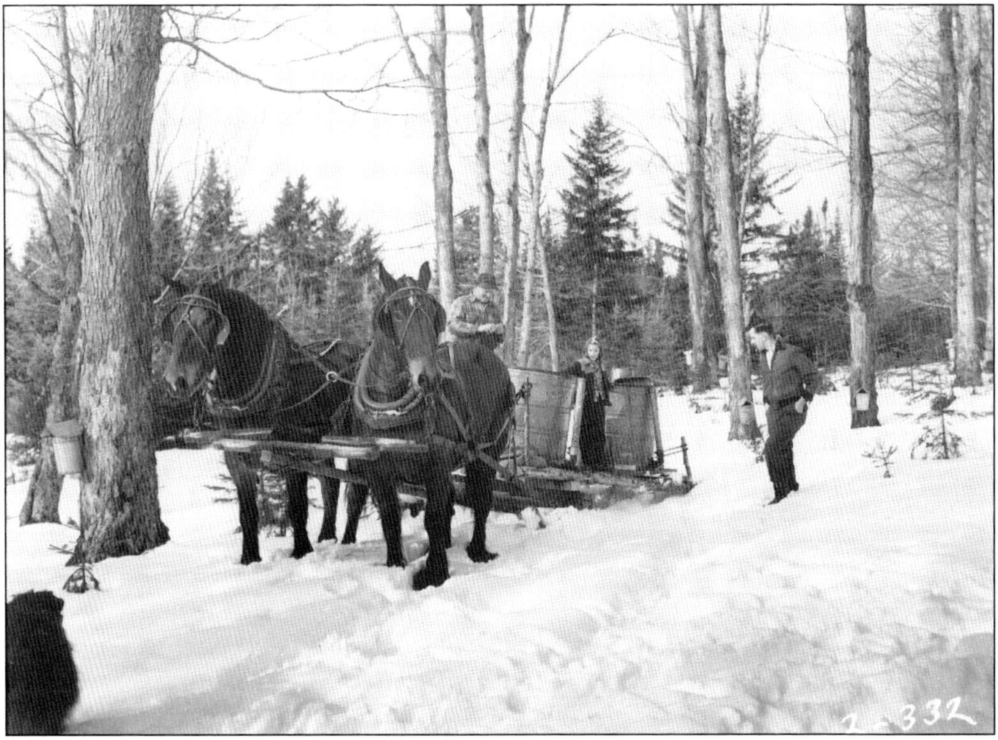

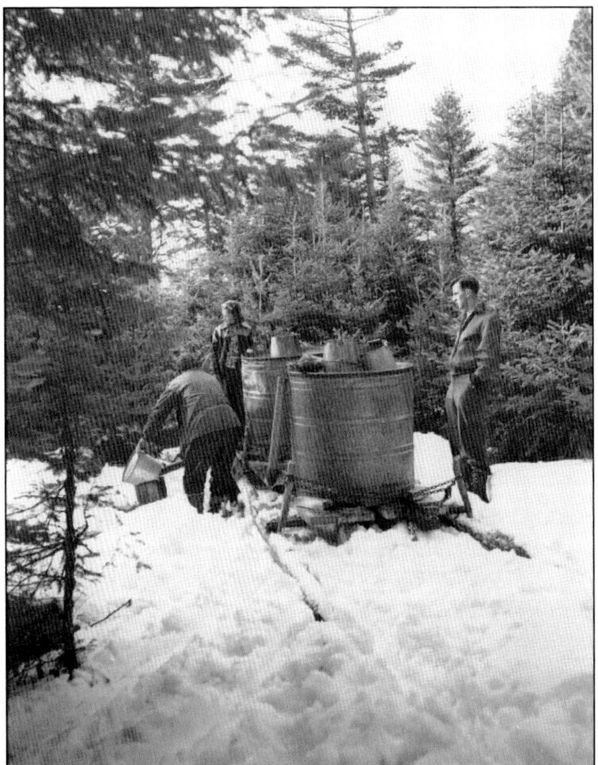

Springtime brings "sugaring" season, which begins when the days are above freezing but the nights are still below freezing. In the sugar bush, the sugar maples were tapped with wooden piles and the sap was caught in buckets hanging from them. Every day, the sap was gathered into larger tubs and taken by horse-drawn sleighs to the sugarhouse to be boiled down in evaporators to make maple syrup. Depending on conditions, it takes about 40 gallons of sap to make one gallon of syrup.

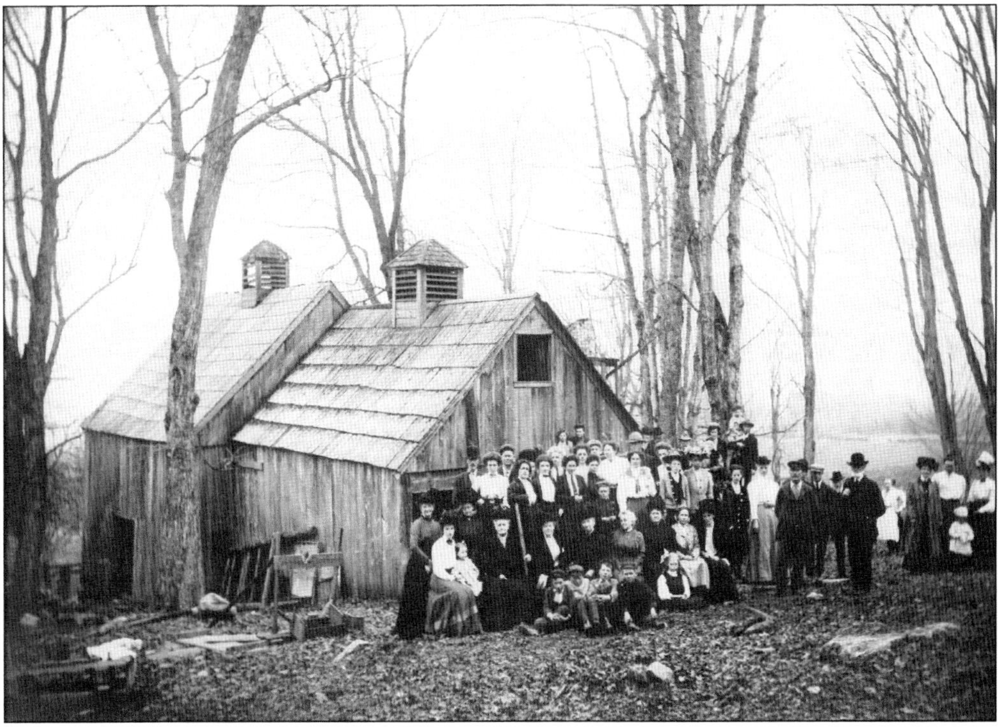

The sugaring-off party was looked forward to for both the sampling of the newly boiled syrup and because it meant the end of winter. It provided a time for the townsfolk to gather and look forward to the coming of spring and warm weather. The sugarhouse usually had a vent on the roof for the steam to escape, giving a nice sweet smell to the air. The treat was "sugar on snow," with thick syrup drizzled over "corn" snow and eaten with a fork. This was usually served with doughnuts and sour pickles.

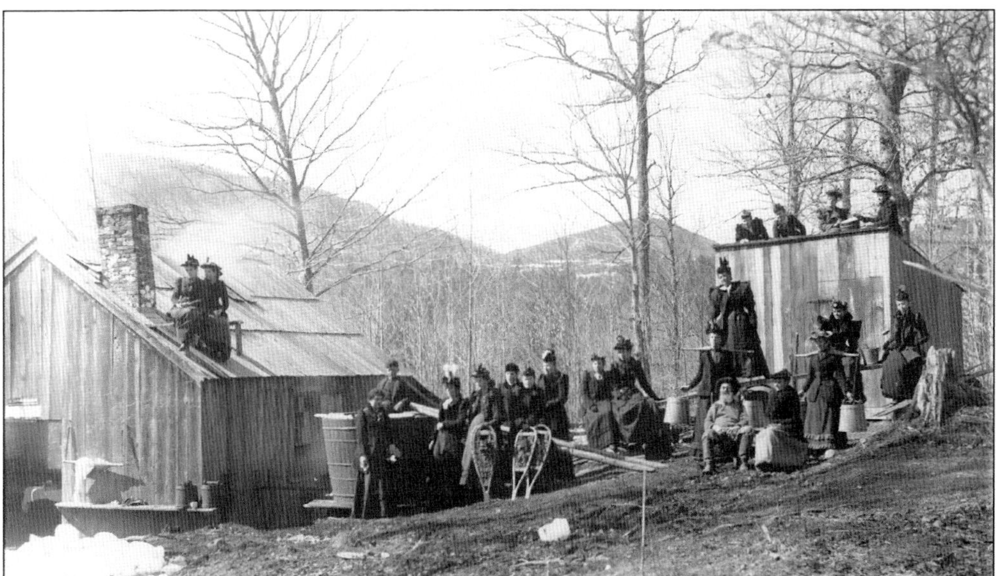

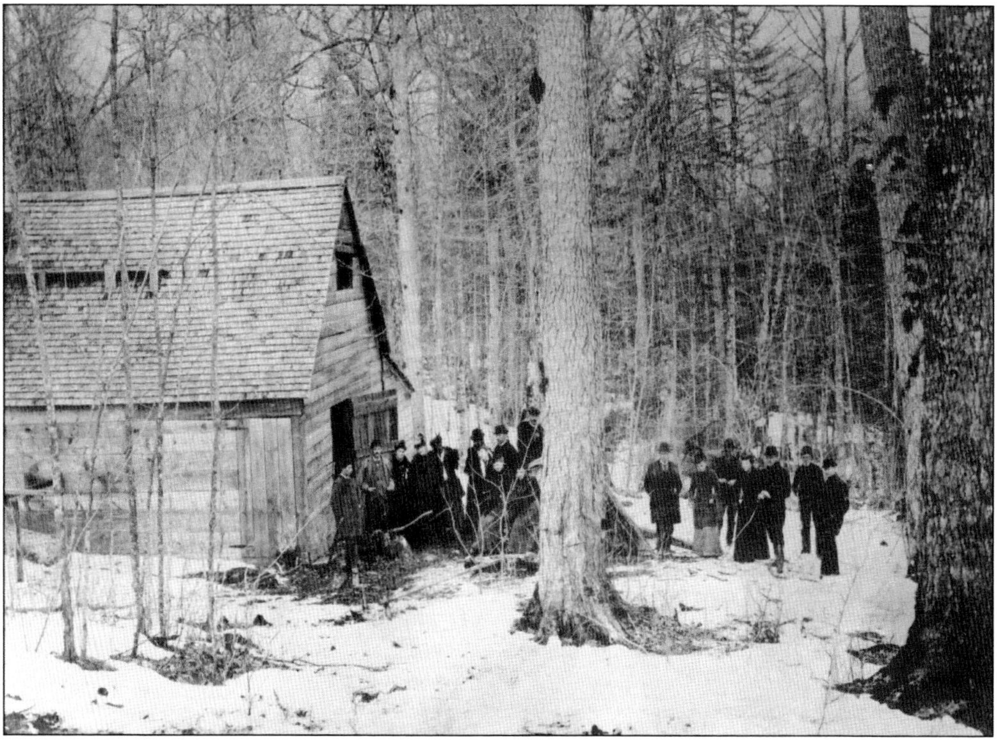

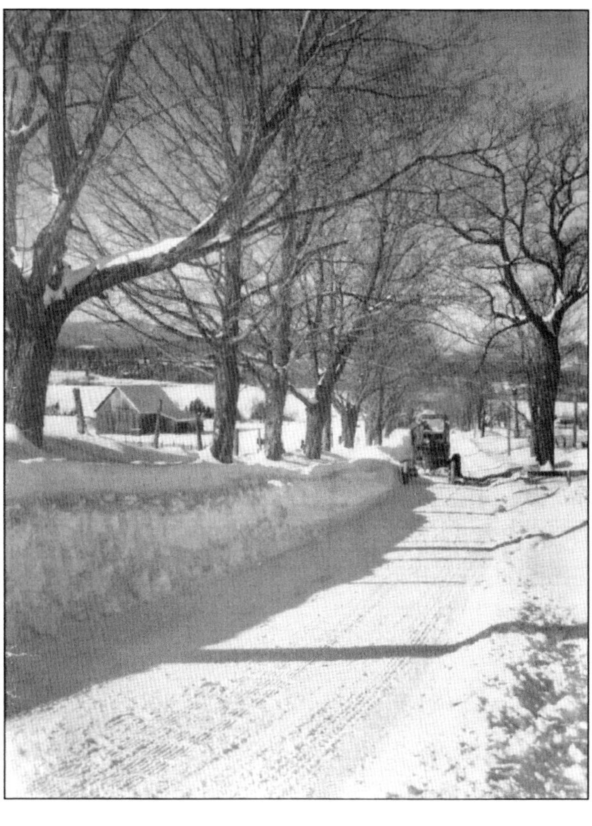

A sugaring-off party is seen above in progress in the late 1890s "out east" on the Way farm. Cynthia Alice Nelson of Barnet, Vermont, is the third young woman to the left of the tree. She was a niece of the Ways.

Lancaster's snowplowing crew did a good job keeping the roads open for passage in the outlying areas. However, as winter went on, the roads became narrow, as seen here. Nevertheless, winter has its own beauty, especially out in the countryside.

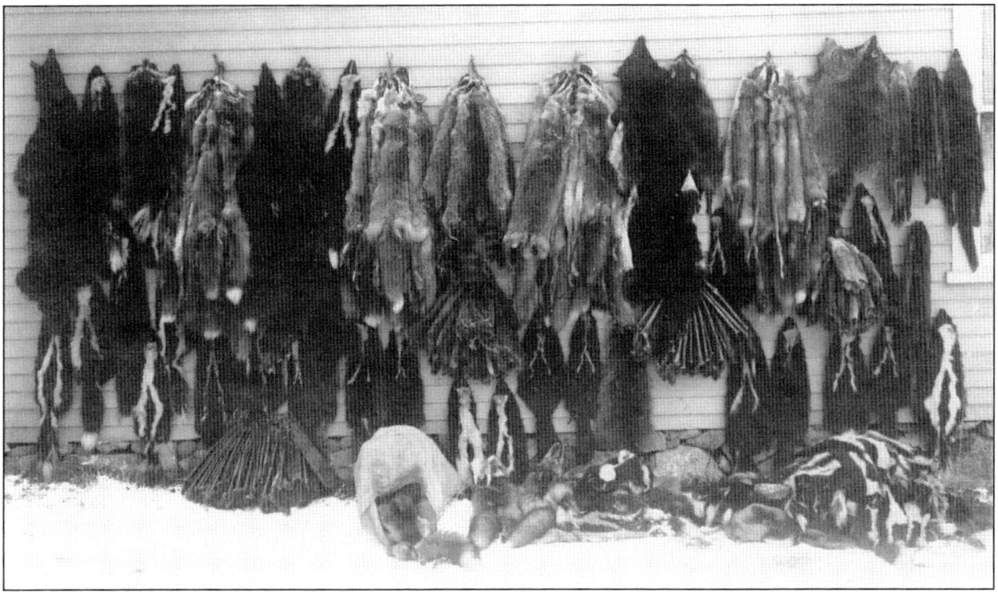

Trapping brought men to the area, including Samuel Martin of Lisbon, long before the first settlers arrived around 1764. Throughout the years, residents supplemented their income by selling the pelts of animals they trapped during the year, as seen in this undated photograph. This also shows the variety of animals in the area—note the skunk pelts in the lower right corner.

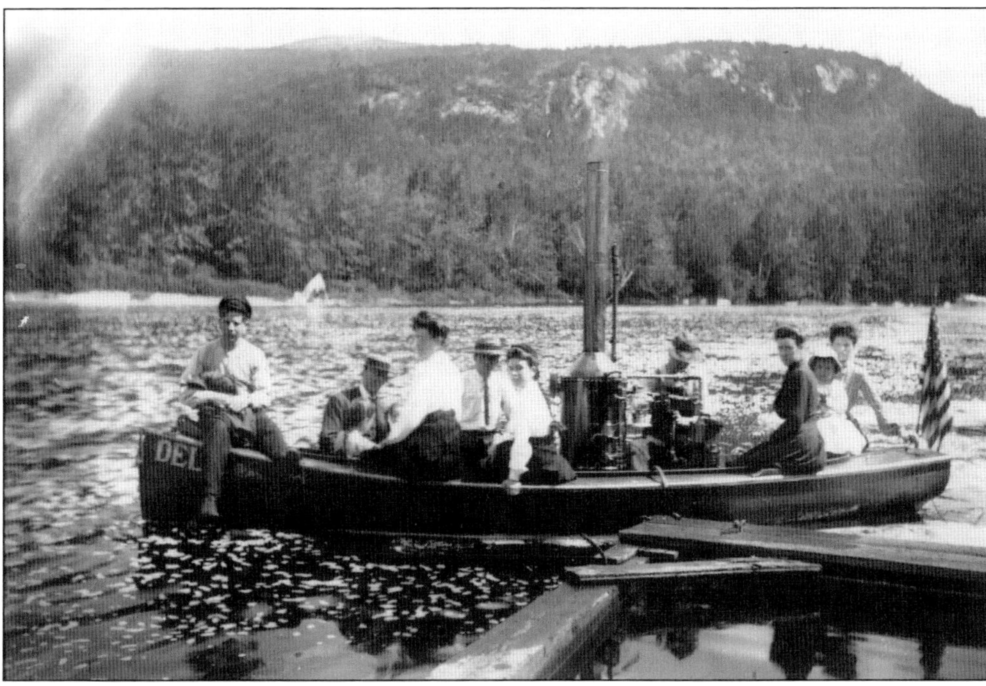

A familiar sight on the Connecticut River were the miniature, or "family size," steamboats, which were modified versions of the Robert Fulton steamboats. These were used for transporting cargo and, on occasion, passengers from one point to another, as well as for excursion cruises up and down the river with stops for picnicking. A typical excursion or pleasure party is seen here, with Mount Orne in the background.

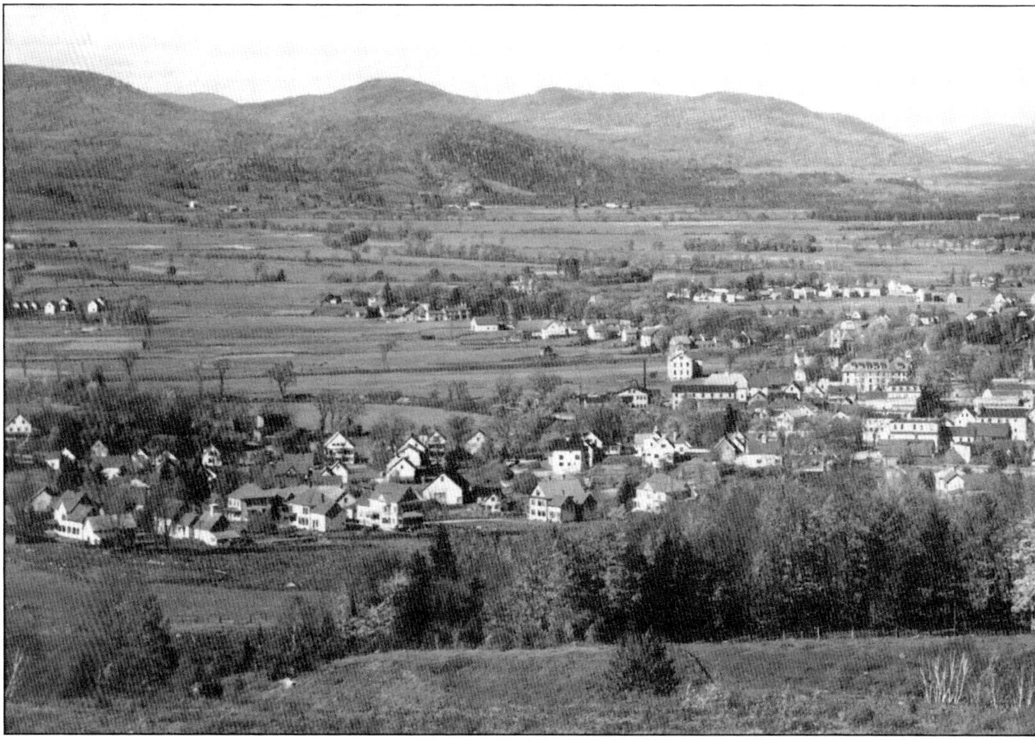

This bird's-eye view of Lancaster was taken looking north from Holton's Hill. Lancaster sits in a river valley surrounded by mountains, with Israel's River running through the center of town.

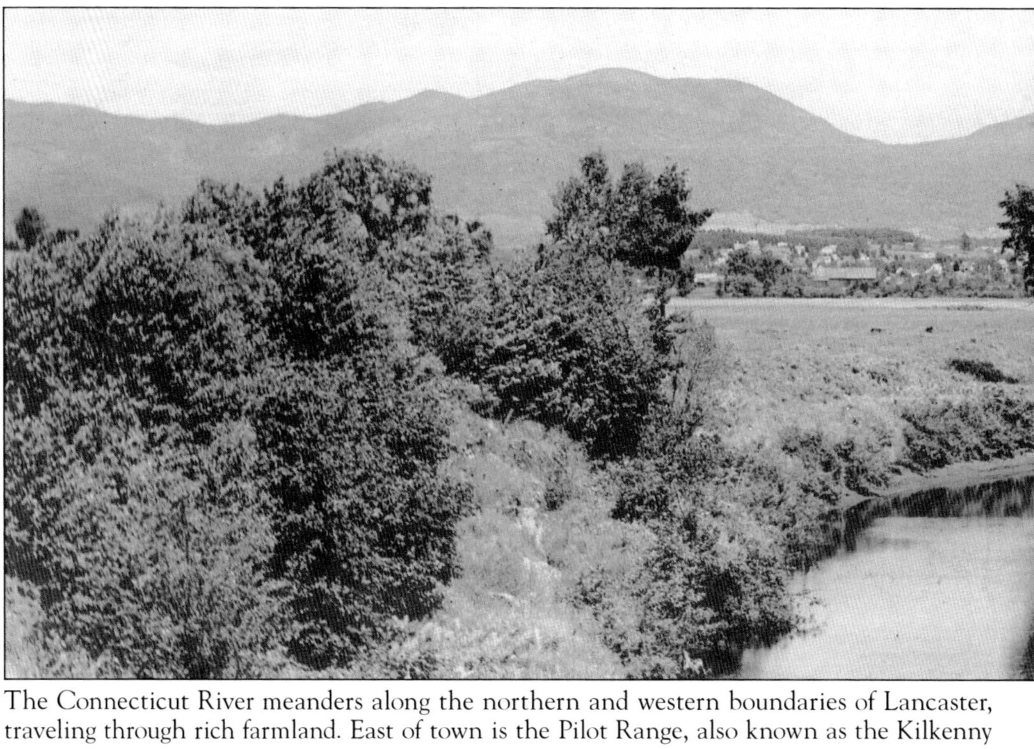

The Connecticut River meanders along the northern and western boundaries of Lancaster, traveling through rich farmland. East of town is the Pilot Range, also known as the Kilkenny

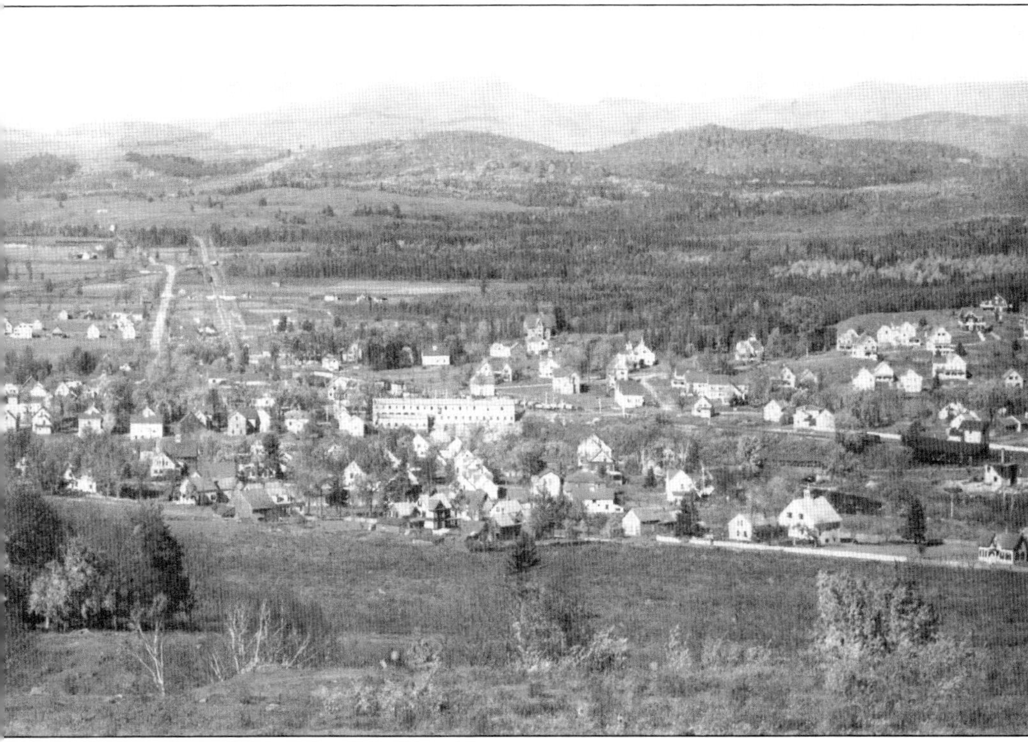

The mountains in the background are on the other side of the Connecticut River in Vermont. In the fall, their colors add a beautiful background to Lancaster.

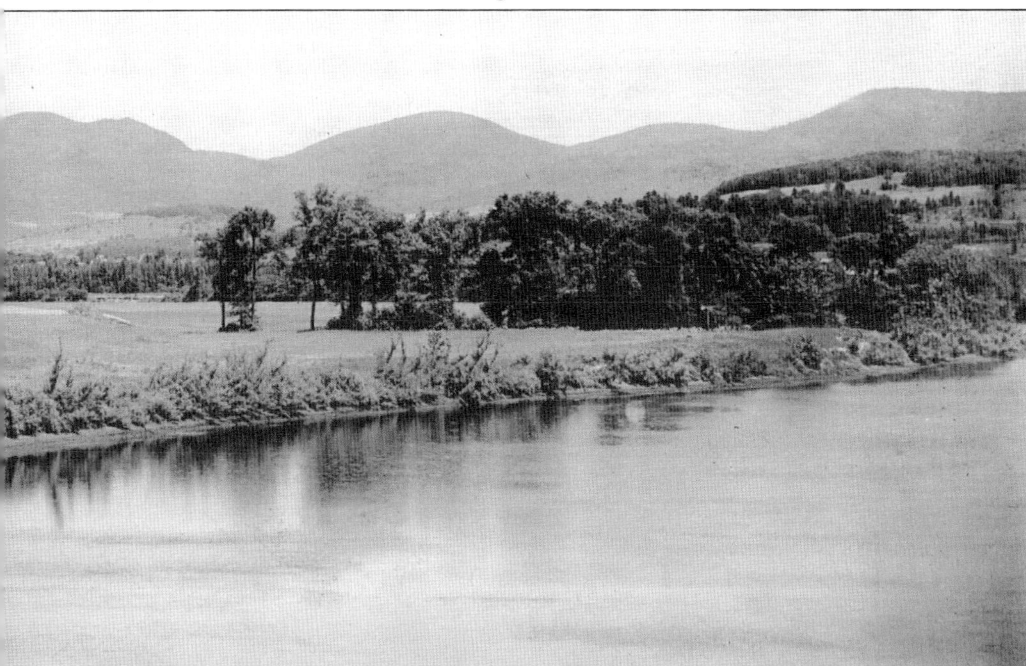

Mountains. It is also the site of the famous logging wreck in 1890. Cabot Mountain is part of the Kilkenny Range and is one of New Hampshire's forty-six 4,000-footers.

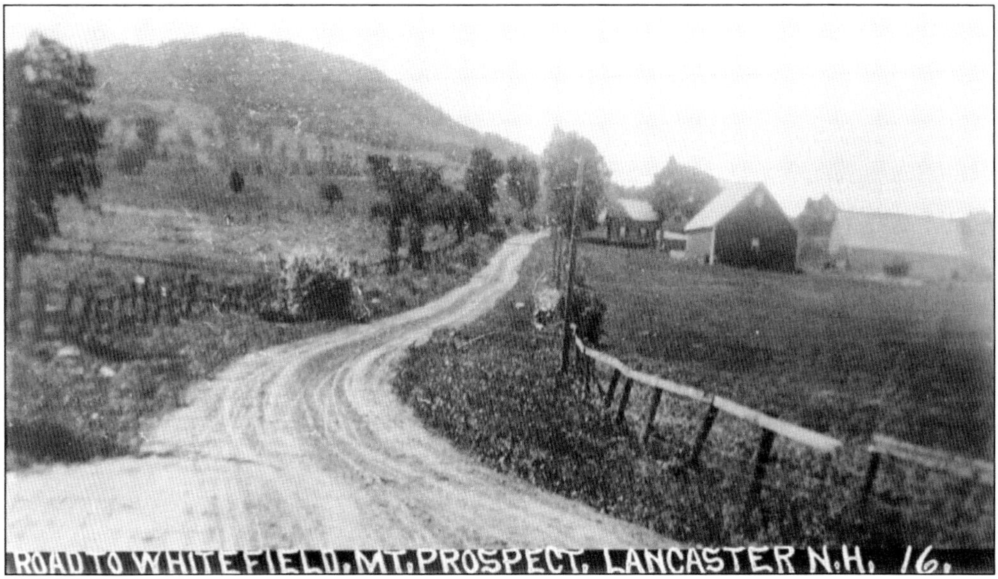

The traveler going south from Lancaster in the early 1900s found the roads going through farmland and over the shoulder of Mount Prospect, seen here on the left. Lancaster is surrounded by towering mountains, with the Presidential Mountains to the southeast, the Franconia Mountain Range to the south, the Pilot Range in the east, Vermont's Lunenburg Heights to the west, and the Vermont Hills to the north. This picturesque valley is completed by Israel's River running through the town and the Connecticut River as its border.

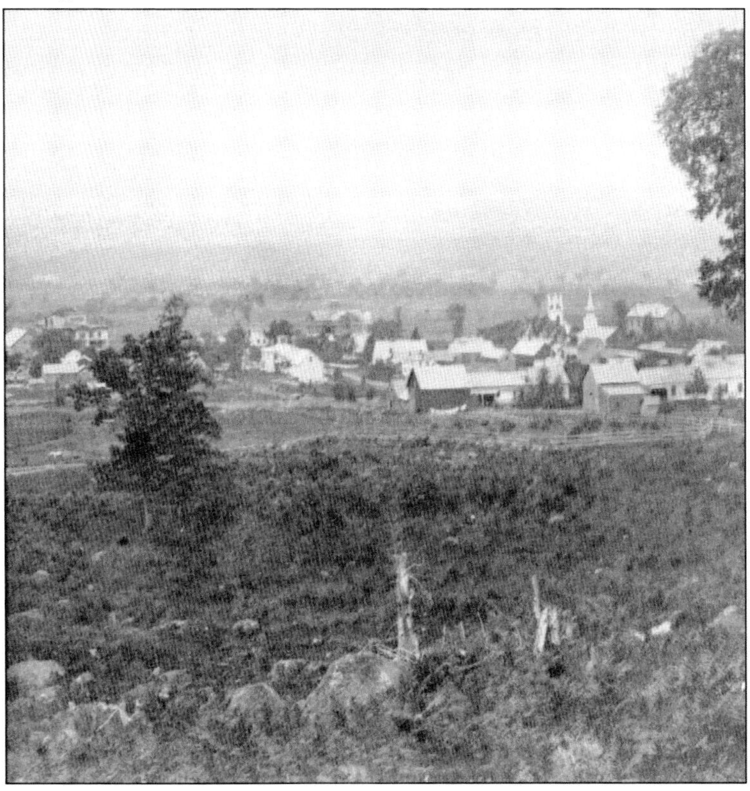

This view from the top of High Street was taken when Lancaster was a young village.

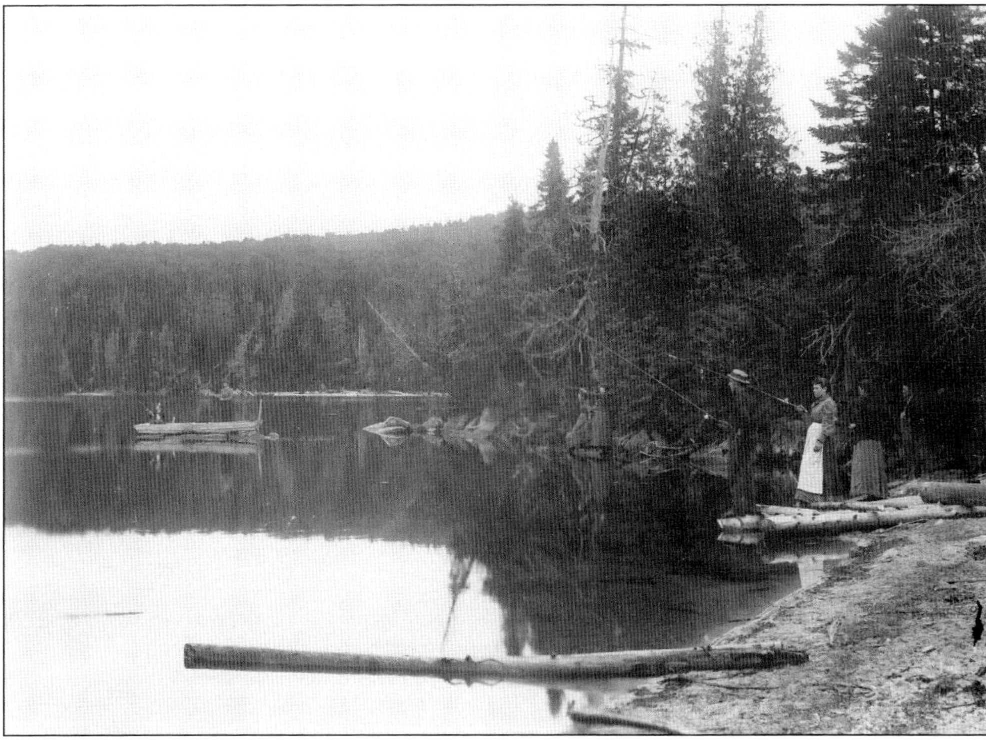

Martin Meadow Pond became a popular local fishing spot both during the winter and in warmer months, with camps along much of its shoreline. The most notable of the residences in the area is Cat Bow Farm, the home of Sinclair Weeks, the secretary of commerce under President Eisenhower. The president visited Weeks there in 1955.

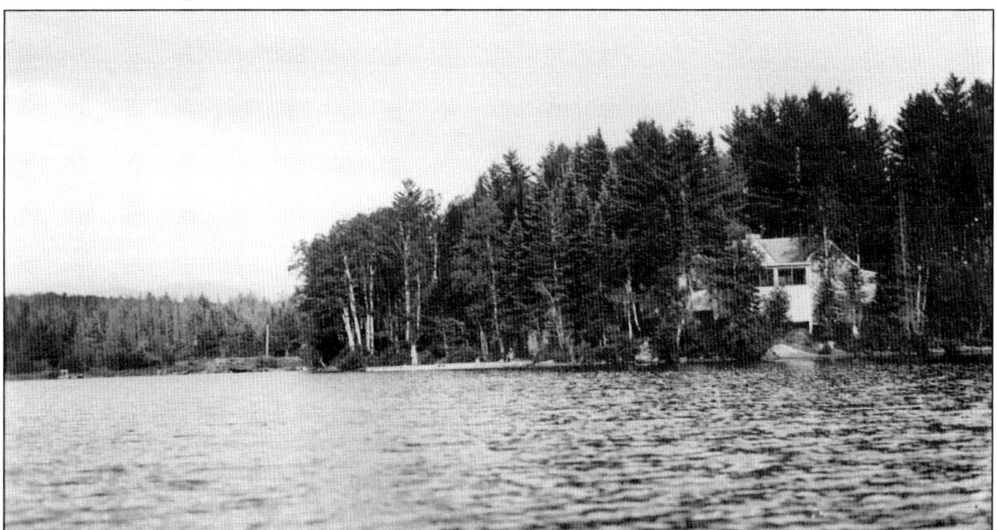

Martin Meadow Pond is a pretty pond southwest of Lancaster, just off the road of the same name. No one really knows who Martin was, but a Lisbon source says that a Samuel Martin traveled from Lisbon in 1753 on a hunting and fishing expedition. It is told that he ventured as far north as Lancaster and built a small shack on the pond.

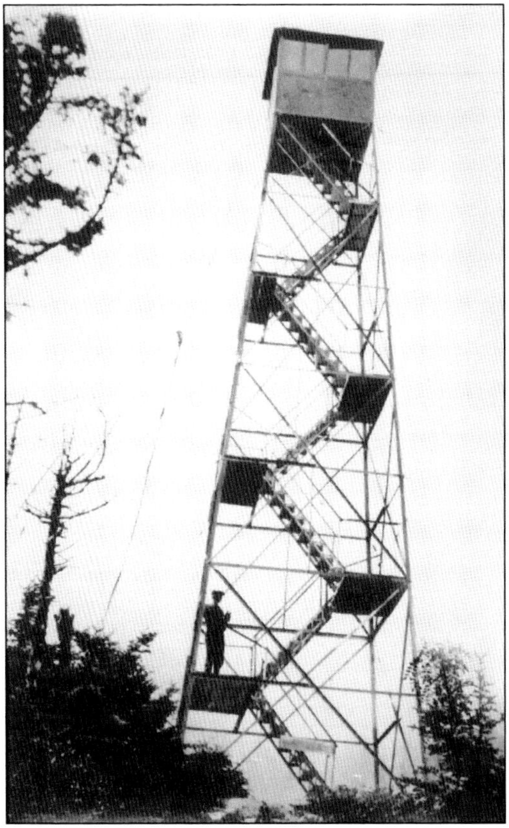

With the logging operations in the mountains, the danger of forest fires was very strong, and it was felt that fire lookout towers were needed. The Cabot Mountain fire lookout tower was built in 1924 to replace the first original tower, a pole with a platform on it. The new tower was 50 feet tall and built on a concrete base with a six-foot-square glass-enclosed structure on top. All the materials were hauled up the mountain by horse. The third and final tower built on the mountain was taken down in 1965.

The forests covering much of the town were of great value as a source of building materials and for the game found within them. Lumbering became an important industry for Lancaster, with several sawmills both in the village proper and in the countryside. Logging was a winter job, performed when farmers did not have their crops to tend to. As seen below, the cut logs were drawn out to a log yard by horse or oxen, then gathered on sleds and pulled to the sawmill or rivers.

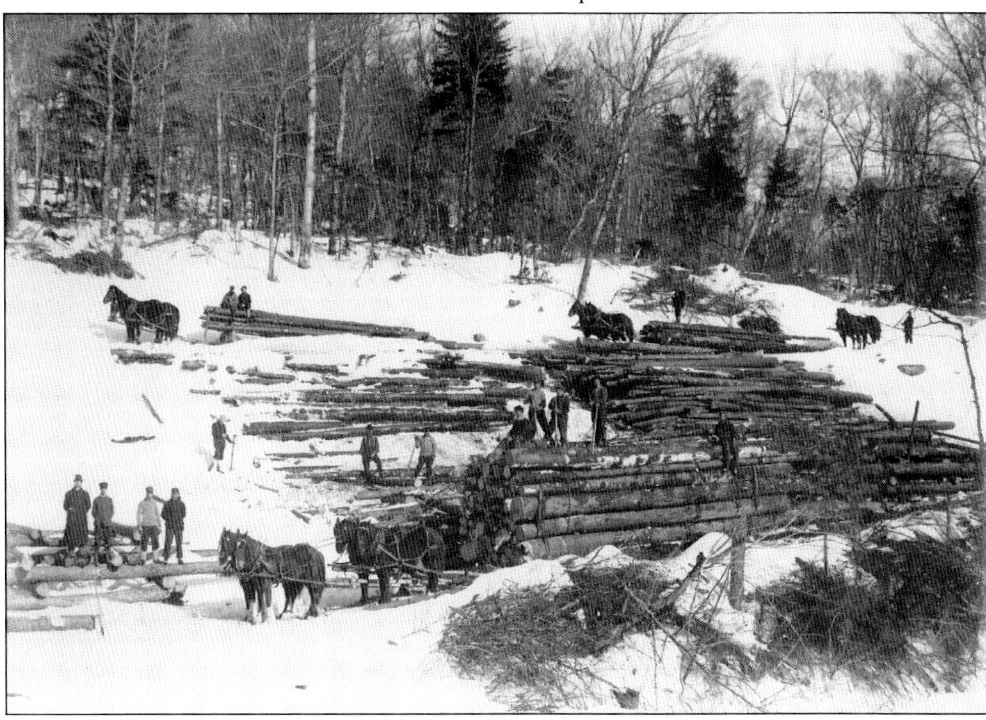

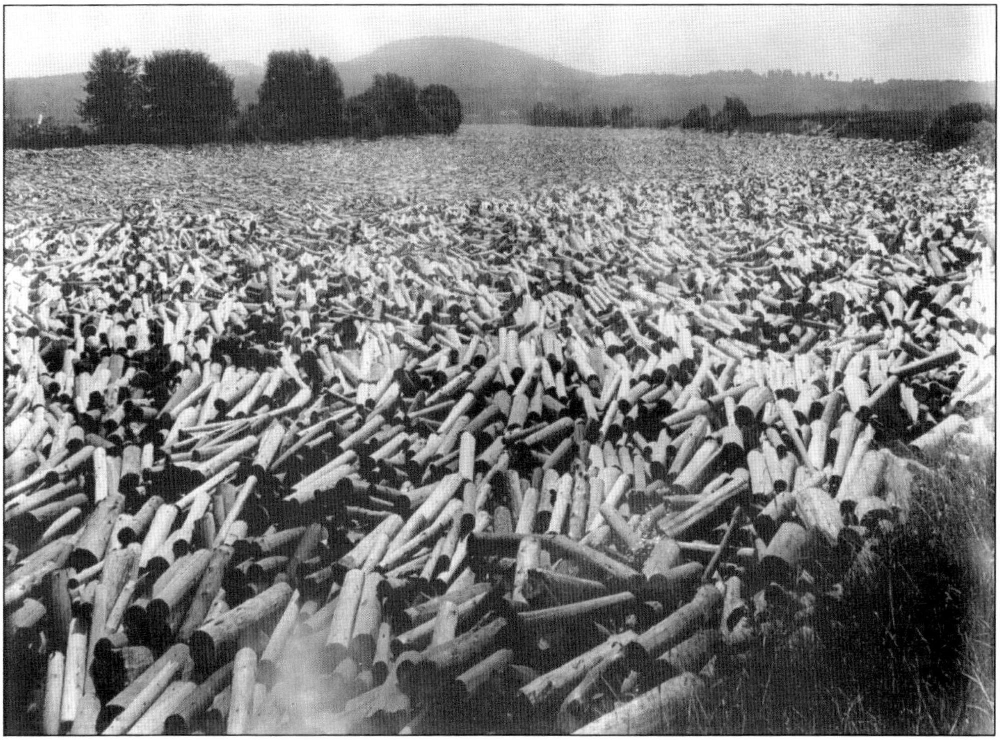

Both the Connecticut River and Israel's River were used to float logs to the sawmills. Log drives were exciting to watch; they were also dangerous for the men who rode the logs to keep them from jamming up. This pulpwood was waiting on the Connecticut River in South Lancaster to be started down river. The concentration of logs was so great that a person could walk across them from one side of the river to the other.

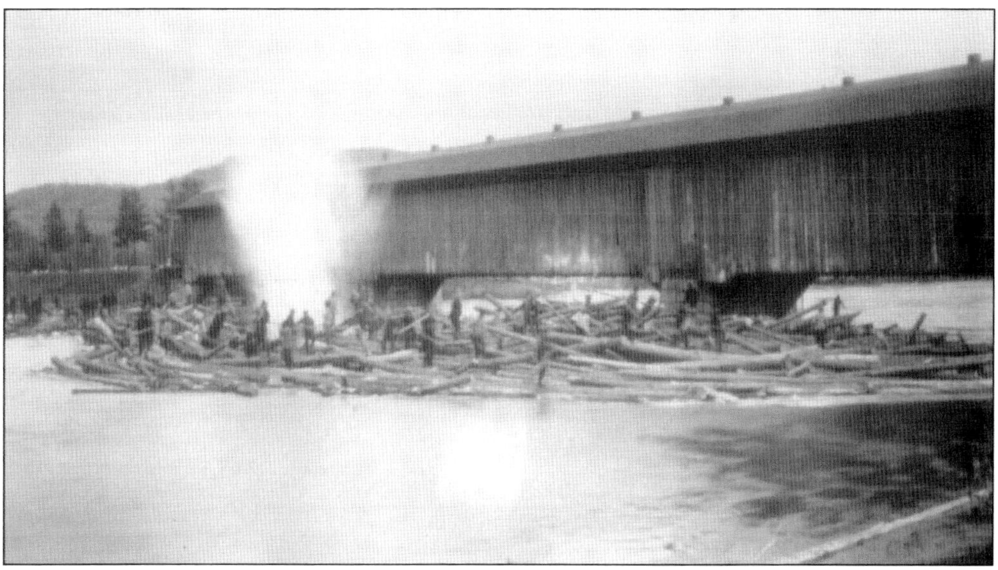

Occasionally, logs jammed at bridges creating the possibility of damaging or even destroying them. Dynamite was often used to break up log jams, as seen here, generating a large plume of water and ice.

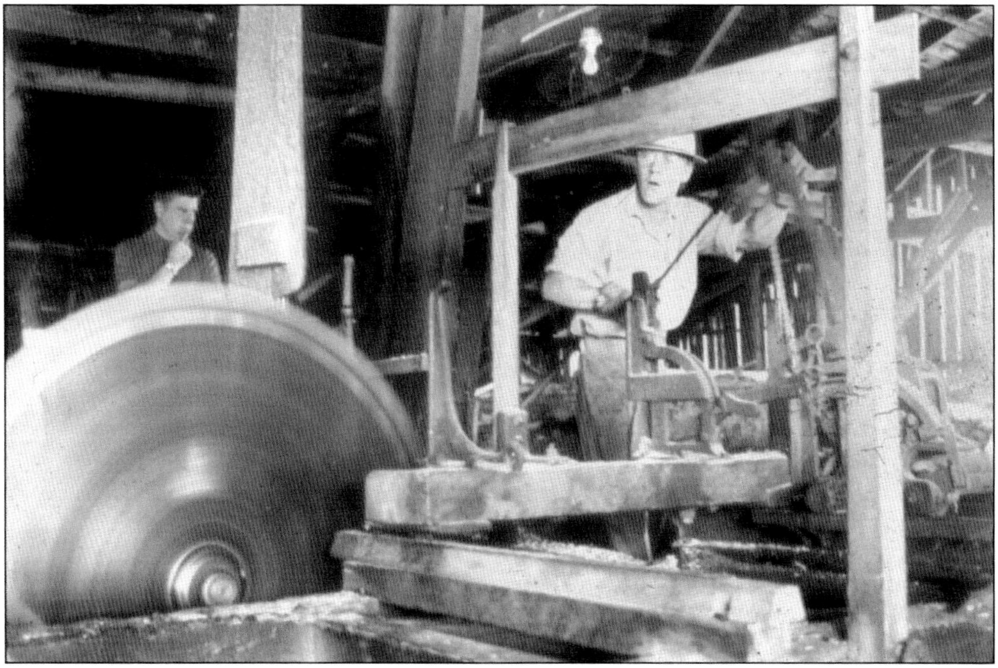

Built by Eban C. Garland, the Garland Mill has been operating in Lancaster since 1856. Garland had a sawmill and a shop where tables and chairs were made. It was sold to William Alden in 1888, and he then sold it to his son Harold in 1926.

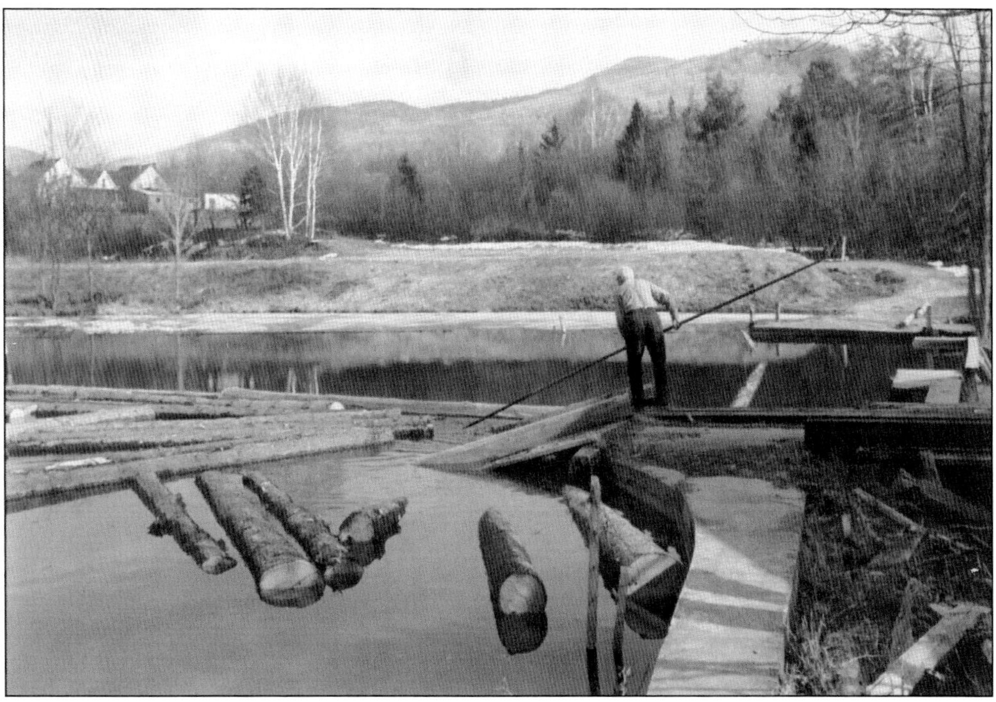

Harold Alden, using a long pike pole, selects the next logs to be sawn into lumber at the Garland Mill in the 1960s.

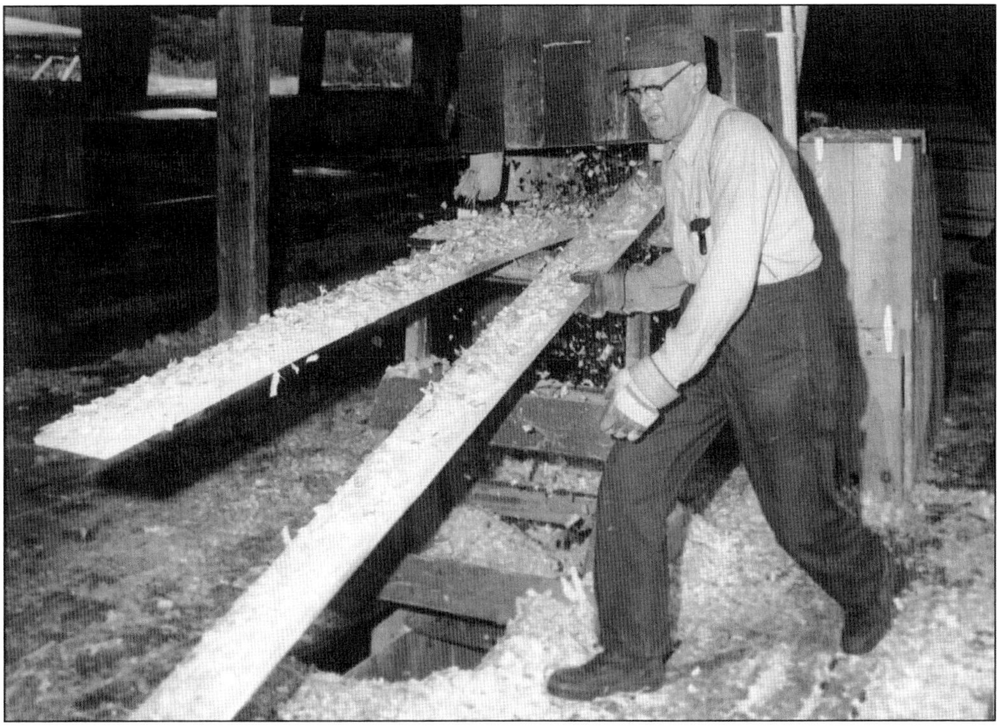

Here, planks coming out of the planer are guided by Harold Alden. Today, the Southworth family operates the mill; they produced the lumber and built the new barn for the Lancaster Historical Society. The Garland Mill is the only licensed, continually operated, water-powered sawmill in New Hampshire. It is listed in the National Register of Historic Places.

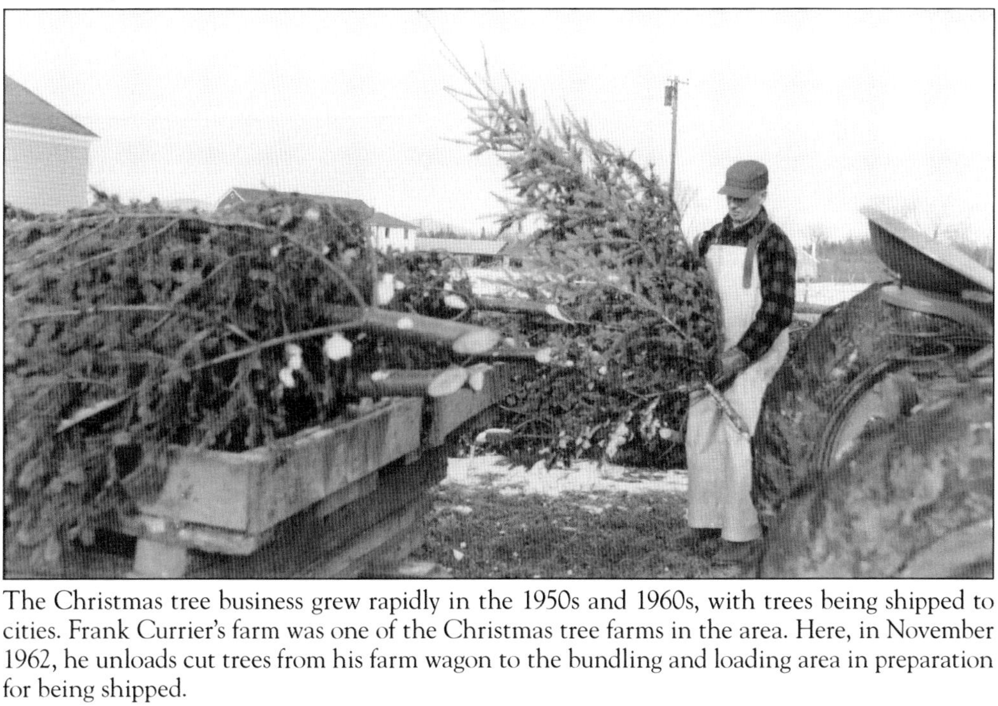

The Christmas tree business grew rapidly in the 1950s and 1960s, with trees being shipped to cities. Frank Currier's farm was one of the Christmas tree farms in the area. Here, in November 1962, he unloads cut trees from his farm wagon to the bundling and loading area in preparation for being shipped.

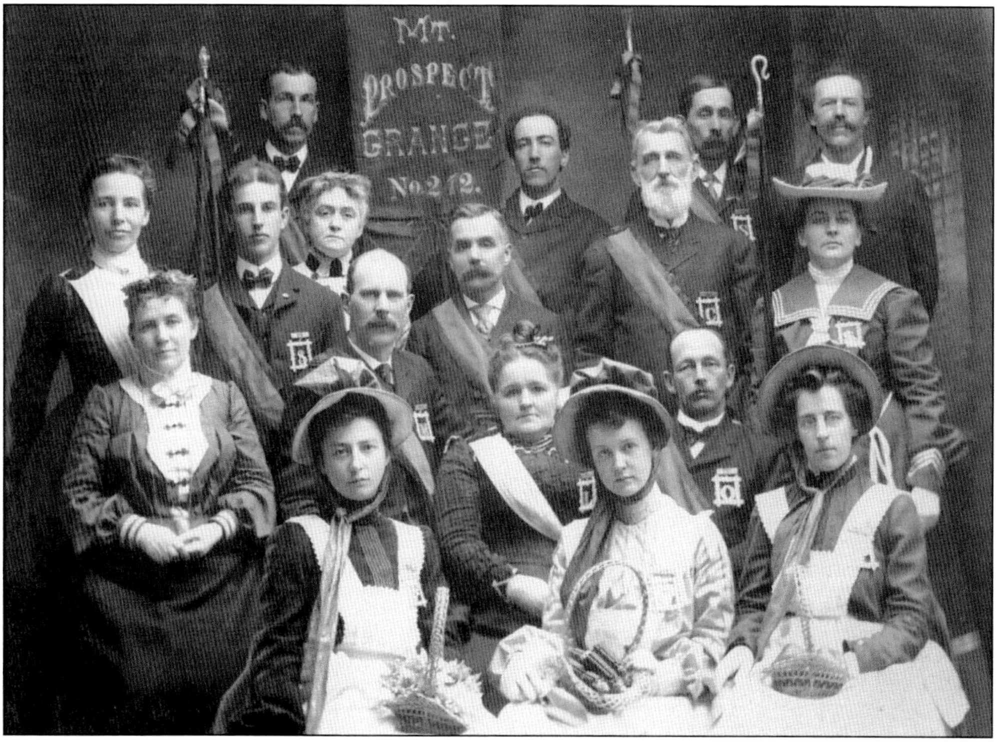

The Grange is an agricultural, family, and fraternal farming organization that was founded in 1867. The Mount Prospect chapter operated in Lancaster for decades.

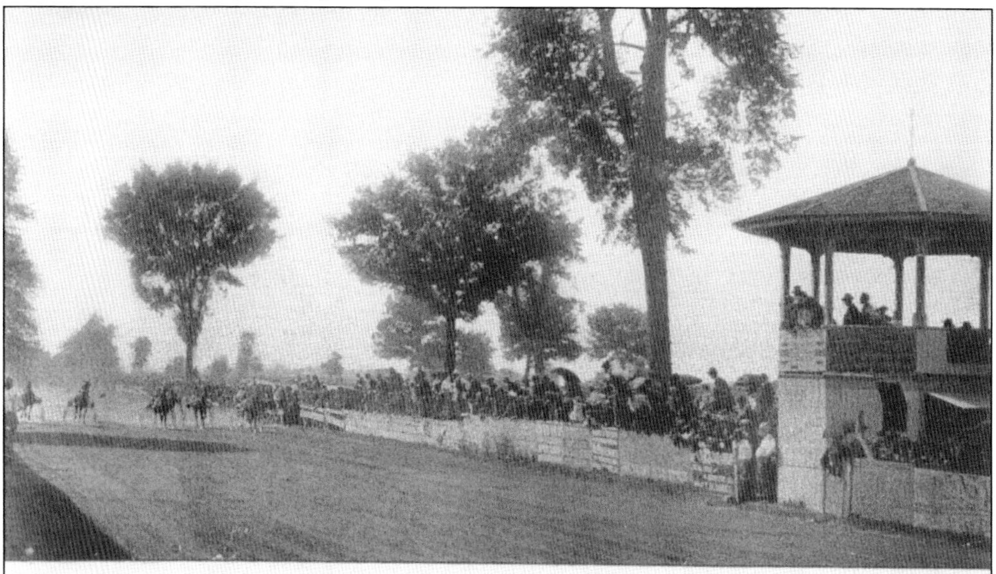

"See you at the fair" is heard throughout the Lancaster area on both sides of the Connecticut River as everybody begins to look forward to the Lancaster Fair, which now begins on the Wednesday before Labor Day and ends on Labor Day Monday.

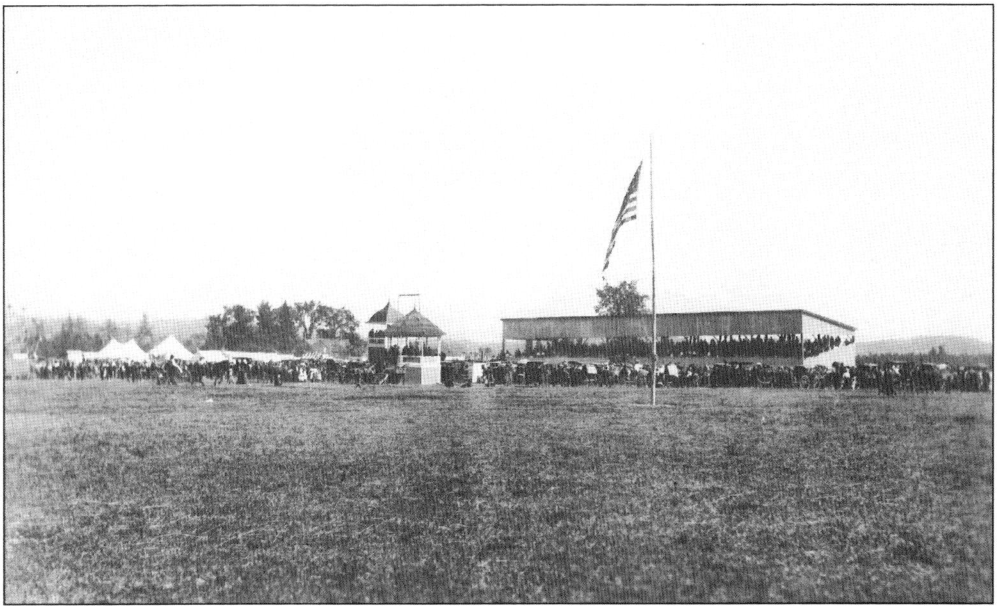

The first Lancaster Fair was sponsored by the Coös County (New Hampshire) and Essex County (Vermont) Agricultural Society in 1902. It was an occasion for the residents of the area to show off produce, farm animals, and handiwork. Eventually, it grew to include horse racing as well. The fairgrounds (above) had once been a gentlemen's riding park.

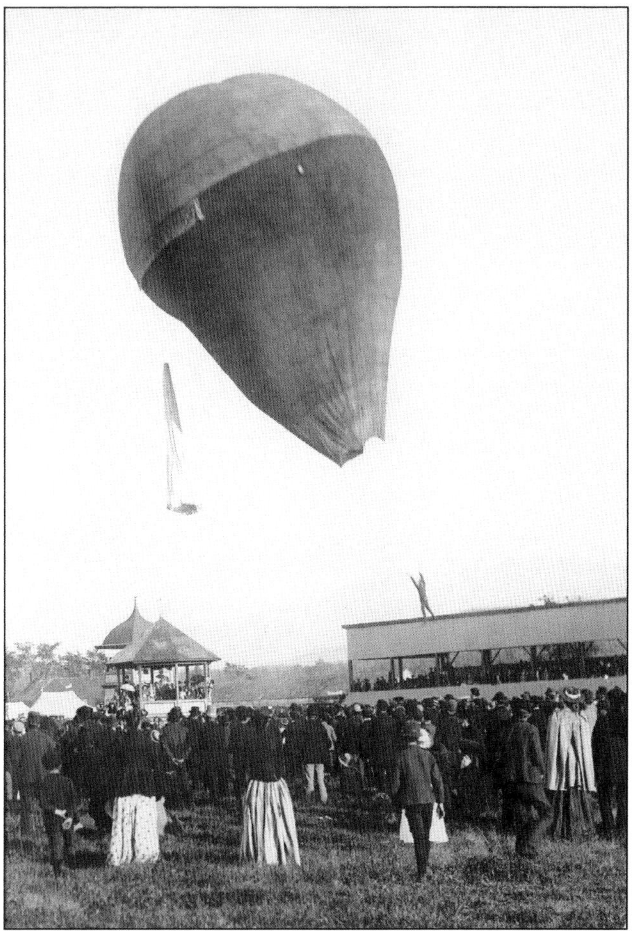

One of the many anticipated events during the early years of the fair was the "flying machines" that made appearances, including balloons like this one.